Journal of a March from Delhi to Peshawur and from thence to Cabul

Journal of a March from
Delhi to Peshawur
and from thence to Cabul

with the mission of
Lieut-Colonel Sir C.M. Wade

including travels in the Punjab, a visit to the
city of lahore, and a Narrative of operations
in the Khyber Pass, undertaken in 1839

by
Lieut. William Barr
Bengal Horse Artillery

**Munshiram Manoharlal
Publishers Pvt. Ltd.**

"The small fort of Ali Musjid has, from its situation, long held the Sikhs in check; and it is not upon record that the celebrated Khyber Pass has never previously been forced." — *Extract from Lord Auckland's letter to the Secret Committee, Simla, August 29th, 1839.*

ISBN 81-215-1095-3
This edition 2003
Originally published 1844
© Munshiram Manoharlal Publishers Pvt. Ltd., New Delhi

Printed in India.
Published by Munshiram Manoharlal Publishers Pvt. Ltd.,
Post Box 5715, 54 Rani Jhansi Road,
New Delhi 110 055.

TO THE

REV. JOHN BARR, M.D.

This Volume

IS INSCRIBED WITH MUCH AFFECTION

BY

HIS BROTHER

PREFACE.

THE following pages were originally written for the amusement of a valued relative, and without any intention of being offered to the public. As the Author of them is not aware that any account of the operations undertaken in 1839, by Colonel Wade's auxiliary army, has yet been detailed by an eye witness, beyond a short and ably-written paper in the *United-Service Journal*, for July, 1842, he has yielded to the suggestions of his friends, and now ventures, with some diffidence, to submit his roughly-penned notes to the consideration of other readers. He does so, at the present moment, with less reluctance, as the increasing importance of our relations with the Punjab renders every information (however slight) respecting that country acceptable; and, for the same reason, an interest may perhaps be imparted to his Journal that he could not hope it would otherwise have possessed.

Dithorn, Staffordshire, 1844.

CONTENTS.

CHAPTER I.

FROM DELHI TO KURNAL.

CHAPTER II.

KURNAL TO LODIANAH.

CHAPTER III.

LODIANAH TO LAHORE.

CHAPTER IV.

LAHORE.

CHAPTER V.

LAHORE TO R HOTAS.

CHAPTER VI.

RHOTAS TO PESHAWUR.

CONTENTS
CHAPTER VII.
CAMP AT P ESHAWUR.

CHAPTER VIII.
CAMP AT P ESHAWUR.

CHAPTER IX.

CAMP AT KOULSIR.

CHAPTER X.

THE KHYBER PASS.

CHAPTER XI.

FROM DHAKA TO CABUL

CHAPTER XII.

FROM CABUL TO FEROZEPORE.

FROM DELHI TO KURNAL

T OWARDS the end of December, 1838, when the excitement caused by the assembly and departure of "the army of the Indus" had subsided, and events were once more assuming their usually quiet course, I unexpectedly received an order to join Colonel Wade's mission, with a detachment of Native horse artillery, and two 24-pounder howitzers, fully equipped for field service. The actual march of the army for Affghanistan had, naturally enough, suppressed any hope I might previously have entertained of joining its ranks; and I seemed destined to pass another season, at least, in the "inglorious ease" of a cantonment life, instead of existing amidst the turmoil and bustle of a camp. The command that had now devolved on me opened a brighter prospect, and I looked forward with intense pleasure to the time I should be traversing the rich and fertile plains of the Punjab; that oftcoveted country, whose powerful but politic chief had ever been wise enough to cultivate an alliance with the British, and has thus obtained a position that places him at the head of all the independent princes. I was at Delhi when the order reached me, and Colonel Wade was at Lahore (a month's march in advance), having gone there during Lord Auckland's visit to the "Lion of the Punjab," for the purpose of introducing to the Maharajah, Shah Shoojah's eldest son, the Shahzada Timour, who was to accompany the mission to Peshawur. Now, whether the mission formed a clause in the tripartite treaty between the British Government, Runjeet Singh, and Shah Shoojah-ool-Moolk, or whether it was happily thought of, devised, and put together during the Governor-General's sojourn in the capital of the "Five Waters," is known only to the initiated; but I believe the requisition for the British howitzers was only made to his lordship at *that* time, or orders for their junction with Colonel Wade's force would, no doubt, have been issued earlier. As it was, before the ordnance could be supplied by the Delhi magazine, Colonel W. had left Lahore and advanced some distance on his way to Nowrungabad, a town on the banks of the Jhelum, some 350 miles beyond the Mogul capital, where he proposed spending a short time in furthering the objects of the mission, and where I *hoped* he would remain until I should be able to join him.

On the 18th January, 1839, all was reported to be in readiness, and I was directed to commence my march on the 19th; but, in consequence of the very heavy rain that fell the previous day, it was necessary to postpone it to the following morning, as the tents and camp equipage were so saturated with water as to be too heavy for the camels to carry. This was vexatious, as already much time had been lost in replacing one of the howitzers, pronounced by a committee to be unserviceable; but the 20th, though a hazy day, was sufficiently fair to admit of a move, so I struck camp a little before dawn, and marched to Allepore, a miserable village, about ten miles from Delhi. On the road we passed numberless ruins, which bore testimony to the grandeur and extent of the once magnificent capital of Hindostan; and a dilapidated serai, about three miles from the city, pointed out the commencement of a series of such buildings, erected at various times and by different Mogul emperors, for the use of travellers from this to Cabul, which was for many centuries included in their extensive domains.

At noon, as the sun was breaking through the mist, a large treasure-party arrived, under the command of Captain C., of the 54th N.I., who is convoying some 20,000 or 30,000 rupees to Lodianah. He pitched his camp a short distance from mine, and after unpacking his treasure, a countless multitude of camels, upon which it had been carried, were taken away to browse. The afternoon was fine, the mist having entirely cleared away, but there was nothing in the surrounding country of sufficient interest to induce me to take a ramble; so, after seeing to the duties and protection of my camp, I adjourned to my tent, and ruminated on the gratification I expected to derive from traversing localities so little known to Europeans, and so celebrated as the scenes of Alexander's conquests.

January 21.—On proceeding to parade at half-past three, A.M., I found a similiar mist to that of yesterday had usurped the clearness of the sky, and the fires which the syces (grooms) had kindled, to see how to put on the harness, as well as for the purpose of warmth, only served to make darkness more visible. The confusion, too, that it occasioned was manifested by the bawling of men, the peculiar and painful grumbling of camels having their loads strapped on, and the neighing of horses, who, coming together in the dark, set to and fought with vicious fury; whilst here and there a steed that had broken from its picket was galloping about, and adding not a little to the uproar. About two miles from Allepore we were obliged to quit the high-road, in consequence of the late rains having swept away the bridge over Ali Murdan's canal, and there being no ford near the spot, we had to make a considerable detour ere we came to one. The aspect of this was by no means satisfactory, the water being above three feet deep, with a steep bank, and awkward turning on the opposite side: however, we dashed through it, surmounted the ascent, and beyond a semi-ducking, got over without any accident. We halted at Barotah, a small village, which has nothing to recommend it but a good encamping ground, and so poor that we had to send to a town several miles distant for our supplies.

January 22.—A beautifully bright and clear sky, in which the starry constellations were displayed with unusual brilliancy, enabled us at the commencement of our morning's march, to pick our way with some feeling of security, and fortunately it happened thus, for in many places the water was so deep, and the road so heavy, as to render it necessary to deviate considerably from the high-way. At sunrise we reached Soneput, which appears to have been at one time a town of some consideration, as its ruins are very extensive, and are still enclosed by a high brick wall, which in former days served to defend it. It is built on a lofty mound, which shows it to advantage; and a few temples situated in gardens, or embedded in groves of trees in its environs, contribute not a little to its pretty appearanee. A good deal of trade still passes through it, and at no great distance there is a ferry on the Jumna, whence roads branch off to the Doab and Rohilcund, where the merchandize is disposed of.

In the year 1036, it was deemed of sufficient importance to cause Musaood of Ghuzani to march against it, when he invaded Hindoostan. This emperor was so celebrated for his strength and prowess, that he obtained the appellation of Roostum (Hercules) the Second; and it is averred he drew a bow with such might that an arrow from it would pierce through the strongest coat of mail, or the hide of an elephant, and that his battle-axe, like Richard Coeur de Lion's, was so ponderous and massive, that, beside himself, no individual could raise it single-handed. Deipal, who was governor of Soneput at this period, did not think proper to await Musaood's arrival, but fled into the woods in such haste that he had no time to carry off his treasure, which, consequently, fell into the victor's hands, and who, on entering the town, gave orders to raze to the ground every temple, and to demolish every idol that should be found within its walls. Having done this he marched in pursuit of the governor, who had in the meantime collected his followers, with a resolution to try his fate in battle; but he was surprised by Musaood before he could well assume the defensive – his army surrounded and taken prisoners, and he himself, with the greatest difficulty, escaped in the habit of a slave. Musaood on his return to Ghuzani left a confidential officer in command of the fortress.

At the eleventh mile we came to Runjaree Burke Chowkie, where troops occasionally half, but there is no village near to it, and the spot is only known by the existence of a chowkie, or guard-house, built close to a banyan tree of great dimensions, and covering a large extent of ground. Numerous blue pigeons obtain shelter under its branches, and the country around being clothed with jungle, game of every description is abundant. The approach to Gunnour, where we halted, is extremely picturesque; a few huts on a rising ground, overhung by some large and drooping trees, bounding one side of the prospect, the other being formed by a large and handsome caravanserai with its embattled wall and towers reflected on the surface of a beautifully clear tank. About 500 yards beyond the village we pitched our tents, and not far from a small pond at which the horses were watered.

The next morning we marched to Sumalka, a village of some size, and possessing the remains of a fine and extensive serai. This, however, is fast going to decay, but a small outlay on the part of Government would preserve it for some years, and at the same time show the natives (who almost exclusively use these buildings) that their comfort and welfare are not always set aside or forgotten by those who rule over them.

January 24.—At half-past four A.M., we commenced our march and after (at the third mile) passing a small collection of huts, thence, till within a short distance of Paniput, nothing was to be seen on either side of the wood, but an uninterrupted jungle. A magnificent view of the snowy Himalayahs before sunrise, in some measure compensated for the loss of the beauties of nature nearer to us: but the glimpse was only transient, as a few minutes after the sun appeared the prospect became fainter and fainter, until at length the haze obscured it entirely. As we approached Paniput the whole of the surrounding country was converted into one mass of cultivation, here and there broken by small clumps of trees, through which are to be seen the spires and cupolas of numerous temples, with their white and polished surfaces, starting from the dark foliage in which they are embedded with an almost dazzling brilliancy.

The town is built on a slight eminence some miles in circuit, most of the houses being constructed of brick, and a few raised to the height of two stories with balconies and ornamented cupolas to the windows. One or two large caravanserais in tolerably good repair are at either side of the city, which is still considered of such importance as to require that a magistrate should reside here. In its environs are numerous tombs of considerable size, but very dilapidated, which point out where the ashes of the nobles in days by-gone have been deposited, as well as where the slain of numerous battles have found a resting place from all their worldly troubles; for Paniput, from its proximity to Delhi, has been the scene of many a deadly contest, and beneath its walls the fate of the capital of Hindoostan has, even to later years, generally been decided.

It was here that the famous Baber, a descendant of the equally celebrated Timour, gained, in 1525, a complete victory over Ibrahim II., by which the latter lost his life and kingdom. The Imperial army under Ibrahim is said to have consisted of 100,000 horses and 1,000 elephants; that of Baber's, of only 13,000 men. The bold Tartar, however, was not disconcerted at the vast numbers opposed to him; but trusting to the hardy valour of his followers, whom he had so often led to victory, he awaited the battle with composure and confidence; first taking the precaution to link his artillery together to prevent his antagonist's cavalry separating his guns, and then dividing his army into two lines and a reserve, the whole of which he commanded in person. Ibrahim, ignorant of the art of war, drew up his forces in one irregular column, and ordered them at once to charge the Moguls, thinking that he would bear down all opposition by his number. But vain was the hope! for Baber, perceiving his folly, ordered the reserve to wheel round in two bodies and the enemy on either flank, which was done in such gallant style that the Patans were forced to retire. Ibrahim, though unskilled in military tactics, was not deficient in courage; and having observed the ill success of his previous manoeuvre, boldly advanced in person, surrounded by the flower of his nobility, and so desperate was the charge, that Moguls recoiled from it; but recovering themself and fighting with desperation, they slew the Emperor and 5,000 of his followers. The fall of Ibrahim decided the fortune of the day. His army, or rather the remnants of it, took to flight, and were hotly pursued by Baber as far as the river Jumna; and it is computed the most moderate historians that no less than 16,000 Patans fell in this action, which transferred the empire of India from the Affghan tribe of Lodi to the house of Timour.

Numerous other actions of consequence occurred here after this, but the last battle of Paniput was fought in 1760, between the Affghans under Ahmed Abdallah, the founder of the Dourranie empire, and the Mahrattas, commanded by Sewdasheo Rao, the Bhow. The sceptre of Hindoostan was at this time feebly swayed by Ali Gohur, eldest son of Alumgire II., and the throne of the Mogul was the prize that would be awarded to the victor. The Mahrattas having been in two previous engagements thoroughly worsted by their adversaries, were in no hurry to come to an open combat, although they exceeded their enemies three times in number; they therefore formed an entrenched camp at Paniput, and awaited the onset of the Affghans, who far some days merely hovered around their position and cut off their supplies. Abdallah, at last, weary of such dilatory work, made a resolute assault upon their defences, but after fighting valiantly for some time, was forced to retire without gaining any important advantage. This encouraged the Mahrattas, who, being still despoiled of their supplies, resolved once more to try their fate in an open field of battle; Abdallah but wanted this. He immediately drew up his forces, and waited with a stern tranquillity the impetuous attack of his foes, who, in their usual manner, advanced with great rapidity, shouting their terrific war-cry and blackening the plain with their multitudes.

When they came within a short distance of his line, Abdallah give orders for the cavalry to charge, which they did so effectually that the light horse of his antagonist were forced off the field, and a general rout immediately ensued. 22,000 prisoners, 56,000 horses, and an immense booty were taken by the victorious Affghans, and Abdallah advanced to and entered Delhi; but nobly contenting himself with his acknowledged superiority, he left Ali Gohur in possession of his kingdom, and returned to Cabul.

We left Paniput on the 25th, and soon found that rich cultivation only extended its influence in the immediate neighbourhood of the city; for as we advanced, jungle claimed the tracts on either side of the road for its own. We reached Garondah at eight o'clock, where our camp was pitched in a very pretty grove of date-trees and not far from the village, which though merely a collection of mud huts, can boast of possessing in its environs an extremely handsome caravanserai. A lofty gateway, flanked on either side by very peculiarly constructed towers surmounted with cupolas, points out its entrance, its area being enclosed by a high embattled wall with bastions at its angles. The whole, though built of a reddish freestone, is considerably dilapidated, but the bastions more so than any other part, and their remains testify that in former days they had been adorned with open circular galleries covered in by domes. A high mound stretches out in front of the caravanserai, from whence a good view of the country is to be had; but beyond a few clumps of trees, interspersed amongst the dense jungle, there is nothing to break the monotony of the scene.

26th January.—We reached Kurnal this morning after a march of about twelve miles over a very excellent road, though it became swampy as we neared the city. At the eighth mile we crossed Feroze Shah's Canal by a good bridge overhung by a few handsome peepul trees. The glimpse I got of the town of Kurnal as we wound beneath its walls rather disappointed me; for except one handsome mosque, I did not see another building to attract my curiosity; nor do the cantonments appear much more prepossessing, as the bungalows are inferior to those at many other stations, and the compounds are bare, and in most instances guiltless of having anything approaching to the semblance of a flower-garden. Our camp was pitched on the parade-ground in front of the foot artillery quarters, which are excellent and not far from the church, which is almost opposite to them. The cantonments are of considerable extent, having barracks for the horse artillery on the left flank, and others for a Queen's regiment on the right. At present, however, the number of troops in the station is far short of its full complement, as the whole of the artillery, both horse and foot, one regiment of cavalry, and one of infantry, have either joined "the army of the Indus," or are on duty with the Governor-General, who is now returning by the way of Khytul from his interview with Runjeet Singh. Colonel Shelton, who arrived three days ago with the 44th, at present commands.

Kurnal, though an ancient city, cannot boast of much celebrity, except as being the spot where the cruel Nadir Shah gained a victory over the Moguls in 1739, chiefly through the instrumentality of traitors in the camp of the dissolute Emperor Mahomed, as the army of the latter under the orders of the brave Dowran, was gaining the day when that general was obliged to withdraw from the field on receiving a wound which soon after proved mortal. The command then devolved on his brother Mozuffir, who attended by a train of valiant nobles, charged through the Persians so gallantly that they penetrated even to the very tent of Nadir Shah. Here, however, for want of being supported, they were cut to pieces; twenty-seven officers of distinction falling on that small spot, and 10,000 of the common soldiers being slain on the field of battle. This event gave Nadir Shah the possession of Delhi, where he soon after issued orders for that fearful massacre, in which no less than 100,000 persons of all ages, sexes, and conditions, were unmercifully butchered.

During the two days we remained at Kurnal, the weather was extremely fine, and the atmosphere so very clear that the snowy and lower ranges of the Himalayah were visible from dawn of day to nightfall. The view of these majestic mountains from our encampment was superb; the mighty peaks of Gungootri and Jumnootri, which I had visited with such intense pleasure in 1835, forming the most conspicuous part of the prospect, and deserving from their very lofty appearance to be the sources of such magnificent rivers as the Ganges and Jumna.

KURNAL TO LODIANAH

W E struck camp on the 28th a little before sunrise, and, even with a guide, had at that early hour some difficulty in gaining the Lodianah road, which was at first but very indistinctly defined from the surrounding open country; it was afterwards better marked out, and on passing the village of Azimgurh was raised some feet above the neighbouring plain, which in the rainy season must be a perfect lake. Azimgurh is enclosed by a high brick wall, pierced with loopholes for musketry, with a tower bastion here and there to add to its security; and opposite to the principal gateway is a large tank with a flight of steps leading to its then unruffled waters, received on their glassy surface the reflections of the village and surrounding scenery. At its northern extremity is a large and fortified caravanserai, with four handsome turrets at the angles of its lofty embattled wall, and defended by a deep ditch which encircled it, though at present only partially filled with water. We reached Leelokeerie, which is about eleven miles from Kurnal, at half-past seven, and pitched our camp just beyond the extremity of the village, which is small and protected by a mud wall. Two or three lofty buildings stand in the centre of it, and are evidently intended as watch-towers whence a good look-out may be kept.

In the afternoon, I strolled to a village situated on an eminence about a mile and a half distant, as I expected I should have from it a good view of the surrounding country; nor was I disappointed, though little was to be seen but the Dhak jungle, except where here and there a few patches of bright green verdure adjacent to a village pointed out the cultivated spots and relieved the prospect. Circular towers, similar to those at Leelokeerie, constructed either of brick or mud, overlooked the neighbouring district and stood in the midst of every collection of huts, which as far as I could observe was invariably enclosed by a mud wall; thereby plainly indicating that the protected Sikh states, which we had entered this morning, are or have been at no distant period subjected to the nightly prowlings of predatory marauders. Captain C.'s treasure party, with an addition of half a troop of cavalry to its escort, is again encamped alongside.

29th.—As there was a considerable march before us this morning, we were early in our saddles, and fortunately had an excellent road, over which the guns rolled without much exertion to the horses. It continued to be raised above the adjacent lands, in some parts higher than in others, and a deep ditch on either side served to drain off the water. The country around was still a repetition of the same Dhak jungle and long grass until we approached Thanesur, where it was lost amidst rich cultivation and extensive groves of mango trees. In one of the latter, on the opposite side of the town, our camp found a refreshing shelter from the rays of the noon-day sun.

As we passed through the city, the road led us immediately beneath the walls of a curious and antiquated fort, with numerous lofty towers, both circular and square, almost close to each other, and which, from their irregular appearance, imparted a wildness to the building that carried us back to the ages of barbarity. Thanesur, however, has the reputation of being not only one of the most ancient cities in Hindoostan, but also one of the most holy; and it was its far famed sanctity that in the year 1011, brought down upon it the vengeance of the mighty Mahmood, who, it is asserted, delighted more in the name of the "Destroyer of Idols," than in all the numerous victories he gained. When the Hindoos heard that this great conqueror was on his way from Ghuzni with the avowed purpose of despoiling their temples, they were seized with consternation, immediately sent deputies to assure him that he should be paid the annual revenues of the city if he would but spare their images. Nothing, however, could deter Mahmood from his purpose, and the only reply he deigned to give to the ambassadors was that, with the help of God, he was determined to root out of India the abominable worship of idols. On hearing this the whole country, from Delhi to Lahore, rose up in arms; but Mahmood was too quick for them, and before they could collect in sufficient numbers to oppose his progress, he had entered Thanesur, plundered it, and demolished all the idols, with the exception of Jugsoom, the largest and most holy, which he sent to Ghuzni, where, after stripping it of all the ornaments, he ordered the head to be cut off, and the body to be cast on the highway.

Independent of the interest excited by the antiquity of the place, Thanesur can boast of possessing prettier spots in its vicinity than are usually to be met with in this part of the provinces. One of the most beautiful is a large tank, crossed at its extremity by a dilapidated bridge, having on one side a small green island, covered with trees, whose autumnal tints were reflected on the water; and on the other an elegantly shaped temple, dedicated to Mahadeo, where, at the time I visited it, several devotees were performing their religious rites. Close to our encampment, too, was an old Mussulman tomb in ruins, surrounded by a few palm-trees, whose tops were upreared high above the dark foliage of the mango grove in which it was embedded: whilst remains of fallen shafts and columns were strewed around, and betokened that, at one time, it was deficient neither in beauty nor elegance.

30th.—Soon after quitting Thanesur, we forded the river Sarsutty, now merely a small stream, but which, in the rainy season, swells to an impassable torrent that subsides as rapidly as it rises. Pursuing our course along a tolerably good road, in an hour we reached rather a deep nullah called the Choorah, which we crossed, and from thence quietly pursued our way for some miles, until we fell in with a couple of ragged Mussulmans, driving a low platform cart, to which was harnessed a regular Rozinante. Being a little in advance of my detachment, and perceiving their horse was inclined to be restive, I cautioned them to keep out of our way, but, instead of attending to my advice, or, not being able to guide the animal, they all at once took up a position in the very centre of the road. The guns by this time had come up, and the troop-horses no sooner saw a strange face, than they set up a tremendous snorting and neighing, which, added to the clanking of the chains on the harness, so dumb-foundered the spare steed, that he in his bewilderment dashed against our leaders, who, nothing loth, immediately prepared for action, and launched out at him most unmercifully with their heels. Rozinante, not approving of this warm reception, reared up, whirled round, tilted out one of his fare, and then scampered off as fast as his terror allowed him. The other, who kept his seat uncommonly well, after a short time succeeded in pulling up his racer, and just in time too, for one more step would have immersed them both in the ditch. At this moment, the individual who was capsized, having been rather more frigh-tened than hurt, jumped up and joined his friend with all the alacrity he was master of, and they both, on the guns again approaching, had the precaution to lay hold of their nag's bit until we were safely out of reach. Not long after this adventure, we met a double-bodied ruth (car) covered with bright scarlet cloth, and drawn by a pair of horses, handsomely harnessed in the Hindustani manner. It was preceded by a couple of armed outriders, fancifully accoutred, and the turn-out evidently formed the equipage of a wealthy native. As the curtains had loopholes, and were closely drawn, it was apparent the conveyance was occupied by females, and being unwilling another scene should occur, similar to that I have just related, I directed them to draw up on one side of the road, till we had passed by: which they did, though with no very good grace, as the outriders seemed to think it was an act unbecoming their dignity. A mile from this we wound round the city of Shahabad, which is large, and possesses some good houses. Amongst the most prominent are the residences of four rajahs, whose domains overlook the whole of the town, and are so polished with chunam, that from a distance they glittered like marble. Our march was one of fifteen miles, and the country, as we passed along, showed more cultivation than we had seen for many a day: but, notwithstanding, the villages have greatly increased in number. Much of the Dhak jungle and long grass still exists, and affords shelter for game of every description. At one spot, where it was rather denser than usual, we disturbed a couple of antelopes, who dashed out of their cover, bounded aloft, and apparently happy in their liberty, were soon lost to sight. Our camp was pitched close to the river Morkunda, now a small and silently flowing stream.

January 31st.—At half-past four we left Shahabad, this morning, but had scarcely proceeded a mile when rain fell; gradu-ally increasing in heaviness until we reached the town of Amballa, sixteen miles distant, and then, down it poured in torrents. Fortunately, our march was over a very excellent road along which cultivation extended its cheerful aspect on either side, with scarcely an exception. A young plantation of trees, many being covered with straw to protect them from the frost, lined the approach for two or three miles before we reached the city, and close to the gate by which we entered it, is a large pucka tank, in excellent repair, having a flight of ornamental steps leading to the clear and translucent water with which it is filled. The bazaar is some miles in extent, and composed of two streets at right angles with one another; most of the houses in it being of late construction, and their uniformity, except where a few of the richer Baboos have increased their residences to the height of two stories, is considerable for a native town. These latter are plastered with the finest chunam, decorated with paintings of various devices, in much better taste than is usually displayed on such occasions; and in front of almost every shop are richly-carved wooden verandahs, with fretted arches beneath which the merchants can display their wares, without being exposed to the influence of the sun, or the vicissitudes of the rainy season.

A mud wall and parapet, in excellent repair, surrounds the city, through which we passed, and found our encamping ground marked out beneath a grove of mango trees, close to the western gateway. Not a tent, however, of any description, had arrived, and I had to wait a considerable time in this anything but comfortable plight, before my advanced marquee, well soaked, the camels weary and drooping under its weight, slowly appeared in sight, and was, after some delay, unpacked, and eventually pitched. Cheerless and uncomfortable, however, was the prospect its interior afforded, for, the ground being low, a pool of water occupied each of its corners, in spite of all the baling that had taken place. It was, nevertheless, some degrees better than the shelter of a dripping tree, under which I had been standing for two or three hours, perusing, as well as the large drops of rain would allow me, various letters I had received, one of the number being an official from Colonel Wade, informing me of his having left Lahore on the 13th instant, and enclosing a route of ten marches from Lodianah to that place, which he wishes me to take. At twelve o'clock the treasure party, looking as miserable as half-drowned fowls, reached their encampment, having been eight hours accomplishing this march. Their tents and baggage had arrived before them; but the greater portion of the latter was so well drenched, that on going over to see the officers in the evening, after the rain had been blown over by a strong wind, I found an unfortunate ensign strutting up and down with his nether man encased in a *table cloth,* for want of a drier article to put on, and their canvass abodes, inside and out, covered with counterpanes, sheets, and dresses, hung up to catch the last ray of a watery-looking sunset.

February Ist, 1840.—I had not long betaken myself to rest last night, when I was disturbed by an animal of some kind or another sniffing at my face; and on opening my eyes, I descried, by the light of a small lamp, a huge Pariah dog staring at me with the most perfect nonchalance. A boot being the nearest missile at hand, was forth-with hurled at the offender's head, and it had the effect of driving him out of the tent, at least for a time; but I had no sooner composed myself to sleep, than in he came again, and awoke me by his exertions to get at some meat which was stowed away at the bottom of a kajour. The other boot having quickly followed the course of its predecessor, out bolted the dog once more; and being now in hopes that my tormentor had taken his departure for good, I was soon in the arms of Morpheus. Next morning, however, my khidmatgar (table attendant) come in with a long face to report that a round of salted beef (which I had always regarded as a stand-by in case of provisions falling short) had disappeared, but in what manner he did not know, as he had carefully put it away the previous evening, and to ensure its safety, had placed my writing-desk and other heavy materials above the package in which it was kept. I was now aware that my friend of the canine species must have paid me another visit; but how he could have removed such ponderous articles, as well as have carried off the beef, which much itself have weighed some fourteen or fifteen pounds, is a mystery to me: but I have considered Pariah dogs capable of perpetrating any theft ever since I caught one in the act of running off with my milk-jug, while marching between Cawnpore and Agra, in 1832. My neighbours in the treasure escort had been still severer sufferers; for Captain C. had been despoiled of a ham and a leg of mutton, and Lieutenant S. of half a dozen loaves of bread, and there is no doubt but the robbers all belonged to one tribe.

The troopers' hackeries (carts) did not arrive till ten last night; and as their culinary utensils and drinking vessels were packed on them, they were obliged to go without any food, except a little "cherbeena," or parched grain, with which they managed to stay the cravings of their appetites. I was therefore necessitated to defer my march till one in the after-noon, that they might cook something of a meal; and whilst they were busy at this operation, I walked to the gates of the town, where crowds of people were passing to and fro. The traffic at Amballa must be considerable, as most of the in-goers and out-comers I observed were mahajuns (cloth-merchants), and buneas (dealers in grain), the greater number being on foot, though a few of the richer and better dressed indulged in the expense of a half-fed tattoo, whose strength was scarcely equal to carry the fat load under which it laboured. As I was amusing myself scanning the features of the various individuals who came across my observation, two handsome Hindustani Ruths, with the purdahs closely drawn, entered the city. They were preceded by a couple of horsemen gaily caparisoned, and armed with matchlocks, and followed by a large sawarrie similarly accoutred, and who, with their prancing horses and glittering weapons, formed a very imposing cortege. I could not ascertain to whom they belonged, but most probably to the Patialah Rajah, whose capital is situated fifteen miles to the south-west.

The troopers having at length dispatched their meal, the "mount" was sounded, and we proceeded on our march to Rajpoora. Nothing could be more beautiful than the day: the sun shone brilliantly, the atmosphere was perfectly clear, and the late heavy rain having washed the dust off the trees, imparted a freshness to their leaves which was truly delightful. As soon as we left the environs of Amballa behind us, a lovely view of the lowest range of the Himalayahs burst upon our sight, and appeared as near as the Mussoorie hills do from Deyrah. About the third mile we forded the river Cuggur, now considerably swollen and of some breadth; but we crossed it without any accident, and shortly afterwards passed, on our right, in the distance, a very picturesque ruin situated on a slight eminence, and not unlike a dilapidated English castle. A small bridge surrounded by trees was close to it, and the prospect being backed by the magnificent mountains, formed a scene which will not be easily effaced from my memory.

At Rajpoora we encamped in a pretty spot, close to a large pond fringed with peepul and other trees. The town is surrounded by a lofty brick wall, with only one entrance; and opposite to this, and at a short distance off, is a very fine and extensive caravanserai, ornamented with numerous turrets and bastions, and having in front of its gateway a circular brick tower, which seems to block up all entrance, whilst its uncouth and heavy appearance contrasts strangely with the light and elegant architecture of the Serai. Soon after the duties of my camp were concluded, the tahseeldar, or head man of the village, came to pay his respects, attended by a large posse of people armed with spears and matchlocks; and so considerable was his train, that, together with the stately manner in which he advanced, I was led to suppose he was a man of considerable consequence, if not a rajah. However, I was soon set to rights on this head, and received him according to his station. He was a well-dressed, stout little man, with very handsome features, and extremely polite and civil; but his language was at first so intermixed with Persian that I had some difficulty in understanding him: this, however, he no sooner perceived than he brought his conversation into Hindustani. Amongst his followers was a Sikh in Runjeet Sihgh's service, — a fine-looking man, with an aquiline nose, a large and flowing black beard, and moustaches, who told me he had just returned from Lahore, where he had been to join the Maharajah's grand camp, formed to receive the Governor-General; that he is an officer with sixty-seven horsemen under him, and that he is allowed two rupees per diem for his pay and subsistence. He was in the action at Jumrood, near the entrance to the Khyber Pass, in which Hurri Singh, one of Runjeet's chief omrahs, lost his life a few years ago; and he there received a desperate sabre cut on the head, for which he obtained a large present. "The Maharajah," he added, "is extremely liberal to those who are wounded in his service; and if he hears of a sirdar failing to reward such, he immediately disgraces him." As he had been to Peshawur, I ascertained from him that it is 250 koss, or a month's march, from Lahore; but he could give me no information about Colonel Wade's movement.

February 2d.—We had a short and uninteresting march of eight miles and a half to Putarsie, where our camp was pitched on a slight eminence, and whence there was a pretty view of the country, which seemed to be covered with extensive jungle, broken here and there into patches of cultivation, and groves of large trees. In the afternoon a dapper little self-conceited Sikh, with a happy good-humoured countenance, came up to me as I was inspecting my stables, and made a low salaam. He was dressed in a bright Madras chintz, closely fitted to the body, with a crimson and yellow silk sword-belt slung across his right shoulder: and in place of a turban a loose piece of crimson silk was tastefully disposed on his head, and so managed that a portion of it hung down his back, and fluttered in the breeze. He introduced himself by telling me he was a servant of the Patialah Rajah, and owner of a village two miles distant, adding, he hoped he might be permitted to look at the troop horses, whose size and strength he appeared much struck with, remarking "a few such might be picked out of the 4,000 sowars in his Prince's service, but certainly not many." After conversation on different subjects he took his leave; and in spite of his being so very well satisfied with himself and his appearance, I must do him the justice to say, he was a civil and merry little fellow, and did no harm with it all. Towards evening four of the rajah's sepoys came to take part of the night duties of the camp, being stationed here by his orders for the express purpose of forming a guard to the sahib-log (European gentlemen) when they travel this way.

February 3d.—We moved this morning to Sirhind, about

nine miles distant: the road after leaving Putarsie being a perfect swamp lined on either side by a belt of thick jungle, only broken in one place by an inconsiderable village of the meanest order, and this continued until we approached our encampment, when fields of cultivation usurped its place. We entered the town by a large bridge which spanned an extensive jheel, and as there were some fine trees, and a few ruined tombs and temples scat-tered around in its neighbourhood, the scene altogether was extremely picturesque. We found our tents pitched in an open area, surrounded by small plantations of trees, through which might be seen cupolas and domes erected over the ashes of departed greatness, and covered with the mouldering stains of age.

Sirhind is of great antiquity, and during the days of the Patan and early Mogul emperors was always the seat of a government which controlled a large tract of country; its surveillance being invariably entrusted to omrahs of tried fidelity, and of the highest rank. It was also a city of the largest magnitude, but the few houses now inhabited might be comprised in a very small circumference, and they are surrounded by a melancholy scene of ruins. Mausoleums, almost in as mouldered a state as the remains which they cover, are innumerable; and though some are, from their prodigious solidity (one close to the road having a wall of masonry no less than eight feet thick) still standing, their dilapidated state tells that ages must have elapsed since they were first erected, and time is fast levelling even these with the ground. In the outskirts extensive brick-kilns, from long disuse, are now covered with verdure, and on some, large trees having found sufficient nurture for their growth, have converted these once ugly and bare masses into, comparatively speaking, beautiful knolls.

February 4th.—This morning we marched to Kunha-ke-serai, and a more uninteresting country than that we have left behind us can scarcely be conceived. Nothing was to be seen but a flat and sandy plain, covered occasionally with scanty herbage; and as for trees, it would have been no difficult matter to have counted all that came within the sweep of our vision. We, however, fared better where we halted, our encampment being close to a very pretty grove of baubul trees, whose yellow-scented blossoms threw a sweet fragrance around. The village of Kunha does not possess many houses, but has nevertheless a small fort, situated on a slight eminence. To this I walked in the afternoon, but the dirt and filth in its neighbourhood disgusted me so much, that I was fain to make a hasty retreat, and remove from odours not quite so pleasant as those thrown forth by the baubul flowers.

February 5th.—A long march of fifteen miles, over a road at times extremely heavy and sandy, brought us to Dowra, where there is a caravanserai situated on a hill; and below, on one side, a collection of small hovels, scarcely deserving the appellation of a village. A few old ruined tombs and, temples are scattered towards the south, from which it appears that in former days a town of, some kind or another existed here; but the remains are of no magnitude, nor is there much to remark about them. On our arrival, a slight shower of rain fell, and soon after blew over; but in the evening we had a violent storm of thunder and very vivid lightning, accompanied for several hours with such a deluge of rain that the tents could scarcely ward it off, and indeed through some it actually forced its way.

February 6th.—We quitted Dowra-ke-serai at five A.M., the rain of last night being succeeded by most lovely weather, and having rendered the atmosphere so clear that we had a beautiful view of the snowy range to the north of the Kooloo Hills, which differ greatly from that to the eastward, inasmuch that there are fewer peaks and a more solid wall-like appearance about it. It continued visible for some hours after sunrise, displaying new and fresh beauties as the rising orb of day gradually touched with a crimson light the more prominent ridges, and threw them out from the greater retiring mass. On approaching Lodianah, the road became as sandy as the most thoroughbred desert camel could have wished for; and on descending to what seemed to have once been the bed of a river, (most probably an old channel of the Sutledge,) we found the accumulated waters of last night's rain to be above knee-deep. Entering Lodianah we passed through the bazaar, which is new and good, but not to be compared with that at Amballa, either for its cleanliness of appearance or neatness of construction. Its inhabitants are chiefly Cashmerians and Affghans, who migrated to this spot when Shah Zeman and Shah Shoojah, the ex-kings of Cabul, fled for protection to the British government, and the latter of whom is now on his way to be restored to his throne by the Army of the Indus. Leaving the bazaar, we came to the cantonments, which are not very inviting; the bungalows in general being small, and having nothing about their exteriors to recommend them. Our camp was pitched in front of the horse artillery lines, and not far from the burying-ground, which is already well crowded with tombstones. During the course of the day I made some requisite official calls, and have ascertained I am to be joined by two companies of the 20th native infantry, who are to escort 250,000 rupees to Colonel Wade's camp, and the whole detachment is to be commanded by Captain Ferris* of that regiment.

*Now Brevet Major Ferris, C.B.

February 7th.—Received instructions to be in readiness
to march to-morrow, with discretionary power to choose
my own time for leaving Lodianah.

FROM LODIANAH TO LAHORE

February 8th.—AFTER a most flat, dull, and unprofitable march, we reached Ghonspore at four P. M., having left the cantonments of Lodianah at half-past one, and encamped opposite to a small but unfinished temple, covered with thatch to preserve it from rain, and situated in the midst of a pretty clump of trees.

February 9th.—Another uninteresting day's journey to Siddum, twelve miles and a half, the monotony of the march broken only by the road, as it neared the village, winding through a small plantation of trees, many of which were growing on a slight eminence, and imparted to the scene so truly an English aspect, that it was impossible to regard the spot without pleasure.

February 10th.—A continuation of the same uninviting country brought us to Dhur'm Kote, the road leading to it being execrably bad, and not less than sixteen or seventeen miles in distance from Siddum. We arrived at the termination of our fatiguing journey just in time to witness a marriage procession depart, for the purpose of fetching and escorting the bride to her future home. It consisted of a band of drums and cymbals, two ruths crowded with silks, and several gaily caparisoned horsemen, who displayed their equestrian qualifications to the amusement and gratification of the bystanders. One of these sowars was a particularly well dressed and fine-looking fellow with a short red tuft tastily adjusted in his turban, and a leathern shield studded with brass bosses slung across his back, and half concealed by his snow-white flowing vestments. Being by far the most imposing-looking individual in the cortege, we at once decided that he was the bridegroom, and we were somewhat confirmed in our opinion, as immediately behind him followed a man bearing a chattah or umbrella, covered with coloured paper and talc, and having long pendants hanging from its circular edge, the "tout ensemble" being somewhat in semblance to a crown. This elegant (!) piece of workmanship, intended to be held over the bride as soon as she makes her appearance, was borne aloft with an air of pride and display that plainly showed it was regarded as no ordinary production. The approaching Benedick, however, seemed so well satisfied with himself that there was no doubt he considered his *own person* to be the centre of attraction; and indeed so much occupied had he been with decorating himself that he had quite forgotten the condition of his steed; which was dirty in the extreme, and looked as if it had lately enjoyed itself by taking a good roll in the mud, whereby nearly every vestige of its primitive hue, white, was obliterated. In this array, and followed by the admiring gaze of the multitude, the procession moved on, and was soon lost behind some trees that concealed its further progress.

Dhur'm Kote is of some size, but contains no building of any interest. Opposite to it is a mud fort, defended by bastions, with a lofty building in the centre, which overlooks the county, and may be called the keep. In the evening Lieut. Rattray*, Ferris's subaltern, joined us, having ridden out from Lodianah.

February 11th.—We were not a little annoyed this morning to find our guide, instead of taking us towards Harike, as he was engaged to do, was quietly piloting us along the high road to Ferozepore; and our mistake, unfortunately, was not discovered until we had advanced many miles beyond where we ought to have turned off. The fellow, moreover, on being interrogated, candidly confessed his ignorance of the direction in which Harike lay, and indeed appeared to have been thrust into his present office without any trouble being taken to ascertain if he was capable of performing its duties or not. Nay, it is more than, probable the Jemadar of Dhur'm Kote pressed him for the service, and considered, that by supplying a *man*, no matter what his qualifications were, he had done *his* part towards furthering us on our journey. On questioning some residents of a village near at hand, they told us of a cross road that would eventually lead us into the desired route; and, unpleasant as this appeared to be, we had only the alternative of proceeding by it, or else of retracing our steps nearly all the distance to Dhur'm Kote. Everything considered, we resolved upon trying the former plan and, having obtained a fresh guide from among our informers, we recommenced our march. The bye-road was by no means so bad as we expected; but after some time, its marks gradually became fainter, and less distinclty defined, until, on descending into a hollow, (evidently an old bed of the Sutledge,) it terminated

*This was my first acquaintance with poor Rattray,—a most brave and gallant officer, with whom I afterwards lived on terms of the most friendly intimacy. On his arrival at Cabul he was appointed a political agent in Kohistan, where, at the commencement of the fatal insurrection in Affghanistan, he was most cruelly and treacherously murdered. For particulars, I must refer the reader to Lieut. Eyre's admirably written work, pp. 70,71.

in a foot-path. On ascending the bank, nothing was to be seen but an extensive plain, covered with tall grass, into the depths of which we could trace the meandering path losing itself. Conceiving this to be utterly impracticable for wheeled carriages, the detachment was halted, whilst Rattray and I, taking a trumpeter with us, scoured the country in the direction our guide showed us we were to go. After much difficulty, we found a sufficiently wide opening for the guns to pass through: so ordering the advance to be sounded, the troops moved on, and, after numerous twistings and windings we succeeded in creeping through this belt of jungle grass, which must have been nearly a mile in breadth. After quitting it, we had to make a direct cut across the country; but the impediments we met with were few, and not difficult to surmount. At last we reached the high-road, which in a short time led us to Futtehgurh, a large fortified village, with a lofty keep, three stories high, in its centre, and close to which we found our tents. The inhabitants, who, it is evident, have seldom seen Europeans, crowded the walls as we passed by, and greeted us with a dialect, which even sepoys had some difficulty in understanding.

February 12th.—Last night the thieves paid us a visit; but our sentries being on the alert, they were scared before any thing of value was stolen. A Bunnea, however, lost his drinking vessel, in spite of the the strenuous efforts he made to recover it, for, being aroused, he had scampered after the rascal who took it, and seized him by the head. The rogue's turban being greasy, it slipped off, and he made good his retreat with the stolen article, which was of more value than the dirty headpiece proved to be on examination. Such a row was made in the camp, that it disturbed us all; and the hubbub consequent on the conversation arising out of this adventure was long in subsiding sufficiently to admit of our again sleeping.

We left Futtehgurh at a quarter to six, and had a capital road the whole way to Makhoo, which may be about eight miles and a half distant. It is a considerable village, surrounded by a mud wall, with a broad street running through the centre; and nigh to it is a cutcha fort, with large bastions, in good repair, and capable of making a stout resistance against anything but artillery. The interior wall of this is about twenty-two feet high, and pierced with loopholes for musketry; and before it is a covered-way with a parapet, some twelve or fourteen feet in height, and with apertures for defence also. We had to wind round the covered-way for nearly half the extent of the fort before entering the gateway, through which we were admitted by a wicket of small dimensions, to a roofed passage that evidently forms part of the shelter which the place affords to man and beast. In the centre of the fort there is a large mud building, to which access is obtained by means of a ladder, and as it is also pierced for musketry, it may be regarded as the citadel to which the inhabitants would retreat as a last resort. One side of the area is occupied by a long range of stables, and the other by circular huts, in the shape of gigantic bee-hives, constructed of straw bands firmly tied together, and covered with mud to keep out the rain. These contain the supplies of the garrison, and under the bastions are small apartments for its accommodation. It belongs to the Aliwoola rajah, as do many of the forts and villages we have seen since our departure from Lodianah.

In the evening, Ferris and I rode down to the Ghat, to see what facilities there were in readiness for crossing the Sutledge tomorrow; but on our way we met with a sepoy, who had been despatched early in the morning to collect the boats, &c., and who was returning to inform us that the authorities on the other side of the river have refused us a passage, as no "purwunnah."*

* A written order.

from the Maharajah, directing our admittance into the Punjab had been received by them. We, nevertheless, rode on, and on our reaching the banks, we sent a message to the chief at Harike, the village situated opposite to the Ghat, requesting him to cross and confer with us; but, after waiting an hour, our messenger came back, accompanied by a common sowar, whom the insolent fellow had sent over in his stead, and to whom, beyond a question, F. would have nothing to say. We accordingly returned to Makhoo, and a letter was immediately despatched to the assistant political agent at Lodianah, informing him of the treatment we had met with, and the delay that was likely to ensue. Game both yesterday and to-day was very plentiful, and the black partridges were particularly numerous.

February 13.—Moved our camp this morning to the banks of the Sutledge, that we may be in readiness to cross immediately the purwunnah arrives. The commandant (as he is called) of Harike is evidently afraid we shall attempt a passage before the order reaches him, as he has kept all the boats on his own side of the river, and will not allow even one to be used for transporting the merchants' hackeries across, and which, in consequence, are collecting on either bank in vast numbers. The chief of Makhoo, a very civil man, who accompanied us to our present halting ground, constructed a raft of reeds and other such frail materials, and wafted himself across to Harike, where he had an interview with the "commandant," and pointed out to him the incivility of his conduct, in not waiting upon us in person yesterday. This brought him over, attended by a numerous train, carrying spears, bows and arrows, and other weapons of defence, he himself being accoutred in a suit of yellow silk, with buff paejamahs, or trousers, made from the skin of a deer. During the interview, he excused his previous behaviour by pleading illness, but this we had every reason to believe was a mere pretext got up for the occasion, as our sepoys who were sent across, saw no symptoms of sickness about him, nor did he then, though he spoke to them, allude to it. He was soon dismissed with instructions to acquaint us immediately he got the Maharajah's "purwunnah," and he was told his conduct had not only been reported to the British authorities, but would most likely reach his Highness Runjeet Singh's ears also; information he was by no means grateful for, especially the latter part of it, as he knew if it once got to Lahore, he would, more than probably, lose his present appointment. As he was leaving, he asked permission to ply his boats across; but with this he was acquainted we had nothing to do, and that he might please himself on the subject. Accordingly, in the afternoon, *one* solitary boat was to be seen travelling backwards and forwards, which shows the old fellow is still suspicious and afraid to send more, lest we should make use of them ourselves.

Evening closed in with a lowering sky, and shortly after sunset, a severe storm of thunder, rain, and lightning set in, and lasted two hours. It was, however, very grateful to us, as during the whole day, thick clouds of sand were incessantly driving into our tents, and powdering every thing as if with salt. The rain effectually put a stop of this.

February 14.—We are still on the same encamping ground, and no message as yet, has been sent from Harike, to inform us we may proceed: so how long we are to be detained in this unpropitious spot there is no guessing at. The single boat still plies across the river, which is now about five hundred yards broad, the Beas flowing into it a short distance above; but, in the rainy season, it must average from one mile and a half to two miles. Porpoises are to be seen playing in its waters; and to while away the tediousness of our detention, we are fain to amuse ourselves with watching their antics, as well as to observe the embarkation and disembarkation of passengers from the solitary ferry-boat. From the specimens it has brought over, we have unanimously pronounced the Sikhs to be a fine handsome-looking race, with a cast of countenance resembling that of the Jews; their manliness of appearance being increased by the magnificent beards and moustachios which they wear. Their fondness for showy and gaudy colours is excessive, especially amongst the higher class; and usually consists of a yellow, orange, crimson, or other bright-coloured robe, with a turban to correspond: most of these articles being composed of silk stuffs. The majority carried a spear or sword, and shield; and a few wore a curious sort of plume, about a foot high, the top of which, from its arrangement, very much resembles the flower of the cockscomb, but the remaining part being bare, gives it too much of a ragged appearance to look well. Of the females we saw but few, and from the carefulness with which they enveloped their faces, as well as from the stiffness of their gait, we concluded they were but too happy to conceal their age behind their mantles.

February 15.—Near 4 P.M., yesterday after-noon the welcome purwunnah, containing orders for our admittance into the Sikh country, was received, and we instantly commenced the passages of the Sutledge, which, after a lapse of three hours, was accomplished without any loss or difficulty. We reached our encampment at Harike a little after seven, it being situated about a mile and a half from the Ghat, and the road leading to it being for the first quarter of the way exceedingly heavy and sandy. Our baggage, tents, and such like articles, did not come up till past nine, at which fashionable hour we sat down to dinner; and a sumptuous one it was, too, considering time, place, and circumstances, though perhaps a *leetel* too much of the river's sand formed one part of its ingredients; but this was to be expected, as our kitchen, constructed on the bank, with only the shelter of a thin mat, had been exposed to a windy day; to hungry men, however, it did not much matter.

At ten A.M. a Sikh chief, attended by a large rabble, and mounted on a white horse, visited the commanding officer. He was dressed from top to toe in bright green silk, edged with gold lace, and across his body was slung an embroidered belt of the same costly material, to which a sword was attached, whilst a shield hung negligently behind his back. He was considered of sufficient importance to be entitled to a chair, and accordingly one was given to him; but two of his followers, men of venerable appearance, with long white beards, took their seats behind him on the floor of the tent, the others remaining on the outside. In the course of conversation we learnt he is, by the Maharajah's orders, to accompany us as mehmindar to Lahore; but being a man of taciturn disposition, and his language somewhat difficult to understand, we could not gather much information from him, and he was soon permitted to take his leave. He, amongst other things, told us it was the Maharajah's gracious intention to feed the whole camp whilst in his territories.

About noon it became very cloudy, and threatened to rain; but it afterwards cleared up, and the afternoon was beautifully fine, though rendered unpleasant by a strong wind driving a large quantity of dust into our tents. This annoyance, however, abated sufficiently in the evening to admit of Rattray and myself taking a stroll to the village, which consists entirely of mud huts, and is of some size. It is situated close to the banks of the river, the cliffs of which are about forty or fifty feet in height, and very precipitous. Ravines run into the country for some distance, and one is made to answer the purpose of a ditch to the fort, which is hexagonal, with very short curtains, and built of unburnt bricks. It has in the centre a small mud building with a square brick erection on its summit, which serves as a watch-tower.

We were amused here at observing a man making pottery, which he performed in the most simple manner possible. In the centre of a circular hole, two feet and a half deep by as many in diameter, a wooden staff was inserted, and upon this, close to the bottom, but not touching it, was a solid wheel of wood, whilst another of smaller dimensions was fixed nearer to the top. The whole of this apparatus was planted perpendicularly into the ground, and the man, sitting on the edge of the cavity, worked the larger wheel with his foot, whilst with his hands he moulded the clay placed on the smaller one (which was turned with the former) into whatever form he required. We saw him construct a utensil somewhat in the shape of a flower-pot, and he finished it in a very neat manner in less than five minutes. The poor fellow, who was miserably clad, complained bitterly of the cold; but this was not to be wondered at, for, independent of his ragged costume, he had to dip his hands into water every fifteen or twenty seconds, and the weather was very much inclined to be more than chilly in its influence.

February 16.—We left Harike, or Hari-ke-puttum, as it is indifferently called from its ferry, at half-past five, and proceeded along a capital road to Putti. As the night had been frosty, we had a beautiful clear morning without a cloud; and to the north-east there was the magnificent snowy range towering high into the pure air, and forming a prospect that can never satiate the eye by being too often looked at. About the third mile we came to a large baoli, or well, at one end of which a building is erected for the accommodation of travellers, and from whence a flight of steps leads down to an arcade close to the surface of the water. This arcade is finished in a neat and somewhat ornamented style, being decorated with pilasters, and having recesses for lamps, &c. We passed several villages, which became more numerous as we approached Putti, where we halted, and which is a large brick town possessed of many houses two stories high. A lofty wall surrounds it, and where this has fallen into decay it has been repaired with huge lumps of clay carelessly cemented with the same material, and which, together with the tottering state of several of the residences, clearly indicates that the place is gradually being deserted. Close to the city is a fort consisting of square brick enclosure, with bastions at the angles, and surrounded by a mud wall of an hexagonal shape, very similar to that at Harike.

After breakfast Rattray and I walked round the environs of the town, and the first thing we fell in with of any interest was a Persian waterwheel, worked by two bullocks, (though not then at labour,) which must raise a large quantity of water at a time, as the vessels affixed to its circumference were of some size, and very numerous. From this we proceeded to a burying-ground, but whether for Mussulmans or Hindoos we could not make out, as it bore indications of belonging to both. Some of the larger tombs were very neat, and constructed of good materials, and one was peculiar, from having a dome erected on the ground, within another and a larger dome; the inside of the latter being decorated with paintings, or rather devices in colour. Around these, again, were evidently the fresh ashes of burnt bodies, (Hindoos,) on which spots small sticks were placed at the four corners of the graves; those of an older date being marked out by low erections of mud, with a recess in each, sufficiently large to hold a lamp. Leaving the cemetery we ascended a brick kiln, from whence we had a very good view of the city and surrounding country, which is not so highly cultivated as I expected to have seen it; but as trees and brushwood covered it in every direction, it wore a pleasant aspect, and was an agreeable change for the unceasing barrenness that we had latterly been accustomed to on the other side of the Sutledge.

We were joined by an intelligent fakeer, who told us the district belongs to Lena Singh, one of the Maharajah's sirdars, and that the town is composed of nearly half Mussulmans and half Hindoos, with a sprinkling of Sikhs. "Its inhabitants," he concluded, "are peaceful and well-disposed, but the neighbouring villages are infested with thieves and robbers." Two or three ponds of some size lie close to the town, and in the one immediately fronting us was a party of grown-up women bathing themselves without a single article of covering on; nor did our presence seem at all to disconcert them, for they went on with their ablutions as if quite unconscious of the indelicacy of the act. Such, however, is a common occurrence in the Punjab.

We walked in the evening to the shrine of a celebrated saint, who lived in the time of Akbar the Great, and which is kept in excellent repair. An old woman has charge of it, but beyond a word here and there we could not understand her, nor she us. She permitted us to enter the building, and pointed out a tomb nine yards in length, as the spot where his bones are interred, but we could not ascertain from the lady whether this extraordinary grave-stone was also supposed to mark the height of the individual! At the head, and a little to the right, is a large niche with a diminutive balcony, and surmounted by a semicupola, and from the manner in which it was discoloured, there is no doubt but it is used as a receptacle for lamps when the shrine is illuminated. The interior elsewhere is quite plain, and possesses a magnificent echo, and the exterior on the whole is pretty, though disfigured by devices in colours, but these are small, and not to be distinguished from a distance.

February 17th.—Marched to Sursing, which cannot be less than twelve miles and a half over a road not nearly so good as that of yesterday's, though still fair. The whole of the surrounding country was enlivened by cultivation, and the crops appear to be thriving most admirably. Many of the fields which were sown with a grain that bears a flower very similar to that of the mustard, were one sheet of golden yollow, and diffused an odour most fragrant to the olfactory nerves. Occasionally the road became confined, and enclosed with hedges of dry brushwood, which reminded me somewhat of Old England, and more so as the weather is peculiarly mild and pleasant. We passed several villages, and in one place a few buildings that to us appeared to be the country-houses of the wealthy, some of them having large gardens enclosed with high brick walls attached. Our encamping ground to-day was any where but in a pleasant situation; the best spot the camp colourman could select for the purpose being a recently ploughed field, as dusty as one could well wish it.

The village is large, and possesses some lofty brick houses, and near to it are some magnificent bere-trees, the largest by far that any of us had seen in India. As there is a good deal of wood and water in its neighbourhood, there are many pretty spots, and one which would have answered admirably for our camp, we afterwards learnt, is close to the road we take to-morrow. On one side of the town a number of gipsies had taken up their temporary abodes, and were busy at their usual avocation of basket-making. They solicited alms of us, as a matter of course; but as they appeared to be a strapping and thriving race, we did not deem it expedient to accede to their request.

February 18.—We struck camp this morning at 5 A.M., and we had a good road, though one that winded a great deal. Cultivation was even, if possible, more extensive than we had yet seen it, and the villages more numerous. About half way we passed through one which was very regularly built; the mud huts having, at a few feet distance in front, a brick wall some eight or ten feet high, with a low doorway leading to each house, but, strange to say, in no other way connected with the dwellings.

Manihala (where we halted) is situated on an eminence, and has many lofty and narrow houses which appeared from a distance more like towers than anything else, and looked extremely pretty as we approached it. It is divided into two portions by the main road running through the centre, but both are similar in character. We encamped close to a clear tank, in which there is a diminutive island covered with a species of fir-tree, and with so light an appearance as to make one fancy it floated on the surface. An elegant mausoleum is erected near it, and covers the remains of a jemadar of the town, who died four or five years ago, and always resorted to the island as a retreat from the hot winds. The garden, in which is the tomb, is still in good order and now belongs to his son, who, at the time we visited it, was seated in an arbour, and enjoying himself with a party of his friends.

February 19.—We left our ground earlier than usual this morning, that we might enter Lahore an hour or two after sunrise; and as the road the whole of the way was excellent, we accomplished our object. For three or four miles before arriving at the imperial city of the Punjab, the country around presented one scene of ruins, nothing being visible but confused heaps of brick, with here and there a mosque or a mausoleum in a half decayed state, but still bearing traces of former magnificence, and pointing out where one of the most ancient cities in Hindostan had existed. In one of these tombs of a large size and in better repair than the majority, a gang of Akallies (a tribe of religious fanatics peculiar to the Punjab, and of a character approaching to the fakeer of India) had taken up their abode. These people are of low caste; but somehow or another have contrived to obtain a degree of power which renders them formidable; and as on account of their sacred character they are nearly, if not totally, exempted from all punishments for their misdeeds, they have become insolent and over-bearing almost beyond endurance. As we passed by, some of them hurled at us a vocabulary of words which no doubt contained epithets of a most disrespectful nature; but being in a language unknown to us, we were perfectly content to remain in ignorance of their meaning. Captain Ferris seeing a fire in the place, directed his Syce to procure a light for his cigar; but on the man's attempting to take one, the Akallies vociferated loudly and turned him out *sans ceremonie*. They dress somewhat like the fakeer, occasionally besmearing themselves with ashes; but the generality wear more clothes and a conical turban of a peculiar but elegant shape, which they don with much taste; and several suspend on it two or three sharp quoits, which they throw with such great dexterity as to render them at close quarters most formidable weapons.

A mile or two from this spot we reached the Delhi gate of the city, where we intended to have halted; but the total absence of water in its immediate neighbourhood obliged us to move on till we came to a spot that would suit us, and this we found outside the city wall and in front of the Maharajah's place, which consists of a confused but magnificent and extensive heap of buildings, each so different from its fellow that it is impossible to describe its general appearance.

LAHORE

As soon as our camp duties were concluded and the guns parked,
R. and I walked to the palace gateway, which was but a short
distance from our ground, and approached by a long bridge
plastered with white chunam and embellished with several hideous
representations intended for peacocks. At one end of it also, a
bird of the same description with expanded tail is cut out in wood,
and occupies a conspicuous place. As we saw several in their
wild state this morning running about unmolested, I conclude they
are here, as in most other parts of Hindoostan, regarded as sacred.
The gateway, which consists of a tolerably lofty archway with a
tower at each side, is also covered from its summit to its base with
paintings, the greater number taken from the history of Crishna as
related in the Prem Sagur, though a few describe the habits and
peculiarities of the wandering fakeer. The figures are almost all
about one-third the size of life, but with proportions as ludicrous
and absurd as they can well be. In some the eye occupies nearly
the whole side of a face, and in others the head appears as massive
as the body. Here fakeers may be seen with their hands clasped
above their heads, and with finger-nails two or three inches long;

there others standing on one foot, their bodies besmeared with ashes, and their long lank hair streaming over their shoulders in the most offensive state of filth. Crishna's exploits occasionally partake of the ludicrous and disgusting. In one compartment he is portrayed with a milkmaid shampooing his great toe; in another, he is perched up in a tree, from the branches of which depend various articles of dress he has stolen from some *fair* damsels who are refreshing themselves in a limpid stream below, and whose heads and hands, clasped in a supplicatroy manner, appear above water beseeching him to return their apparel, but to no purpose, as he is only laughing at their distress. In a third, he is dashing out the brains of a man with his club; and in a fourth, tearing out the entrails of a prostrate foe with the most brutal ferocity. Having satisfied our curiosity at these wonderful (!) embellishments, we passed beneath the archway and came to the inner gate of the palace; but here we were stopped by a sentry, who forbade our further progress. We remarked, however, that it is *enriched* with paintings of a similar character to those on the first, and though no doubt considered in good taste by the Punjabees, to Englishmen they have a most ridiculous appearance.

Close to the palace there is a large mosque covered in with domes of white marble; but fearing we might be prevented gaining an admission, we deferred visiting it until we shall be accompanied by an influential person with power to pass the numerous guards who are to be met with on every side.

The wall which surrounds the city is constructed of burnt brick, and is in excellent repair. Its height is between thirty-five and forty feet, with circular and angular bastions at intervals, and has in front a covered-way with a brick parapet, and a tolerably broad ditch with a counterscarp of twenty feet. The wall is also pierced with loopholes for musketry, and I believe is further defended by cannon, though I did not observe any. Its circumference must be two or three miles in extent, if not more; and a double set of gates, which are always shut at eight or nine A.M., debar all ingress and egress after those hours. A branch of the river Ravee (the ancient Hydraotes) runs close to it on the west side, but as in the rainy season the main stream unites with this, Lahore may be truly said to be built on the left bank of the river.

Shortly after returning to our tents, Captain F —, who had ridden to Anarcolly to visit a friend of his (Colonel Foulkes) in the Maharajah's service, came back, bringing that officer with him, and who before taking leave insisted that we should all dine with him in the evening. He told us, the salute we had heard as we approached Lahore, were minute guns firing in honour of General Allard, who lately died at Peshawar, and whose body had been brought to the capital for interment, had this morning been removed from his house at Anarcolly to his country residence in the neighbourhood, where it will remain until a suitable grave can be prepared for its reception. On the occasion six regiments of the Maharajah's were paraded for the purpose of paying respect to the memory of the deceased, who was beloved both by natives and Europeans, and whose death has cast a gloom over the city. He breathed his last on the 23rd of January, having suffered for some time from a diseased heart, and his body, wrapped up in numerous cloths, but not embalmed, was placed in a coffin and brought from Peshawar in a conveyance that may be termed a double tonjon. He had numbered fifty-two years, and has left a wife and large family, to whom he was greatly attached, and who are all at present residing in France. His last words were, "What will become of Madame Allard?" His amiable manners had endeared him so much to Runjeet Singh, that his attendants have not yet dared to inform that monarch of his death, lest, as he is still in a precarious state, it might produce a relapse or even more fatal results, for his health has considerably suffered since the Governor-General's visit during the last month. He left Lahore a few days ago to visit Amritsir, and as he travels by very short and easy marches, accounts have been received of a decided improvement having taken place, but he is yet very far from being recovered. During five days he could not lie down to rest for fear of suffocation, his tongue and tonsils having been so weakened by a paralytic attack as to prevent his throwing off the phlegm brought up by a cough except with the greatest difficulty. Intelligence arrived this morning that he had passed a most excellent night, and had derived great benefit from it; and it is a source of great regret to us that he is absent from Lahore at the present time, as another opportunity of seeing and conversing with so celebrated a character may not occur to us.

In the afternoon the Governor of Lahore, who reigns supreme here during the absence of the Maharajah, paid a vist to the commanding officer, and, being a man of consequence, was received with marked attention. His approach being announced, we walked about twenty or thirty paces to meet him; and his alighting from a palanquin, and salaaming, we bowed in return, shook hands, and led him to our tent, where we deposited our worthy burden on a cane-bottomed chair, as no costly ottomans formed part of our camp equipage. He here presented Capt. F. with a "ziafut" of 250 rupees; and after having inquired respectively concerning our healths, the conversation turned upon our march, the state of the Maharajah, and such like topics. Our visitor was a short, elderly, and rather plainly-dressed man, with an intelligent and somewhat amiable cast of countenance; and, as he was the perfect gentleman in his manner, we were altogether much pleased with him. He remained rather better than half an hour, and took his leave with same ceremonies as above mentioned; his palanquin being attended by a number of foot soldiers, carrying matchlocks, and accoutred in a demi-sort of European costume.

In the evening we rode to Anarcolly, the military cantonment of Lahore, to dine (as was agreed upon) with Colonel Foulkes;* but it was so dark when we reached his residence, I had no means of judging of its exterior, further than that it is of some extent, and had the never failing Eastern luxury of a fountain, or, I should say, row of fountains, in the garden. The visitors invited to meet us consisted of nearly all the European officers in Runjeet Singh's army present at Lahore, amounting to five or six in number, with whom we passed a pleasant evening, and from whose conversation I was glad to learn they, in general, thought so well of the Maharajah and his service, though it was not always sunshine with them. Their chief complaint against him, I must add, a very natural one too, is the dilatory manner in which they are paid; for though each officer commanding a cavalry or infantry regiment. receives, or ought to receive, 500 rupees per mensem, months elapse between one payment and another, and they are at this moment several thousands in arrears. For this they do not blame the Maharajah so much as the ministers by whom he is surrounded, and through whom they trace any indifference he shows to them. The same system is pursued towards the men; and Captain S. complained bitterly of the state his corps was, in consequence, reduced to; many of his soldiers being only able to afford a meal every third day, and numbers being without shoes to appear in on parade. These latter he invariably passes into the rear rank, to be out of sight; but he has not yet found a remedy to conceal the attenuated forms of the others. Notwithstanding these

---

*The termination of this officer's career was melancholy in the extreme. During the troubles that ensued on the death of Runjeet Singh, he was sent to Mundi, where, eventually, the troops under his command mutinied. He was warned of his danger, and urged to make his escape: but, with a spirit worthy of his English birth, he resolved to remain at his post, and abide the consequences. During the night, he was attacked by the Sikh soldiers, who cut him down, dragged him from his tent, and with demoniacal ferocity, threw him on to a blazing fire before life was extinct!

deficiencies and drawbacks, he was anxious we should see his regiment paraded, and we have promised to attend for that purpose at half-past three, to-morrow afternoon.

Anarcolly, which is in the centre of the Lahore cantonments, was the joint property and built by the Generals Allard and Ventura. On their first entering the Maharajah's service they lived together in a large adjoining mosque or tomb, where the family of the latter, with about forty or fifty female slaves, have resided without once moving out of doors since the General took his departure for France, now two years ago. He is however, daily expected here, as he arrived some months ago at Bombay, and the intelligence of his friend's death will no doubt hasten his movements. In the room where we dined there was a portrait of General Allard, which bespeaks him to have been a handsome and benevolent man, possessing much firmness and decision of character, tempered with mildness. He wore, at the time it was taken, a uniform similar to that of our horse-artillery, and was decorated with two orders; one, the "Legion of Honour," the other the "Bright Star of the Punjab," lately instituted by Runjeet Singh. Another picture of the General and his family, taken by a French artist when he returned home some three or four years ago, was pointed out to us, and though not finished, being merely the design from which a larger drawing was made the group is well arranged, and the pretty faces of his Cashmerian wife and his children, who were dressed in the costume of their mother's country, drew forth the admiration of us all. Adjoining the dining-room is another of some dimensions, lined from top to bottom with looking-glass, and which, when illuminated, must have a brilliant effect, as it looked extremely pretty and dazzling even with the two candles that were brought in with us. With the exception of wanting the bath and fountains, it reminded me much of the "Sheeshah Khanuh" in the palace at Agra. We were subsequently shown into what may in truth be termed "the

Painted Chamber," as it is adorned with pictures of battles in which the two Generals were engaged, and executed on the chunam walls by native artists. The perspective of these scenes is most ridiculous; and at the siege of Moultan the cannons are turned up on end to enable the gunners to load them! the figures overtop the fortification, and the cavalry seem to be manoeuvring in the air; and absurdities of a similar nature are perpetrated throughout them all, and no doubt afford much amusement to their gallant owners whose poilcy has led them thus far to assimilate their dwellings with those of the native population; for it can hardly be supposed their taste is so far vitiated as to regard these embellishments as ornamental.

Wednesday, 20th February.—We left Colonel F.'s a little before midnight, and were escorted to camp by a guard of a dozen Sikh sepoys, as our host did not consider it advisable for us to pass near Lahore without them, lest we should meet with insult from the Akallies or others who might be prowling about at that untimely hour. The moon, which was not very far from setting when we started, gradually became so obscured by thick clouds that we had some difficulty in tracing out our way, and on reaching the town it required more than ordinary caution to keep clear of the ditch that yawned on one side of us, and the edge of which was on a level and not to be distinguished from the road itself. Flashes of lightning, which, when we left Anarcolly were indistinct, and near the horizon, now became vivid, and flickered above our heads, momentarily brightening our path and casting an unnatural hue over the surrounding scenery, and then leaving us in a thicker darkness than before, whilst the thunder from a low rumble had increased to a majestic peal that reverberated through the heavens. A few portentous drops caused us to hasten our steps as we approached our tents, and we had no sooner reached the shelter they afford than the clouds opened their sluice-gates and poured down a torrent of rain which lasted without intermission for ten hours. Our camp, in consequence, presents this morning a most miserable spectacle, and to-day's halt, which I had gladly hoped would have proved most beneficial to the troop-horses, affords any thing but a comfortable rest to them, and is even more injurious than a march in fair weather would have been. With their clothing wetted through, the ground beneath them flooded, and their heads drooping towards the earth, they present a picture of misery in unison with the rest of the camp, where, here and there on the higher ridges, are to be seen a few hungry followers vainly endeavouring to puff into a blaze some half-ignited sticks, which, soon smouldered by the dampness of the turf throw forth a thick smoke that slowly ascends and curls over the tents before it dissipated. With such examples before us we saw there was no possibility of getting any thing cooked for ourselves, and a kettle of water being with difficulty heated we were fain to content ourselves with a biscuit and a cup of tea for breakfast, a meal we soon found to be quite insufficient for three hungry men; we therefore, as soon as it was fine, and a few nags that had been standing nearly up to their knees in water had been removed to more elevated and drier spots, rode over to Anarcolly, as we knew there must be something in the larder *there*. Two of us, however, arrived rather late for the matin spread, but an early tiffin being ordered, we in the mean time, with Mons. Benet, the Maharajah's doctor, as our "cicerone," went to Allard's country-seat, where his body is at present lying in state.

Crossing the parade ground, we entered on a road that winds through a very pretty grove of date-trees, celebrated for their exquisite fruit; and at the termination of this, on the right-hand side, the late general's retreat is situated. A large garden surrounds it, but is not laid out with any particular taste; and the residence itself, two stories high, is built in a half European and half Native style of architecture; the whole, inside and out, being embellished with paintings of dragoons, lancers, and foot-soldiers, nearly half as large as life. The coffin, covered with a black velvet pall, was placed on a raised platform in the centre of the lower apartment, and around it large waxtapers were kept burning night and day. On its top laid the general's cap, his two orders, some valuable cashmere shawls (the offerings of natives) and a Persian sword, presented to him by the Maharajah, who paid 5000 rupees for the blade alone; the hilt being of gold studded with jewels, as were also the ornaments of the scabbard outside. Sentries were pacing to and fro at the corners of the building, which is encircled by a broad verandah, (where the same display of paintings is made,) and has fountains at intervals, embedded in its centre for the purpose of rendering the apartments cool during the summer months. We ascended to the upper room, which, similar to that at Anarcolly, is covered with looking-glass, and at the four corners of the roof are small dormitories, very comfortable and airy.

In the same garden, and close to the residence but exceeding it in size, is a large mausoleum, erected by the general some years ago over the remains of a daughter to whom he was greatly attached, but who died in infancy. Its summit, which is surmounted by a dom, is reached by a flight of three terraces planted with orange, pomegranate, and other trees; but as few of them have attained to any height, the building, which consists of one heavy mass of brickwork, is to be seen in all its pristine ugliness, and will be years before it is concealed by the foliage. Entering the interior, we found some labourers busy disinterring a coffin, as it is resolved the corpse of the general shall be buried in the centre of the pile, and that of his daughter removed to one side; but whilst observing their work, a second coffin was discovered, about a foot and a half longer than the first, and which none present knew any thing of. This will therefore be placed on the other side, as there is no doubt it contains another of the general's family.

We had just got beyond the precincts of the garden, when we met the governor of Lahore, who, mounted on an elephant, was also on his way to see the general lie in state; and, as he requested our company, we rode back with him. On entering the apartment that contained all the mortal remains of poor Allard, he appeared much affected at the sight, and felt the solemnity of the scene; remaining for some moments without uttering a word. He then launched out into praise of the deceased, and spoke as if he really meant what he was saying, and not as mere complimentary sentences, which are too apt to be uttered on such occasions. He put several questions to us concerning the customs in use with Europeans when burying their dead; asking whether we had any stated times for praying at their tombs; whether we offered flowers on their shrines, or ever burnt them; with many more interrogations of a similar nature. He returned with us to Anarcolly, where he sat some time, and in the course of conversation appeared anxious to know the reason I wore spectacles, remarking with a smile, "he was sure it was not on account of old age." The doctor explained it as well as he could, and he seemed greatly pleased at the ingenuity shown in rectifying short-sightedness by means of concave glasses. Nothing would, however, satisfy him until he had tried them on; but, being an elderly man, he could not, as was to be expected, see any thing with them. He remained upwards of an hour, and on his departure the doctor showed us a magnificent shawl made at Cashmire by order of poor Allard, which cost 3000 rupees, and which, with another he intended to have presented to the queen of France. I think Mons. B. said it was three years in being made; and the Cashmirians are now working one for General Ventura, which will cost double the above sum.

We dined with Foulkes again this evening, and met at his table nearly the same officers as we did yesterday. We heard from them that the Maharajah is about to advance an army to Peshawur under General Tezie Singh, who will command fourteen regiments of infantry, and sixty or seventy pieces of ordnance: part of the force being already encamped at Shahdera, on the opposite banks of the Ravee. His lieutenant is General Ram Singh, quite a young man, and the person who not long ago murdered a favourite youth of Runjeet Singh, for which he was mulcted in a fine of 20,000*l*. Report says the lad had made rather free with the general's character, which annoyed him so excessively, that he was resolved to have his revenge; and the better to effect this, he, with others, watched his victim as he was returning from durbar, and slew him; some say giving the first blow himself. No other penalty than the fine was inflicted on the very *gallant*! officer; but life is held cheap at Lahore, and a murderer may always escape justice by paying 1000 rupees; unless he happens to kill a person of rank, in which case, as in the above instance, the sum is proportionally increased.

Some of the party again spoke of the kindness which the Maharajah shows to his European officers, and mentioned that whenever they visit him, he invariably asks them to be seated on a chair.* I fancy, in these instances, they allude to private durbars, for I have heard it stated that Runjeet Singh, on public occasions, considers it his best policy to throw the "Sahib-log" (*Ang.* gentlemen) as much as possible into the shade, that he may appear to be pefectly independent of their services, and show to the world how easily he could do without them; and I understand also he is particularly jealous lest the more powerful of his generals should gain any undue influence or ascendancy over the minds of his nobles. However this may be, he treats the most of there well, and often makes them presents of pistols, matchlocks, handsome saddle-cloths, horses, &c.; and to the doctor he not long ago gave a most valuable medicine-chest, which had been presented to him by Lord William Bentinck, during their interview at Roopur,

* A mark of high respect in Eastern courts.

in 1831. Before communicating his intentions to M. Benet, he showed it to him in open durbar, and apparently out of mere curiosity, asked him what he thought it was worth. After a cursory examination, the doctor replied, "Five hundred rupees at the very least," "It is yours," added the Maharajah, "do with it what you please." But the sirdars around, jealous of this mark of favour, hinted that if a bottle was taken out occasionally, and given to Mons. B., it would be sufficient at a time, and the gift would last longer. (!) To this Runjeet replied, "No, no; it cannot be in better hands than of the doctor's, who shall keep the whole."

As an instance of his partiality for, and forbearance towards them, the following anecdote may suffice:—On a certain occasion, the Maharajah had issued an order that no horses should be allowed to enter the precincts of the palaceyard; but this Captain La F., who commands an infantry regiment, did not hear, or did not attend to; and one day, on his riding to durbar, was, of course, stopped by the sentry on duty; he, however, instead of dismounting, as was requested, felt nettled at being opposed by a *native*, and in the heat of the moment, and in a most unmilitary manner, laid his whip rather smartly across the soldier's back. Intelligence of this outrage was immediately conveyed to the Maharajah's ears, by persons ever on the alert to throw odium on the Europeans; but he, instead of being angry, directed the instant admittance of La F. and his charger; adding, that he did not intend the mandate should apply to Feringhees; he also, in the most delicate manner, waited till his chiefs had withdrawn, and then told La F. of the order he had given; at the same time remarking, he was aware of his conduct; and adding, he was not, on any account, to beat his sepoys again.

His passion for fine horses is notorious, and he has large studs in various parts of the Punjab; the principal ones being at Dingee and Goojrat. The famous Leila, for the possession of which it is well known he indulged in a long and expensive war with its owner, is now quartered at the former place; and as the village is situated on our route, I hope we shall see it.

Of the services, the artillery is his favourite branch; and he spares neither pains nor expense to bring that arm to perfection. The most valuable horses he can buy, or receives in presents, he invariably allots to it; and there is now a magnificent Arab in one of the troops, which was given to him by Lord Auckland, at the same time with a portrait of Queen Victoria, which, notwithstanding the salaam and complimentary speeches he made on receiving it, we were told he has already bestowed on one of his omrahs! He has freaks of generosity which, at times, know no bounds; and the other day, during his illness, he presented to his two gooroos, or spiritual teachers, a lac of rupees (10,000*l*.), 80,000 being in gold ingots, and 20,000 in sequins. Superstition, no doubt, helps him to be liberal on these occasions. After dinner we were indulged with a taste of his celebrated liquor, and, certainly, more fiery beverage never passed my lips. He does not allow it to be stilled for any one but himself, but he presents a bottle now and then to his officers, which accounts for our having got a drop of the "rale nate stuff."

February 21.—Noormahal, the governor of Lahore, much to our surprise, paid us another visit; but we were not long in discovering it was for the delivering certain presents that the "Lion of the Punjab" had been pleased to send us. On Ferris was bestowed a silver-hilted (gilt) sabre, attached to a gold embroidered belt, a chogah of crimson pushmeena, handsomely worked with lace, and a pair of solid gold bangles, terminated at each end by a snake's head, and enriched with emeralds and rubies in their unpolished state. Bangles, of a similar nature and value, and robes of the same texture, but inferior in workmanship and different in colour, were presented both to Rattray and myself; and had we been in durbar, courtesy to the royal donor would have obliged us to have donned them, and we, no doubt, should have presented highly amusing figures, enveloped in the folds of such cloaks. As it was, we accepted the gifts with a salaam, and laid them on one side with an indifference to their worth, as it is more than probable we shall be obliged to give them up, on account of an existing regulation of Government, prohibiting the reception of presents at Native courts, or when received, directing them to be sold for the benefit of the Company. Before taking his leave, the governor informed us, that one hundred of the king's sepoys will accompany us as far as Colonel Wade's camp; and that orders to furnish our detachments with whatever necessaries we shall require, have been issued to the various functionaries on the road.

Intimation of our wish to visit the town having been conveyed to the Maharajah, who is still encamped between this and Amritsir, he was pleased to direct a state elephant should be in readiness to escort us through it, as well as to issue orders that every facility should be afforded us of gratifying our curiosity. As soon as Noormahal had taken his leave, we mounted the elephant and seated ourselves in the howdah, which was edged with embossed silver, and divided into two compartments. Two attendants, clothed respectively in yellow and pink silk, sat behind us, and a guard of five sepoys, attired in red and armed with muskets, cleared the way in front.

Having entered the city by the Musti gate, we proceeded for some distance down the main street, which is filthy to a degree, and extremely narrow, being not more than thirteen feet in width. Situated in it, is Bokhari Khan's mosque, an edifice apparently of late construction, roofed in with three large domes sheathed with gold; and as the sun was shining on the temple with noonday splendour, it looked extremely brilliant and rich, though beyond the domes there is nothing particularly attracting about it. Next in order came the mosque of Wazur Khan, which is large, and very beautiful; but to see it properly, required that we should dismount: we therefore descended from our elephant, and entered the court-yard. Four minarets, covered with enamel painting, the colours being arranged with great taste, and of the most brilliant hues, rise towering towards the sky, and connecting them are forty rooms, where the dervishes were wont to read and reside, but which are now filled with beggars and decrepit individuals, who crawl about in a state of disgusting nudity. The mosque itself is also embellished with pigments, and with numberless sentences extracted from the Koran, the letters of which are inlaid with such neatness and accuracy as to excite wonder. The tomb of the founder, surrounded by a light and pretty screen of fretted work, occupies a small portion of the court, and is, I believe, still regarded as a place of sanctity by the Mussulman population. The building, with its court-yard, covers three biggahs of ground, and is in excellent preservation, though built 215 years ago, according to our guide's information. Many of the beggars lined the gate-way, and solicited alms as we passed; and before we entered, some of the faqueers wished us to take off our shoes, — a proposal we declined acceding to, nor were we asked to comply with it by our attendants.

Leaving the Wazeer Musjid, we returned two or three hundred yards by the same street, the houses of which are, for the most part, two stories high, though some attain to three, and are generally ornamented with wooden balconies, richly carved, and with semicircular domes over the windows to shield them from the sun. Crowds of persons, showily dressed in silks of every colour, thronged the place, and with difficulty got out of our way; and had we met a vehicle of any description, I know not how we should have passed it. Turning down another street, at the corner of which a diminutive Hindoo idol, protected from the weather by an equally small cupola, is erected on a pedestal about fourteen feet in height, we continued onwards, leaving to our right a small temple crowned with bright green domes, and which, strange to say, looked extremely pretty amidst the surrounding houses. We shortly after came to the musjid built by command of Aurungzebe, which we entered by one of the side gateways, and were at once very much struck with the massiveness, simplicity, and beautiful proportions of the building now falling rapidly into decay, but still retaining much of its former magnificence. It is constructed of red freestone, inlaid with white marble; the mosque itself being surmounted by three large domes of the latter costly material, and crowned with gilt spires. Opposite to it stands the principal gateway, which is lofty and fine, but on the side facing the mosque very much dilapidated, and fast progressing to ruin. Surrounding the court are the dervishes' habitations, fourteen feet wide, level at the top, and paved with broad flag-stones, thus forming a parapet, or walk all round the musjid; the wall of which rises about three feet above it, and may be, from summit base, thirty feet in height: it is also pierced with loopholes for musketry, to admit of its being turned into a place of defence, if necessary. The court-yard is 580 feet square, marked out into rectangles by means of bricks inserted sideways into the ground; and in the centre is an excavation now choked with weeds and perfectly neglected, but which formerly received the waters cast up by numerous fountains that still exist. The minarets, which are lofty and plain, are elegantly proportioned, and though shorn of their cupolas, still appear as complete works of art. We ascended one, and had to mount upwards of two hundred steps ere we reached its summit: but the magnificent view of the city and neighbouring country spread beneath us more than compensated for the fatigue of climbing a ruinous staircase, tenanted by bats and pigeons, who flitted and flew by in alarm at the intrusion. The buildings in Lahore most conspicuous for their size were pointed out as the residences of Koi-now-nihal Singh, the Maharajah's grandson, and of Rajah Dhian Singh, his prime minister; but there are many other large edifices, though totally void of any pretensions to taste in their architecture. In the direction of Manihala, the extent of ruins is interminable, but the country to the north-east is extremely pretty; and also about Shahdera, where the white tents of Tezie Singh's army, at present encamped there, contrasted beautifully with the dark foliage of the trees which surround the mausoleum of the emperor Jehanguire.

Quitting this truly magnificent Musjid, we entered the grounds belonging to the palace, one portion of the first enclosure being formed by the wall in which the principal gateway of the mosque (on this side kept in perfect repair) is situated; and was the entrance which Aurungzebe invariably used on going to his devotions, the populace being admitted by the one through which we had passed. In the centre of this square, which is laid out in gardens and terraces, is an elegant little building, erected by the Maharajah, with marble pilfered from the tombs of Jehanguire and his wuzeer, where he transacts business in the hot season. The lower apartment is fourteen feet square, ornamented with looking-glass, gilding, and colours, most harmoniously blended, and extremely rich. Light is admitted through Saracenic arches on pillars, and a verandah, eight feet broad, with a ceiling embellished in the same style of profusion, encompasses the whole, which is built on a chabootra some four or five feet above the ground. We ascended to an upper room of similar size and shape, but even more beautifully and gorgeously ornamented; the four doors being decorated with ivory, inlaid in various devices, each being different from the other, and all arranged with much taste. There is also an apartment under-ground, where the Maharajah takes refuge from the hot winds, and during the hours of recreation admits a few of his most intimate friends.

A small open building, in which he occasionally sits to

enjoy the fragrance of his garden, stands on the left of this, and another similar to it on the right, where some five or six fakeers live, and subsist upon his generosity.

Passing through another gateway decorated with paintings of figures, wild animals, &c., fashioned in the most grotesque style, we were conducted into a large rectangular court, in which the Hall of Audience is situated. Constructed of red freestone, its exterior would have been handsome, but a coat of plaster has obliterated the fine tracery of its workmanship, and imparted to it a whitewashed appearance, anything but pleasing. Although still used as a place of business, little or no care seems to be taken of it, as two horses were stabled under its arches, and marks of others were but too conspicuous. The throne from whence the emperors, in former days, were wont to administer justice, projects from the centre of one of the longer sides, and is raised several feet above the ground: the other three being open, and consisting of lofty arches on pillars: a row also running lengthwise through the middle. Opposite to it, on the other side of the court, is a large building, surmounted by a Mussulman coffin, and erected by order of Jehanguire; with the beautiful idea, that he was to remember, when he distributed justice to others, a time would come when his own actions would be tried by a higher Power.

We were admitted through a low archway beneath the throne to a small court, and close to a building which contains the regal entrance to the hall of justice. The exterior of this is covered with paintings in oil of a very extravagant description, and evidently of late construction, as one subject represents the interview of the Maharajah with Lord William Bentinck at Roopur. The parties are supposed by the artist to be assembled in the audience tent, the Sikhs being arranged on one side and the British on the other. The two great potentates occupy the centre of the scene, and

Lady William, accoutred in white *trousers, boots, and gold* straps, is seated a few paces behind her husband. An uglier set of vagabonds than the man of daubs has made of our countrymen cannot well be conceived; though the people who accompanied us regarded them as likenesses, and were eager to point out "Macnaghten Sahib," the "Bakhshee Sahib,"* and others, who have only to *see* their portraits to be grateful. Another picture represents the Maharajah in the presence of Baba Nanuk, the founder of the Sikh sect: the holy father being most splendidly robed in a suit of embroidered gold, and sitting; whilst his disciple, who has done so much to extend the domains of his followers, is dressed in bright green silk, and standing, with his hands joined in a supplicatory manner. Behind the Baba, keeping guard, is an Akalli with a drawn sword, and with but very little covering. A third represents a similar scene, with the single exception of Runjeet Singh being in a still more humiliating position – on his knees. A few drawings of flowers, which separate these compartments one from another, are extremely well done, and true to nature.

On leaving the picture-gallery, as we dubbed this remarkable building, we were conducted to the king's garden, around which is a handsome stone balustrade, very much neglected, and requiring a great deal of repair. At one extremity, overlooking the surrounding country, is a small kabgah, or holy building (where the "Grunth," or sacred book of the Sikhs, is read) erected on marble pillars, with a very handsomely decorated ceiling and tesselated pavement; and, opposite to it, another of similar construction, but more beautifully, enriched, though exceedingly filthy, and used as a stable. In the open verandah in front of the latter, there is a small fountain, the reservoir of which is ornamented with flowers, constructed of precious stones, let into marble,

---

* Literally paymaster: Colonel Wade, so called from his having had charge, for many years, of the treasure-chest at Lodianah.

but in so dirty a state, that our "cicerone" was obliged to remove the mud ere they were visible; and it was really quite melancholy to see such a profusion of magnificence entirely thrown away, where a little cleanliness and care were all that was required to restore it to its pristine beauty. On quitting this, and passing through a common-looking quadrangle, one side of which is used as a granary, we again emerged into the court where the Hall of Audience is situated, and crossing it, were conducted to the Foundry, which occupies one corner of it. Amongst other pieces of ordnance, we were shown two very respectable-looking brass 24-pounder howitzers, lately cast from the models of those presented to Runjeet Singh by Lord William Bentinck; and the superintendent told us there were ready for service, in and about the immediate neighbourhood of Lahore, 700 guns, of various calibres. We would willingly have remained here longer, but were obliged to hasten back to camp, as dense masses of clouds had gathered overhead, and threatened an instantaneous deluge.

Previous to visiting the city, we were informed it was more than probable we should be insulted by the Akallies; but, beyond one man calling out, "There go a pair of English thieves !" and another comparing us to a couple of pigs, we were allowed to pass unmolested; and as these fanatical gentlemen are privileged in their own country to say whatever they like, we were content to pocket the affront. Ferris, who was here in May last, with Mr. M'Naghten's mission, told me that, on one occasion, when he and M., of the horse artillery (in company with General Lena Singh), were riding through the town, an Akalli made a cut at the latter, with his drawn sword, but fortunately missed him: and, on another, he saw a number of these men attack a person on horseback, apparently of high rank, and after hurling him from his seat, they dragged him into one of the by-streets, up which he was hurried with great rapidity. What became of him F. never heard.

Soon after we had reached our tents the clouds began to discharge their contents, but the rain was neither heavy nor of long continuation; and, as soon as it subsided we rode over to Anarcolly, to inspect Captain Ste–'s regiment, which was unable to parade yesterday, on account of the unsettled state of the weather, and which he promised we should see to-day. The same excuse was, however, tendered on our arrival, and received as a valid objection, the parade ground being a perfect swamp. We had invited the whole party there to dine in camp, but while they were preparing to accompany us, the rain came down in such torrents, and continued so long without any intermission, that there was no moving out, and we were obliged to take that meal with them.

February 22.—Several of the Maharajah's European officers breakfasted with us this morning, after which we visited the doctor's baraderie, or summer-house, presented to him by Runjeet Singh, and situated at no great distance from our camp. It is raised some feet from the ground, and surrounded by a pretty little garden, which, in the rainy season, is so entirely covered with water, that Mons. Benet found it impossible to move out; and, on the Maharajah paying him a visit in his *barge*, told him so, and intimated his wish to live at Anarcolly, which Runjeet Singh very readily assented to.

At ten o'clock we mounted our horses and proceeded along a capital road to the Shalimar Gardens, which are about three miles from Lahore. At every mile we passed a "baraderie," at one of which the Maharajah generally remains to take a meal, or spend the heat of the day, as may be his inclination, when he visits this royal retreat. We entered the gardens by a low gateway, and were immediately delighted with the refreshing coolness of a shady and broad walk, paved with bricks inserted sideways into the ground. Along this we continued for a short distance, and then ascended by a ramp to a higher terrace, from whence a beautiful view of a large reservoir, filled with fountains (its pale blue waters receiving the reflections of numerous surrounding buildings, imparting to the scene an air of enchantment rather than of reality,) burst upon our sight with a suddenness almost startling. This reservior is 240 feet square, and has 160 fountains tastefully distributed in and around it. Its centre is occupied by a raised platform, with a balustrade about a foot high, on which the native girls exhibit the graces of their persons in the voluptuous dances of the East, the monarch and his courtiers surveying their movements from a large summerhouse facing and erected on ground fourteen feet above it, and which is also the height of what may be termed the first compartment of the gardens, comprising a space of 900 by 400 yards, the whole being fronted by a wall of red freestone, inlaid with white marble, and surmounted by a low balcony of fretted-work. A number of very small but pretty minarets on the roof, impart a lightness of construction to this "baraderie," which is thrown open to the front by three large Saracenic arches, and where, beneath the centre one, a beautifully carved piece of white marble is inserted at an angle of forty-five degrees, over which the water from the upper fountains, after passing beneath the building, dashes in a glittering cascade, and unites itself to that in the large reservoir. A "takht," or throne, also of white marble, the lower part being composed of one immense slab, stands immediately in front of this, and in days of yore, when used by the Mogul emperors, was covered with costly shawls or carpets, on which they reclined, and, in the enjoyment of this lovely spot, endeavoured to forget the never-failing cares attendant on the possession of a throne.

On the opposite side are two smaller buildings, and between them a hollow square, about twelve feet below the surface of the second compartment of the gardens, and on a level with the third, which, in extent, is equal to that of the first or upper one, the centre division being only 100 or 120 yards in breadth. In this square five large fountains are arranged, and on three sides, receptacles are constructed for upwards of 200 lamps; in front of which the springs, play, and are to be seen from the lower gardens, through an arcade that forms the fourth side. The effect of this, when illuminated, must be most gorgeous, as each drop of water would sparkle with the brilliancy of a diamond; and the collected thousands of them thus form a blaze of light intensely vivid and beautiful. Other edifices are on the right and left of the large reservoir, which is surrounded by broad terraces, divided into walks by parterres, and filled with various coloured and sweet scented flowers.

From the large "baraderie," in the upper compartment, a line of fountains, with terraces on either side, extends to the north wall of the garden, where there is a very pretty building, possessing a richly ornamented and painted ceiling; and a like range of founts stretches from the hollow square with the arcade to a similar erection at the southern extremity. Midway, however, conser-vatories of water, with numerous fountains, break the lines, and from these broad walks branch off to other parts of the garden, which is thickly planted with citron, pomegranate, and other trees, and enclosed by a high embattled wall, with, at intervals, a tower crowned by open galleries, and two large gateways, now in a dilapidated state. There was one other and small but elegantly furnished building, which attracted our attent- ion, and is situated apart from the rest, having a small reservoir with fountains in front, and a large but plain marble seat close to it. Under-ground are apartments, to which light is admitted through a doorway, constructed in the shaft of a well, the water of which is seen some twenty feet below.

Tradition assigns the completion of this almost earthly paradise to the Emperor Shah Jehan, the great patron of architecture, who, for the last seven years of his life, was so barbarously imprisoned by his son, Aurungzebe, in the fort of Agra. Monuments of his taste exist all over India; and the Shalimar Gardens of Lahore and Cashmire have attained a celebrity even throughout Europe. So delightfully pleasant were they to us, that we quitted them with regret; and could we have seen them as they are prepared for the reception of the Maharajah, with the fountains playing, the lamps burning, and all the pomp attendant on Eastern display, I doubt not but we should have lingered on its walks beyond the bounds of prudence.

On returning to our tents we visited some merchants who had for sale a batch of horses, just brought from Cabul, and the neighbouring countries. Some of them were exceedingly fine-looking animals, but they asked extravagant prices, and though we offered what we considered fair sums for two, they declined accepting our terms.

The weather which had continued turbulent and stormy till near midnight, had been succeeded this morning by a cloudless sky, whose clear azurs contrasted beautifully with the verdant turf, to which the late rain had imparted an unusual brightness; and as the evening continued equally fine, the people emerged from the city to perambulate the numerous gardens situated in its environs and—for natives—laid out with considerable taste. Crowds of well-dressed persons, very few being without one or two articles of silk, hurried by our camp, and as their costume consisted of the gayest colours, the scene was altogether lively and animated. At one moment, a noble of the land, mounted on a richly caparisoned elephant and surrounded by a train of matchlock-men, passed by; at another, a horseman carrying a bow in his hand, and a quiver of arrows slung behind his back, was to be seen curveting and caracolling his steed, to attract the gaze and admiration of the multitude. Here, a Sikh artisan, habited in his holiday costume, comprising a yellow silk turban, with "paejamahs" of the same material reaching to the knee, and a crimson robe wrapped round his body, was hastening to the fashionable rendezvous, and with him another, enveloped in the folds of a scarlet cloth chogah embroidered with gold, green silk trousers, and a pair of ornamented slippers peeping from beneath them. There was here much to remind one of Oriental magnificence; the stately elephant carrying the sumptuous howdah; the prancing war-horse with its costly appointments; the glittering arms of the guards attendant on the omrahs,* and the rustling silks of the more peaceful inhabitants, carried one back to the days of Bernier, whose descriptions of the Mogul's court were considered to have the truth; occasionally, however, the more closely-fitting dress of an officer belonging to one of the Maharajah's regiments pointed out that European customs had been adopted to some extent, but the existing head-dress of crimson or other bright-coloured silk still attests the unwillingness of the Sikh soldier to wear the chako, under the impression, I believe, that it is constructed, or at least kept together, by leathern bands formed from the sacred hide of the bull.

The ruins of Lahore attest its great antiquity, but there are some grounds for conjecture that it existed even so far back as the time of Alexander, and was the city of the Second Porus, whom that great Conqueror subdued.† In extent and grandeur it rivalled the Imperial towns of Delhi and Assa, and in the year 1015 was reckoned in some measure to be the capital of Hindoostan, as the seat of government was then transferred to it from Ghuzni, by the Emperor Musaood III. Subesequently, however, it does not appear to have been a favourite abode of the Mogul sovereigns until the reign of Jehanguire, who resided here, as the purity of its atmosphere, agreed better with his constitution than that of any other place, and it was also near to his oft-visited retreat in the

* Nobles.
† Vide Dr. Vincent's "Voyage of Nearchus."

vale of Cashmire. Much of his time was spent in beautifying both
the town and its environs, which were also greatly improved and
added to by his son Shah Jehan, but who, though born here, lived
in it only casually, as, he considered it too far distant from the
southern and more extensive portion of his dominions. The bigoted
Aurungzebe, *his* successor, merits praise for being the founder of,
perhaps, the most magnificent pile in the city – the Badshah's
mosque, of which mention has been made before, and on which
the eye is never satiated with gazing; so simply grand is the building,
and so elegantly proportioned are the minarets.

The present ruler of the Punjab, who gained possession of
Lahore at the close of the last century, fixed upon it as the seat
of his government, but lately he has become more attached to
Amritsir, an equally large and populous city, and which owes its
greatness entirely to his partiality. Apparently anxious his name
should be transmitted to posterity as a firm supporter of that
faith in which he was brought up, he has endowed there a costly
temple, which, strangers can only approach by making large
offerings of money, and submitting to various ceremonies imposed
upon them by the officiating priests. The most wealthy of the
merchants and tradespeople, with the keen-sightedness ever
attendant upon those engaged in the pursuits of traffic, foreseeing
the rising greatness of the new town, are gradually leaving Lahore,
and removing to it: and as all the valuable shawls and other fine
fabrics of Cashmire have also been transferred to the mart there,
the commercial importance of the metropolis is much inferior to
what it once was. Still it is considerable, and amongst a population
of from 80 to 100,000 persons, whose pride and vanity consist
in the fineness of their apparel and beauty of their ornaments, it
may readily be supposed a thriving business is driven in silks,
jewellery, and such like articles. During our sojourn here, very

*About 3*s*. 4*d* to 4*s*.

excellent descriptions of the former were brought to our camp
and offered for sale at one rupee ten annas to two rupees* per
yard; though the colours, generally speaking, are rather bright
and gaudy, yet there is something attractive about them, and
they are admired even by our own fair countrywomen – than
whom who can be better judges on subjects relating to dress?
Silk strings for sleeping trousers sell for their weight in silver,
and are celebrated all over India. Pattoo, such, as we can buy
in our provinces for twenty-four to twenty-six rupees a piece to
be had here for sixteen or eighteen, and coarse blankets of a
strong texture for a mere trifle. Paper inkstands, inscribed with
sentences from the Koran, and lackered over in the manner
practised at Banilly, are well made, and fetch from one to five
rupees, according to the size and style of the article. Ear-rings,
bangles, and other ornaments of jewellery are worked
uncommonly well, and the gold embroidery of Lahore equals
that of Delhi. Ivory figures are carved with care, but have a
stiffness about them assimilating closely to those produced on
canvas, and also a sameness in the design that detracts much
from their value. Wood, strange to say, is not to be bought, nor
could I ever get sufficient for a small frame; which appeared so
extraordinary that I concluded my servant was either misinforming
me, or had not made sufficient inquiries; however, on asking the
Maharajah's officers about it, they told me it was true, and that
Runjeet Singh will neither allow a tree to be felled until it is
actually required for use, nor grass to be cut within twenty-four
miles around Lahore. The troop horses have consequently been
supplied with a sort of strawy stuff, that contains little or no
nourishment, as all the "moth-bhoosse,"* to the extent of a lac
of maunds, (8,000,000lbs.) was consumed when the Governor-
General's camp was here last month.

* The chaff of a species of vetch.

Of the Maharajah's health we have had no accounts to-day; but it is not expected he can survive much longer, as numerous attacks of paralysis have already brought him to the verge of the grave. His constitution, naturally most robust, is now sinking beneath the excesses of which he has been guilty, and the quantity of spirituous liquors he has imbibed, even to later days, (for he has now limited himself to six pice* weight in the twenty-four hours,) has aided in the ruin of his once iron-bound frame. His nobles, imitating him in his depravities, have set an open example of immorality in the court of Lahore, which has been eagerly followed by his subjects, who have carried their infamous orgies and impurities to a height unknown, it is to be hoped, in other cities. His son, Kurruck Sing, pronounced to be half-witted, is heir to his kingdom, and will succeed him without opposition, unless objected to by Rajah Dhian Singh,[†] the most influential person in the state, besides, being prime minister and possessor of an army numbering from 25,000 to 30,000 men, with a fine body of artillery. The individual whose opinion perhaps has most weight with Runjeet Singh, is the faqueer Aseemut-oo-deen, the physician, interpreter and general transactor of his business. He has two brothers, also faqueer, one the Governor of Lahore, the other the Governor of Amritsir and of the Fort of Govind-ghur, where the Maharajah keeps his treasure. The other persons, whose names we became familiar with, are Shere Singh,[‡] a reputed son of Runjeet's, who is a fine soldier, fond of Europeans, and will even eat with them; and Now-ni-hal Singh, son to Kurruck Singh, a high-spirited lad, about twenty years of age, and just appointed commander-in-chief of the army, now on its way to Peshawur. The Rajah Dhian Sing has also two influential brothers, both noblemen possessing large tracts of country, and almost as ambitious as himself.

* A small copper coin
† Mudered by Sirdar Ajeet Singh, in 1843.
‡ The late Maharajah, who was murdered, in September 1843, by Ajeet Singh.

FROM LAHORE TO RHOTAS

February 23.—We quitted Lahore this morning with feelings akin to regret, as there were many places in and around it worth seeing, which the shortness of our time had compelled us to leave unvisited; and as our sojourn there had been rendered very agreeable, through the kind and polite attention shown to us by the Maharajah's officers, to whom we, with the exception of F., were perfect strangers. Having started our baggage at an early hour, we recommenced our march towards Peshawur at 8 A.M., passing beneath the city walls, and subsequently crossing a branch of the Ravie, just fordable and no more. About a mile from this, we reached the river itself, which was much swollen, running rapidly, and above 400 yards broad. Here we found but three boats to transport our troops, baggage, horses, and ordnance, and these were occupied by a detachment of the Maharajah's horse artillery on their way to join General Tezie Singh's encampment. They had two guns with them, both brass six-pounders, highly polished and covered with red cloth to preserve their brilliancy, a point apparently of great consideration. The native officer in charge allowed us freely to inspect them, and pointed out on the breech of one a deep indentation caused by a cannon-ball which struck it when in action. They were not, however, much to be commended, and the carriages and wheels were infamously bad and rattled marvellously loud when shaken. The ammunition-boxes, too, were but indifferently constructed, and but ill calculated to keep out water. Those of the limbers, in the present instance, were filled with clothes, drinking vessels, and such like things, instead of powder and shot; which necessary articles, from there being no immediate want of them, were carried in tumbrils drawn by bullocks. The majority of the horses had crossed over, but the few remaining on the bank were in good condition, and seemed smart, active animals, though rather undersized: of the harness, it can only be remarked that any in a worse state, and still in use, cannot be conceived, and the men were slovenly dressed, filthily dirty, and appeared to be under little or no control.

At the Ravie, we had a specimen of the manner in which a Punjabee ferry is conducted, and where anything but order and regularity was observed. As soon as the artillery had finished with the boats, a regular scuffle ensued for them, and of course strength and might won the day; those who had gained possession of them retaining it, by thrashing unmercifully any individual who attempted to enter the boat except of their own party. One little fellow I observed making dexterous use of a short thick stick, with which he belaboured the heads and legs of those who being no acquaintances of his endeavoured to secure a seat, and the gentler sex, I am ashamed to say, were treated in no better manner; for those who got on board (and many did) had, after receiving their portion of thumps with the rest, to tumble in head foremost, or were dragged in by the feet or hands, whichever limb was nearest to their friends, who had previously obtained a footing. Children, too, were in danger of being crushed, and I understand it is not a rare occurrence for two parties to draw swords and have a regular set-to for the precedence; indeed, Foulkes mentioned that not long ago, a man deliberately levelled his matchlock and shot another who had disputed his right to a passage. As it was not our wish to enter into squabbles with the Purijabees, Ferris halted and sent a message to the Governor of Lahore to say he should remain where he was until the boats were cleared for our use. In about an hour, Noormahal, accompanied by General Tezie Singh, came down and directed that they should be immediately made over to us. On this being done, we commenced transporting the ordnance, which, with about thirty horses, was crossed before nightfall, and an encampment formed on the right bank of the river, in an extremely pretty spot, shaded with large trees, amongst which the graceful date flourished, and with its feathery leaves added much to the beauty of the scene. Close to this wood, is a "baraderie," erected on a piece of ground which juts into the stream, and being of two stories high, and constructed with some pretensions to taste, looks extremely well from the opposite side. A small party from the Maharajah's regiment, and sixteen men from the companies, afford protection to my camp during the night, Ferris and Rattray remaining on the left bank with the treasure.

24th.—We are obliged to halt to-day to admit of the rest of the horses, the treasure and the companies of the twentieth crossing the Ravie; and Rattray and I made use of the opportunity thus afforded us to visit the celebrated mausoleum erected over the remains of the Emperor Jehanguire. It was situated about a mile from our camp, and occupies the centre of a large enclosed garden, which we entered after passing beneath a very fine gateway, in however, so ruined a state that the action of a few more monsoons will level it with the ground. The garden is laid out in the usual Eastern style, with a range of fountains running down the centre, and broad terraces separate it into compartments, now overrun with a rapidly increasing jungle. The tomb itself reminded me much of the lower story of that at Secundra over the great Akbar, being divided into various rooms, where holy men in former days read the Koran and performed religious ceremonies is honour of the deceased; but who with the numerous attendants ever watchful to preserve a prepetual flame suspended above the emperor's tomb, have passed away without their places being filled up; and their deserted abodes have now become the dwelling places of bats and pigeons, who are seldom disturbed, either by the intrusion of a devotee or the curiosity of a stranger.

A long and arched passage paved with marble, arranged into ornamented circles and diamonds by the insertion of valuable and various coloured stones, led us to a small room, where in the centre lies a sarcophagus of pure white marble richly ornamented with flowers, composed of precious stones so beautifully selected that the very colours blend together with a harmony closely approximating to their originals in nature. Sentences from the Koran in Arabic also aid in its embellishment; and the sepulchre, both in size and shape, as well as in costly profusion and magnificence, is very similar to that over the emperor Shah Jehan in the Taj Mahal at Agra, the most sumptuous edifice perhaps ever reared to perpetuate the memory of a deceased individual. We ascended by a narrow and steep staircase to the roof, which is entirely paved with white marble marked out like the passage into various devices, and was formerly enclosed by a low balustrade of the same material, now only remaining on one side; the rest having been removed by the Maharajah to adorn his palace at Lahore and the temple at Amritsir. Its surface measured seventy yards square, and in the centre there is a raised "chabootra" or platform fifty-four feet long and the same in breadth. Marble minarets, with mosaic work inserted at intervals in broad zig-zag lines, rise from the corners of the building and are divided into four stories, opposite to each of which had once been balconies, now despoiled by the same hand and for

the same purpose as the balustrade. Fifty-five steps led us to
the summit of one of these (which including the height of the
mausoleum would give an elevation of about seventy feet) from
whence we had an extensive view of the surrounding country
and of the city of Lahore; the large and populous, but dirty
town of Shahdera, so named from its proximity to the tomb,
being spread out beneath our feet.

Shah Jehan built this magnificent pile over the ashes of
his father, as an atonement, it may be presumed, for the
numerous rebellions he had formented against him,) who died
on his return from Cashmire on the 9th of November, 1627,
aged fifty-eight years; and opposite to it he erected a smaller
mausoleum in commemoration of the wuzeer Aziph Jah, and
connected with Jehanguire's by a range, of dervishes'
habitations, once the abode of piety and learning, now by a
strange perversion of their original use, converted into barracks
for Tezie Singh's soldiers, who are generally quartered here.
The ruthless hand of the despoiler has forestalled conquests
due to time alone, and the once grace-fully swelling dome of
marble that protected the remains of a Mahomedan noble
has been shamefully removed to enrich the Sikh shrine at
Amritsir, leaving in its stead an unsightly mass of brick-work,
to remind one of the uncivilized deeds perpetrated by the
present Maharajah.

February 25.—Having received intimation that the road
in advance was in some parts completely under water, and in
others rendered extremely heavy by the late rain, we could not
commence, our march till daybreak, and for the same reason
were compelled to take a circuitous route to avoid a stream,
now quite impassable, that cuts the direct road to Nungul, where
we ought to have halted. We were, therefore, directed to the
village of Bucka, where there is a bridge that spans the turbulent

river, and which cannot be less than twenty miles from Shahdera; we, consequently, did not reach our tents till long past noon, the companies with the treasure arriving about an hour afterwaids, much fatigued, and many of the sepoys quite overcome by the long journey. Our encampment; situated near the village, was almost encircled by the river before passing beneath the bridge—a work attributed to Shah Duolut, and which from its extent must be most useful in the rainy season, though the water is now confined to two or three of its arches. A total want of cultivation was observable throughout the march, the country being chiefly covered with a long swampy kind of grass that attains to the height of ten feet; and the villages we passed were neither numerous nor of any size. In a small hovel, close to our camp, the sepoys killed two "biskopras," a species of lizard of dusky grey colour and about eighteen inches long, which they asserted to be poisonous. Our second set of tents did not arrive till sunset, and our servants having been exposed the whole day to the heat of the sun, which was excessive, were thoroughly fagged and fit for no work. Baba Luchmun Singh, who accompanied us from the Sutledge to Lahore, is again with us, and will continue to act as our mehmindar until we overtake Colonel Wade.

26th.—It was our intention to have halted to-day at a village called Kammokie, but our guide, who appeared to know nothing whatever of the road, and who we afterwards learned was an unfortunate travelling beggar, pounced upon for the occasion, took us to Emminabad, a large town built of burnt brick, and about eleven miles from Bucka. This, as we are not far from the direct road to Peshawur, does not much signify beyond the inconvenience we were put to by our advanced and breakfast tents having proceeded to Kammokee; for as we had to despatch a man to recall the servants with them, it was long past noon ere our morning repast was spread before us. The road throughout was a succession of swamps, and in many parts so much under water that we were compelled to leave it and strike across the fields. At Emminabad, we encamped close to, and partly in a Mussulman burying-ground on the north side of the town, where there are several pretty groves of trees. A Chupar, or mounted messenger, belonging to Colonel Wade, joined us here, and will accompany us to Peshawur.

February 27.—We left Emminabad at daybreak, and found the road for the first two miles a perfect lake, the water seldom being below the horses' knees and oftener higher. It was afterwards, with but few exceptions, very good the whole distance to Gujranwala, where we halted and had our tents pitched close to the late Sirdar Harri Singh's fort, which contains his tomb and dwelling-house. Within a few yards of our encampment, we had a specimen of Eastern barbarity, in an individual who was hanging: by the heels to a tree, and who had apparently been left to die in that dreadful situation. He seemed to have been a man advanced in years, as his beard and hair were grizzled; but as he had been suspended about a month, his features were not distinct, and rendered less so through being mutilated by birds of prey. The bystanders told us he had been thus punished for murdering a child and stealing the silver ornaments which encircled its ankles and wrists; if so, he deserved his death, but the method employed to effect it could only emanate from a most uncivilized nation.

In the evening, we walked to the fort and entered it by a large and new, though not quite finished gateway, called the "Nuobut Khaneh," or place where the state drums play. After passing through a second gateway, which brought us to a garden, our attention was immediately arrested by a ridiculous picture representing the battle of Jamrood, in which Harri Singh lost his life. It is painted on the back of an apartment fitted up with receptacles for lamps to illuminate the fountains in its interior, and is about twelve feet long by six feet in height. It is divided into two compartments, the left side being devoted to the exploits of Harri Singh's army, the other to those of Akbar Khan, his antagonist's. The two upper rows tell of the advance of cavalry regiments on either side; the next two, of the formidable array of jinjalls carried on camels' backs, preceded by a few horsemen, who have already come into action; the fifth, which is the centre one, displays the valiant Harri Singh sumptuously clothed, and seated on an elephant, with an attendant behind holding a "chattah" over his head, the renowned Akbar Khan being opposite to him, similarly mounted and similarly attended. Below these, are other squadrons of cavalry and camel sowars, of both nations, facing each other; and the concluding line is occupied by a detachment of Sikh infantry marching in regular order to the sound of martial music, with a gun in front blowing a party of Affghans into eternity. The whole skill of the artist seems concentrated on this spot; for independent of the grape-shot, which *appear* in multitude as the stars of the firmament, he portrays with dignified ease and simplicity the muscular power of an Affghan, who is lifting his wounded comrade from the ground with one hand, and that too with so little apparent exertion as to be seemingly a matter of ordinary occurrence with him. The same display of strength is exhibited among the cavalry in one of the upper rows, where a Sikh, with one stroke of his scimitar, has severed a horse into two equal portions, which, strange to say, in spite of the dismemberment, are capable of retaining the uprightness of their position; and another, of the same nation, has, by a clean sweep of his sabre, cut off the head of an Affghan, which is being returned with the velocity of a bullet into the ranks of his wondering countrymen, whose heads and arms are flying off in every direction, and are parted with by their owners with all possible indifference and utter disregard of their value, whilst the Sikhs are unscathed! Nor ought the dignified complacency and perfect gooodhumour visible in the countenances of the two chiefs, opposed to each other in deadly conflict, to be overlooked; and it would be well if more civilized generals were to diplay equal urbanity of manner and coolness of demeanour when brought in such close contact on similar occasions, and take example from their behaviour, as depicted by the artist, whose skill is only equalled by his impartiality: inasmuch as, though it is a notorious fact that the Sikhs in the end were defeated, it is not so well known that *all* the wounded and slain were on the side of the *victors*. Such, however, we found it to be in this panorama; and it need not be added, that we derived much amusement from the representation of the battle of Jamrood, in which the really gallant Harri Singh closed his career some two or three years ago; the Sikhs at first, from their numbers and better discipline, gaining the day, but who, instead of following up the victory, were observed by the Affghans to disperse in search of plunder; on which they again returned to the charge, took their enemies by surprise, drove them off the field, and recaptured some ordnance which had been taken from them. Harri Singh, indeed, refused to quit his ground, and rallying around him a few horsemen, with hardy spirits like his own, he dashed into the midst of his foes and felt covered with wounds. He was one of the best of Runjeet Singh's generals, and had risen with his master's fortune. His body was burnt not far from the spot where he met his death, and the ashes collected and transmitted to Gujranwala, where they are deposited beneath a plain but neat tomb in the garden surrounding his residence.

This latter is one of the prettiest Eastern houses I have seen. It consists of three stories, each containing a room about sixteen feet square, the lower ones being enclosed by broad verandahs, and below ground there is an apartment to retreat to from the hot winds. A range of fountains extends close, to the entrance-front, and at the corners of the "chabootra," on which the dwelling is erected, are circular ornamented seats, which, when used, are covered with silk carpets or Cashmire shawls. At the top of the second and third stories, similar conveniences are also constructed, those of the latter being made after the model of a lotus flower, and the exterior of the elevation is covered with the finest chunam, free from any of those tawdry embellishments natives are so apt to consider as ornamental to their abodes. We could only gain admittance to the lower apartment, as the individual who had charge of the keys had gone to the city ; and the circumstance was to be regretted, as we were told the second story is very beautifully fitted up, whilst that we entered had nothing particularly attractive about it. The garden is laid out in rather a pretty manner, and, in addition to some very fine cypress trees, can boast of two or three large vineries. We were shown the "devta ke mukam," or abode of the idol, which is situated at some distance from the house and close to a reservoir by which the fountains are supplied with water. It is a small domed temple, built upon a chabootra, in an enclosed area. A flight of three steps leads to it, and immediate on the right of the entrance is the image of a bull in a sitting posture, the hump of which our guide touched and salaamed to with great reverence. On the door of the temple being thrown open, I could not help feeling disgusted at the idea of the glorious Deity being represented by nine oval stones, kept constantly moistened by means of water dripping through an aperture in an earthen pot suspended above them, to which the sepoys who accompanied us commenced praying. When will men cease to worship the work of their own hands?

It was now getting late, and as we had satisfied our curiosity as far as we could, we quitted the fort. Outside, but close to the "Nuobat Khaneh," stands a low range of buildings, with Venetian

blinds, which we were at a loss to guess the use of—I averring
it must be the cook room, and F. that it was a royal pig-sty!
On going up to it, however, a suppressed growl informed us
we were mistaken, being no other than the place in which
Harri Singh kept his tigers. One was all that remained out of
four; and he, though a handsome animal, was not particularly
large, and had only been in captivity two years. A piece of
string was all that fastened a by no means strong doorway,
but the animal was quiet, and allowed us to gaze at him without
taking offence: a goat is his daily portion of food.

Gujranwala is a large and apparently an increasing town,
and is celebrated as the birth place of Runjeet Singh, and his
ancestors. His father, Maha Singh, and his mother are both
buried in its environs, but we did not see their tombs, as they
are situated at some distance from our camp, and at the
opposite side of the town.

February 28.—Reports having reached us late last night
that the hackeries, with the troopers' baggage, had broken
down, and could proceed no farther, a number of camels
were sent to fetch it; and, that no delay might ensue, the
jemadar of Gujranwala was directed to furnish carts, to be
in readiness early on the following day. Morning, however,
dawned before the camels returned, and as the carts were
not forthcoming for some hours after, our march was postponed
till the afternoon, and I took advantage of the delay to pay
Harri Singh's villa another visit, in hopes of seeing the upper
apartment. Nor was I disappointed; and the harmonious manner
in which the gilding and colours are blended, the elegant
arrangements of the ornaments on the ceiling, and the richness
of the chamber throughout, deserved the encomiums we had
heard lavished on it. In recesses formed beneath a series of
Saracenic arches, are a number of glazed paintings on a small

scale, and, omitting the perspective, by no means badly executed. Some of these related to their gods, others to the haram, and the latter, as may be supposed, were by no means most decorous in their description. As several of them have been entirely removed, and many glasses of others are cracked, we asked our guide for an explanation; and he replied that the apartments belonged exclusively to the fair daughters of Eve, who on one occasion had quarrelled amongst themselves, and to settle their difference had resorted to the feminine weapon of slippers, which they heroically flung at each other's heads, and thus caused the destruction apparent in the late Sirdar's property.

On our return to camp, a respectable and intelligent Sikh offered his services to pilot us to the "Sirkani Bagh," where the remains of Runjeet Singh's father and mother are interred. As it still wanted some time before we should march, Rattray and I accepted them, and on our way thither found our guide particularly inquisitive as to the strength of our army; whether we thought it was capable of contending with the Maharajah's; the number of our guns, and other questions of a similar tendency. We were hardly repaid for our walk, as there is, nothing particular about the tombs of Runjeet's ancestors, which are close together, and under separate roofs; but a large and circular, though unfinished building stands near them and is interesting, as our informant told us the Maharajah is having it erected for his own mausoleum, and that at his death he will be buried here: it is, however, for so great a man, a poor monument when compared with the Taj Mahal at Agra, or even Jehanguire's tomb at Shahdera. A "baraderie," or summer-house, covered with paintings in bad taste, and but indifferently executed, is erected in the centre of the garden, which is large, but very inferior to Harri Singh's, though it can boast of a few good trees.

We reached camp at half-past twelve, and soon after commenced our march; the road, which was excellent, leading us through a profusion of cultivation in a forward and thriving, state, and the horizon being bounded by a magnificent view of the snowy Hindoo Koosh, only forty koss distant from our present halting-place, Nattih, which is a mud and tolerably large village, built on a slight elevation, and may be about nine miles from Gujranwala. On one side of it, and close to the road, is a deep excavation, some twenty-four feet long, by twelve in breadth, where the inhabitants were busy stowing, away their grain; but on our arrival, which seemed to cause considerable sensation, they ceased their labours to gaze at us, and the summits of the wall and houses were lined with spectators. It is now, however, the usual reception we meet with on approaching any town, and European faces are no doubt strange in this part of the country. Our tents were pitched in a very pretty spot, and we had everything comfortably settled before sunset.

March 1.—Two hours before dawn we were again in the saddle, picking our way by the aid of a pale moon, across which. a few clouds would every now and then lazily flit, and cast a dark shadow over our road, by no means a continuation of the excellent one which, yesterday, had called forth our praises, but a succession of swamps, equal in extent and difficulty to those on the other side of Emminabad. As day approached, the country gradually became more distinct, and displayed to our view an extensive plain, covered with long jungle grass and a hamlet or two here and there in the distance. Before, however, we reached Wuzeerabad, the villages had become numerous, the jungle was cleared away, and fields of young corn threw a cheerful aspect round the neighbourhood. We passed beneath a lately-constructed and lofty gateway, covered, as usual, with grotesque paintings of all descriptions, the figures being nearly as large as life. The street we traversed was broad, clean, and possessed of some good houses, and is, I should say, a mile, or not far short of it, in extent. A similarly decorated gateway brought us out of the town, and another adjacent to it, under which we also passed, is even more highly embellished — the pictures being stuck as close to one another as they can be put. In front of this was a small encampment of the Maharajah's troops. Descending a slight eminence, we reached a branch of the Chenab river, (the Ascesines,) which we forded, and encamped on its right bank, on the same spot occupied by Colonel Wade and his mission, when here.

Immediately we halted I despatched one of the chupars, or mounted messengers, (another of whom had joined us this morning,) to request the attendance of the Thannadar, from whom we hoped to obtain camels, in lieu of the hackeries which have hitherto carried our men's baggage, and which, from the miry state of the roads, can scarcely be dragged along by the bullocks. In about an hour he arrived, mounted on a handsome roan horse, and seated in a green velvet saddle, edged with gold embroidery. He dismounted to pay his respects to our commanding officer, who had, in the mean time, reached camp; but no sooner had his fiery courser been delivered to the groom, than he broke loose, and dashed in amongst my troopers, who, happily for the intruder, were fatigued by the long and heavy march just concluded, or they would have punished him for his rashness. As it was, a few eager spirits were anxious for the fray, and strove to break from their pickets; but the roan was secured before any mischief was done: though the Thannadar was too great a man to notice the transaction further than by casting his eye (for he had but one) in the direction his steed had gone. He was a well-dressed, fine-looking fellow, but very haughty, and so little inclined to attend to our wishes, that F. at last told him we should remain at Wuzeerabad till the time the camels were supplied. This nettled him, and he impertinently replied, we might stay twenty days if it was our pleasure; though it was very apparent he did not at all relish the idea. He was dismissed with but little ceremony, his behaviour being such as not to merit any; and he retired, surrounded by his train of matchlockmen and attendants, in the same order that he came.

Soon after he had gone, a procession of a very different nature occupied the scene—being a funeral train bearing the corpse of a young woman to the banks of the river, where it was to be burned. The body, wrapped in an orange-coloured piece of cloth, was placed on a "charpaee,"* carried by men—and a few, also, of the male sex occupied the station of our chief mourners, behind whom the women dressed in white, but not of the purest colour, ranged two by two, and followed chanting a dirge. For the completion of the ceremonies they chose a spot not far from our camp; where, having heaped some logs one upon another, the body was placed on them, and then more wood piled on it. The pyre was soon after set fire to; on which the mourners commenced to screech and beat one another at a measured time—this ceasing, and continuing at intervals, until the corpse was entirely consumed.

As this was the principal day of the Hoolie festival, the Hindoos in the detachment, and those in the companies were, as is their custom, flinging a red powder upon every one they met, and nothing would satisfy the native officers until they had bestowed on us a sprinkling, which, however, we insisted should be very slight. My own men, I thought, acted in a more refined manner, as they each brought a rupee or, two on a clean napkin, which they presented as a nuzzur, and with the compliment of which we were contented; though I could not help fancying some of the money did double and even treble duty.

* A sort of light bedstead

During the rainy season, the Chenab must be a most noble river, flowing in a channel from a mile and a half to two miles in breadth, sweeping over the belt of land on which we are encamped, and reaching up to the very walls of Wuzeerabad, a town of some size and extent, and possessing several large buildings; amongst others a lofty house belonging to General Avitabile, commanding very fine views of the country, that to the north being backed by the Snowy Mountains.

March 2nd.—Our suspicions were right; the Thannadar's welcome to stay twenty days at Wuzeerabad was not given with the cordiality such a long invitation demanded, and we were therefore not very much surprised to hear that the camels had arrived during the night, and that we could now prosecute our journey without being delayed. Our departure, however, was not wholly unattended with sorrow for on awakening this morning. R. was much grieved to see a favourite spaniel he had brought with him, lying at the foot of his bed dead and cold, although he was frisking about in the tent when his master went to rest. Being the only dog in camp we had all become attached to it, and we buried it near the ashes of the woman who was burnt yesterday, and not without strong suspicions that poison was used to remove him.

At half-past eight we resumed our march, and for three quarters of a mile the horses had to drag the ordnance through a bank of heavy sand that tried their powers to the utmost. On reaching the river not a boat was to be had, all being occupied by a detachment of Sikh troops crossing with treasure. On their return, however, we got possession of them, and, in the mean time, had been busy preparing ghats to facilitate the transport of our cattle. This was no easy job, as the Chenab was running rapidly, and undermined our labours as fast as they were completed. Many of the horses, when about to spring into the boats, sank with the sand as it gave way beneath them, and were afterwards with much difficulty got on board, being afraid to trust themselves again on such insecure footing. One indeed twice jumped overboard, and was only the third time secured in the boat by his accidentally slipping on his haunches, and being tied down in that position. The camels even gave us more trouble, and threw themselves into such ludicrous contortions to express their anger and disgust at being compelled to embark, that on more occasions than one, all hands were obliged to cease their exertions until relieved of a hearty laugh. It was four P. M. before everything was landed on the right bank of the river, now flowing in a bed about 600 yards broad; and the sun was just dipping beneath the horizon, when, after a march of ten miles, we encamped on the northern side of Gujrat, a town rapidly rising into importance, with a large bazaar and handsome gateway in the course of construction.

March 3rd.—The excessive fatigue incurred yesterday both by man and beast demanded a halt, and as our next march is to be an unusually long one, we remained at Gujrat to recruit for the forthcoming labours, and enjoyed a day of rest. We walked in the evening to a building a short distance from our camp, and which, though unfinished, is evidently intended for a shooting box, as the majority of the pictures with which it is embellished are representations of sportring feats; such as cock-fighting, hunting, wrestling, &c.; and are the only drawings on such subjects that I have yet met with in the Punjab. A range of stables occupies one side of a lately formed garden, and contained forty of the Maharajah's horses, all astonishingly fat, and some upwards of a foot across the withers. Of course they are useless in their present state, and are merely kept for show; their disgusting condition being brought about by chiefly feeding them with the hand, large balls of coarse sugar and butter being crammed down the throats of the steeds, who submit most willingly to the operation, and are always ready to undergo it.

March 4th.—The direct road to Peshawur being impracticable for guns, on account of the steepness of some ghats that cross a low range of mountains, extending through the country, almost parallel with and not very far distant from the river Jhelum; we were obliged to take a more circuitous road, which will eventually bring us to a lower ridge, where the hills are more undulating and less precipitous. Accordingly, a short distance from Gujrat, we diverged to the left; and though we expected to have had a long march, we little fancied it would ever have been the extent it really proved to be. Twelve koss was the distance marked in our route, and as a koss is a measure varying from one and a quarter to upwards of two miles, we thought we would hit the happy medium, and calculated it at one and a half mile, its most general approximation. At the fifteenth mile, a large village appeared directly ahead of us, and as the sun was extremely warm, we mutually congratulated ourselves on the apparently speedy termination of our labours, and pronounced it to be not so long a march after all. As we approached it, however, misgivings shot across our minds, and the total absence of tents or camels proved that we were either mistaken in our calculations, or that our advanced camp had inadvertently been taken to some other place. A resident shortly put us to rights, by saying Dingie was four koss further on, a piece of information we received with but little courtesy, as we could only look forward to a tremendous grilling, and which have been so easily avoided, had we known of the existence of this village; but we had been told all was barren to Dingie. There was now no help for it, and on we proceeded, very soon entering an extensive jungle of the dhak tree, whose knotted trunks and tangled roots were ranged on either side of our track; but whose branches being almost denuded of leaves afforded us little or no shade, and seemed to mock us with their presence. Midway we came to a "baoli," or covered well, one of those constructions that do honour to the pious feelings of individuals who have been thus led to bestow their wealth for the general benefit of their fellow creatures; the weary find repose under its arches and refreshment in its waters. *We* halted and refreshed also, descending eighty steps to reach the surface of the well, where there is a small apartment for the pilgrim to cook his meal, which obviates the necessity of his ascending for that purpose. In a few minutes, we resumed our journey, and after a march of twenty-three miles eventually reached the long-wished for town of Dingie.

As we approached it, our attention was called to a small crowd, principally of women and children, and on riding up to see the cause of their assembling, perceived in the midst of them a man stretched on the ground at full length, who had, half an hour before, been deprived of both his hands, as a punishment for the crime of stealing. A few quiverings about the muscles of his legs were all that betokened he still existed; but he was insensible, and no wonder, as he had bled profusely, and he was thus being inhumanly left to perish, as no one dared to assist him. The block, a rude piece of wood, was lying by his side; but the hands had been carried off for the purpose of being exposed near the spot where he had committed the depredation. We consulted about bringing him into camp, and I directed my native doctor to do so; but on attempting to remove the poor wretch, we were told the sentence was the law of the land, and that we had no business to interfere. This was true; but we subsequently heard with much satisfaction, that a few of his friends had secretly conveyed him away, and that there is a chance of his life, as they would, immediately they were able, insert his stumps into boiling oil to allay the bleeding; I fear, however, the chance is but slight.

Two other executions, though unattended with the barbarous mutilations above detailed, had taken place at the same time; but it will hardly be credited that the punishment of death these unfortunate individuals suffered was awarded to them for the crime of having killed a cow! but such was the case; and the deluded Sikhs consider the blood they have just shed as called for to appease the anger of their deity, insulted in its representative, a four-footed creature of the earth! The road led us nearly beneath a tree, on which the body of one of the offenders was suspended, and where it will remain as a warning to others, until devoured by carrion birds, or it falls to pieces under the influence of time; the other was hanged at the opposite side of the town.

With these scenes of horror around us, we did not find the environs of Dingie very prepossessing, and the town itself has nothing to boast of but its size, being chiefly constructed of mud hovels, promiscuously heaped together in a sort of elegant confusion. We, however, visited the royal stables, for the purpose of seeing the far-famed "Leila," the horse Runjeet Singh waged an expensive war to gain possession of, and which, when brought out for our inspection, rather disappointed us. It was a speckled grey, and might have looked handsome, had it been in proper condition; but it was overloaded with fat, filthily dirty, and its heels, for want of paring and exercise, so excessively high, that it limped along with much difficulty. One of a pair of "Dakhinies," for which the Maharajah gave 9000 rupees, far exceeded "Leila" in beauty; but it was much too grossly fed, and equally ill attended to: the other was dead.

Evening closed in without bringing any tiding of the soldiers' baggage; but we were not kept much longer in suspense, as a sepoy, who had been sentry over it, made his appearance, and reported that the surwans* had suddenly attacked him in the

* Camel-drivers.

jungles, tied his hands behind his back, gagged him that he might not give the alarm, and then tossing the loads from the backs of the camels, had made off. At eight o'clock, a similar report was made of those belonging to my men; but, as all this could not have happened without gross neglect on the part of the sentries, they are to be severly punished. The surwans had evidently concocted the plan beforehand, and it would not surprise us to hear that our *friend*, the Thannadar of Wuzeerabad, had given them a hint before starting, and suggested the depths of the jungle as a convenient spot to carry their deed into execution, being at an agreeable distance from his own jurisdiction. We shall, in consequence of this, be obliged to halt tomorrow; but it is somewhat doubtful whether we shall be able to procure either camels or carts, in so short a time, from the neighbourhood of Dingie.

March 5th.—Late in the evening, as we were about to despair of obtaining any camels, a long string of them entered our camp, which had been procured at a village some miles distant, through the strenuous exertions of our mehmindar, Luchman Singh.

March 6th.—We left our ground at half-past three, and, by the aid of a clear starlight morning, picked our way in safety to the foot of a low range of hills, which we reached at daybreak. These hills appear to be divided into two chains; and a pass, three miles in length, with a road tolerably free from stones, and not very steep, conducted us across them, and eventually brought us to the village of Kohar, where, however, we did not halt, as the river Jhelum was only a mile beyond it: we therefore pushed on to it. After we had breakfasted, and the cattle had been fed, we passed over to the right bank; and as the channel was not very broad, and we had several boats sent down from a large town, about ten miles distant, we got every thing transported in less than three hours. The Jhelum is rich in classical associations, being the Hydaspes of the ancients, where the brave Porus unsuccessfully combated the progress of Alexander the Great, and on which the conqueror of the world embarked on his homeward return. Had time been at our own disposal, we would gladly have dropped down the current in search of the ruins of Nicaea, as well as to have visited the extensive salt-mines at Pind Dadun Khan, from which Runjeet Singh derives a large annual revenue. We were not able to do this, but we enjoyed the luxury of a bath in its clear stream, which, either from its purity, or from having its source in the vale of Cashmere, is sometimes styled the River of Paradise. Never dreaming of alligators, we were delighted with our refreshing ablution: but we subsequently learned that, like other large rivers in India, it swarms with these tyrants of the deep. Our camp was pitched on a tongue of land round which the Jhelum silently flowed; and in front of it, and about four miles distant, a bold mountain (a terminating ridge of the Salt Range) majestically stood forth from the surrounding plain.

March 7th.—The four first miles of our day's march were ascended till we passed the village of Singhooe. Here we got on to firmer ground, and it continued thus for seven or eight miles, when we descended to the valley of the Kuhan. This is very confined, steep hills bounding it on either side, and the stream, though neither deep nor rapid, yet indulges in such a sinuous course that we were compelled to ford it several times. Large boulder stones encumber its bed, and are also abundantly strewed around in the valley, which must be under water during the season of the periodical rains. A sandy track was our road, and being soft and yielding to the foot, the pull for the horses was terrific. We shortly came in sight of the far-famed fort of Rhotas, which, like its namesake in Behar, was formerly used as a prison for state criminals. Our first glimpse of it was very characteristic, and well calculated to fill the mind with gloom, only one corner, forming. the centre of a dismal hollow, enclosed by bleak and barren hills, being visible. Its wall is in a ruined state, and so horribly blackened by time that, had we not known otherwise, we should have pronounced it to have been stained by the action of fire; and the surrounding cliffs, dark almost as itself, hideously harmonized with the whole. A narrow path led up to it; but being impracticable for guns, we had to continue ascending the bed of the river. At length we reached an opening in the hills, and a beautiful view of an extensive plain, backed by lofty and irregular mountains, was displayed to our sight. We expected to have traversed this, but were disappointed—the bed of the stream, here closely hugging the ridge, which turns suddenly to the left, being still our course.

We had just come within hail of another face of Rhotas, and were looking forward to a speedy termination of this toilsome march, when an unfortunate accident delayed us for a considerable time longer. At this precise spot a bend occurs in the river, with a more rapid current than usual, had gradually washed away the road, leaving a perpendicular bank about a foot and a half in height, at the extremity where it crossed the stream. Observing this, I spurred my horse to a gallop, to see if it could not be levelled; and the troopers inconsiderately concluding the movement to be a signal for them to follow, set off at the same pace. Before I was aware of this I had reached the other bank, and on turning round, perceived it would be useless to halt them. On they came, and the leading howitzer had just surmounted the difficulty, when one of the pole-horses slipped, fell, and put a stop to the impetus of the wagons closely following in its wake. An extensive quicksand, unknown to us, was spread beneath them, and in less than ten seconds, three pieces of ordnance and five or six horses, with their riders, were struggling in the sand. For a moment the scene was fearful; but the men being, happily, uninjured, we easily removed them from their uncomfortable position. Jackets and boots were then instantly doffed, and we set to work to cast loose the traces, by no means an easy matter, as several of the horses had fallen on them. At length it was effected, and four of the steeds were got out without much trouble; the other two took more time, being in rather perilous situations, and I was afraid neither of them would be removed without receiving much injury, if at all. One of these had been thrown on his side, in a spot where the ground seemed to be of the worst description, and was gradully being drawn under; the ridge-bone of his back having already disappeared. A rope was, with much difficulty, passed under him; and, eventually, he was hauled out by sheer strength. The other, a pole-horse, had retained his upright position, but its hinder legs had sunk so far that the animal was resting on its belly. A rope was likewise slipped under him, and in process of time he was pulled up.

We then proceeded to the ordnance, which, with the exception of the howitzer, was extricated without much exertion; but this long resisted our utmost and united efforts. One wheel had already sunk half way below the nave, and was *carefully*! feeling for a better bottom to rest on. We hauled, but not the slightest upward movement was apparent; again our strength was applied — the result was the same; again and again were our struggles renewed, but to no effect; and the deceitful nature of the ground would not allow us to remain more than a few seconds in one position, so that our labours were cramped. At this time a wagon belonging to the other section, which brought up the rear of the treasure-party, (the latter having taken the narrow path I before alluded to,) rounded the base of the hills, and directing them to cross the stream a little lower down, a few more hands were available to assist us. Extra drag-ropes were tacked on, and once more we set our strength to the task. A long pull, a strong pull, and a pull all together, was the word, and after some time, a barely perceptible motion was visible. I cheered. The exertions were renewed; every individual threw the whole of his muscles into play; and at last, out rolled the gun from its difficult position; the sand, in five seconds afterwards, assuming the same treacherous appearance of security as it did before we got on to it. Just then the spare horses came up, and I had several of them to replace those who had suffered most on this occasion. A few hundred yards brought us to our halting ground, directly opposite to the fort, whose walls on this side are equally black with those on the other, and its aspect as gloomy. Numerous sepoys of the companies whom Ferris had despatched to our assistance, as soon as he heard of our disaster, returned with us, we having met them as they were hastening to join us.

Rhotas is built on not the highest part of a long ridge of hills, and why the spot was ever chosen as a place of defence it is difficult to say, as in many places it is commanded by neighbouring heights; but the wall, which is stone, is strong, and further defended by numerous bastions. The road leading to the gateway is steep, and by no means calculated for large horses, being nothing more than a bad "puharrie"* track; however, up we went; and though there was a good deal of stumbling over the smooth worn rock, and the gallant captain, a perfect Nimrod at riding, was, nag and all, nearly falling over the precipice, we managed to enter the fort in safety. Ascending a paved causeway; inclosed on either side by lofty walls, we passed beneath a second gateway, over which is inserted a Persian inscription, cut in white marble, purporting, I believe, to commemorate the founder. A decent-looking individual having volunteered to show us the "lions" of the place, we submitted ourselves to his guidance, and he conducted us forthwith to the ruins of the old palace, an edifice constructed of cream-coloured stone, and looking airy and light, after the universal red material of which all public buildings we have seen have hitherto been

* Hill

composed, unless of marble. It is, however, very much dilapidated, and on one side a complete ruin, the rooms being wholly exposed to the influence of the weather; but the other is more perfect, and being built on the edge of a hill, forms a lofty and noble object, and commands an extensive view of the surrounding country from its upper windows. Opposite to it stands a gateway, which probably formed the "Nuobat Khaneh," where the royal band played. Our attention was directed to the key-stone of its arch, which has slipped from its position, and appears as if it would momentarily topple to the ground; but our guide assured us it had been thus for eighty years; and a subsequent examination convinced us that the entire left wing of the building has sunk considerably below the level of the right; it may not improbably have been caused by an earthquake. Crossing a bridge which spans a ravine filled with brushwood and wild shrubs, we were taken to the entrance in southern face of the fort, which is built of similar stone to the palace, and being free from all tawdry ornaments, looks simple, chaste and massive. Two large balconied windows, elegantly and curiously carved above and below; are on either side of the archway, and a smaller one between these stands out in bold relief from the plain surface of the building, and forms a pleasing, contrast to the other unadorned parts. We then visited the city, which is a miserable place, constructed entirely of unburnt brick and, swarming with "kunchunnees," or nautch girls. A well of large circumference, but now choked and useless, is close to the gateway at which we entered; and near to it is the commencement of a subterraneous passage, which tradition asserts runs round the fortifications. We returned to camp descending through a breach in the walls, in the expectation that it would prove better track than the one we first encountered; it did not, however, and much caution was requisite to keep our nags from falling. On reaching the banks of the river, we passed several buildings erected below the fort; amongst others, a large mosque,

and a "madressa," or college; and crossing the Kuhan, we, in a
few minutes, arrived at our tents.

The building of Rhotas was on this wise. After Shah Shere
had firmly seated himself on the throne of Hindoostan, he conquered
the Punjab and issued orders for the chiefs to come and make
obeisance to him. They all did so with the exception of Rai
Sareeng, whose dominion extended over the mountainous tract
of country situated to the west of Jhelum, and his absence so
exasperated the emperor that he was heard to express his
determination "to throw such a wedge into the breasts of the,
Kakurs that it should stick there till the day of the resurrection."
Having obliged Rai Sareeng to submit, he proceeded to put his
threat into execution, by ordering a fortress to be erected on
the spur of a hill suitable for the purpose, and which when
completed, was to keep the surrounding tribes under subjection.
The superintendence of the work appears to have been entrusted
to one Toder Khuteri, who is said to have represented that the
Kakers, the inhabitants of the country, "entertained such an
aversion to work for wages, that they had agreed amongst
themselves, upon oath, to expatriate every person who should
act contrary to it." Sheer Shah in answer, flatly told him, "that
he should nowise be allowed to give up that work, which he
only wished to do in consequence of his greediness for gold."
Toder, on the reception of this new command, fixed first a golden
ashraf* as the price of one stone, which paramount sum induced
the Kakers to flock to him; afterwards, a stone was paid with a
rupee, and this pay gradually fell to five tankas: thus the fortess
of Rhotas was completed.†

---

* A coin that varies srom £1 12s. to £1 18.s in value
† Vide Neamet Allah's History of the Affghans, translated by Dr. Dorn.

6

FROM RHOTAS TO PESHAWUR

March 8th.—We quitted Rhotas at daybreak, and marched to Adriana, where our encampment was formed on an acclivity overlooking and close to the river Kuhan, whose bed for the most part was the only road we had, and was very heavy and sandy. The scenery throughout was pretty; the neighbouring hills being generally covered with a species of dwarf jungle tree or stunted bushes; and the stream formed a delightful little rivulet that rolled onwards with a gentle ripple as it washed the stones impeding its progress, or, flowing beneath some huge rocks, settled into deep pools, where it was hushed in the silence of repose.

March 9th.—We marched to Buckrala through scenery similar to that of yesterday's, except that the hills were of a more lofty and wilder description. Our camp is on the spur of a hill sloping down to the Kuhan, and the village is above and at some distance from us. A few years ago, it was the resort of a noted band of robbers, who infested the pass, and committed such terrible depredations, that no one ventured to ascend it unless in large bodies. Runjeet Singh very properly considered that the high road to Peshawur ought to be rendered safe even for private individuals, and issued orders to root out the marauders by fire and sword; but it was not until the village had three times been burnt to the ground that the desperadoes were driven from their haunts, and the pass considered free from all danger. A shorter road from this to Rhotas strikes across the hills, but is only fit for foot passengers and camels.

March 10th.—A little after sunset yesterday evening it commenced to rain, falling for several hours successively, and pouring down with a heaviness I scarcely recollect to have witnessed before. The Kuban, which opposite to Buckrala had dwindled to a slight and narrow brook, this morning was two or three feet deep and rolled down with an impetuosity scarcely credible, its waters discoloured by a red earthy matter washed from the hills, and presenting a strong contrast to the almost crystal purity it had possessed so shortly before. As our route lies still up its bed, we were compelled to halt; and as the day was fine, the cattle enjoyed the rest after the unusually heavy marches.

About noon, a sudden disturbance arose in the camp, and, on running out of my tent to ascertain its cause, I perceived Rattray in the midst of the Maharajah's soldiers endeavouring to allay the tumult occasioned by one of Colonel Wade's Chupars, a Mussulman, having grossly abused the founder of the Sikh sect, Baba Nanick. The holy man's followers resented this indignity so warmly that they were nigh to slaying his defamer on the spot, axes and hatchets being raised to murder him; and had not R. at once rushed to his rescue the Chupar's life would have paid for the temerity of his tongue. The Soobedar of the company was immediately sent for and directed to punish the men concerned in the affray, but in the evening the almost victimized individual presented himself and sued for their forgiveness — a request he was no doubt led to make after the reception of a douceur to hush up the matter.

March 11th.—We started early this morning and were prepared for a day of laborious toil, as the crowning of the Bukrala pass was to form the conclusion of our march. The river had gradually subsided during the night to very nearly its former stillness; but the narrow valley bore indications of its late violence; the long reeds that had sprung up in it wherever they could find sufficient nurture, being levelled with the ground, and partially covered with a viscous deposit of red mould brought down from the hills. We had hitherto been in some measure indebted to the marks left by cart wheels for the correctness of our road; these had now been entirely obliterated, and we therefore submitted ourselves to the entire guidance of a villager; but the greatest evil arising from the rain was the numberless and extensive quicksands, formed through its agency, and which required extreme caution to avoid. We had not proceeded very far from camp, when we fell in with one of these, stretching from bank to bank, which would have stopped our further progress, had there not been a sloping rock that just allowed a passage for the ordnance and no more; still it was necessary to remove some of the horses, and the pieces had to be dragged across by manual labour.

As we ascended, the hills on either side became more prependicular, and the stream was confined to a narrow channel obstructed by huge stones. The farrier had been sent twenty yards in advance, to point out the situations of quicksands; but, when about half way, I perceived him of a sudden sink into one of them, out of which his steed floundered with some difficulty. I followed, and to avoid his error, took a direction more to the right, where the ground appeared firmer; but I soon found I was not beyond its influence, for my horse was immediately up to his knees, and seeing the farrier's nag standing a little to the left, he struggled, notwithstanding all my opposition, towards him, and thus led me into the very spot my predecessor had occupied. Here he at once sank up to his belly, and feeling his exertions relax under me, I thought nothing but the drag ropes would have removed him from his critical position, and was about to dismount, when, making a last and strenuous effort, he succeeded in regaining *terra firma*. The guns halted until the ground still further to the right was pronounced practicable, when we moved forward, and soon after, turning sharply to the left, entered a defile with huge rocks. Here not the most indistinct trace of a road was to be seen, and we unanimously concluded we had come the wrong way; an opinion however, warmly combated by our guide, who assured us it was erroneous. Nothing could therefore be done but *make* a passage for the guns, and the sepoys and troopers were soon busily at work with hand spikes, pickaxes, and fowrahs.* Having completed something of a clearance, we proceeded, but were soon brought up by several huge rocks, too large to be removed in the short time we had at our disposal, or with the means at our command. We consequently inclined to the right, where there was a narrow passage, with an awkward turning in the middle, and just the breadth of the carriages; but on one side it was overhung by an immense projecting rock, and on the other it was obstructed by a fragment of stone about four feet high. There was no alternative but to attempt this; and as the whole was on a steep slope, the leading gun advanced to the trial at a smart gallop, the men ducking their heads as they reached the overhanging rock, and the near wheels rising high into the air, as they passed over the stone on the left.

Success crowned the undertaking as far as regarded the first gun, but the second, by turning too soon, stuck fast, and was, after the horses had been taken out, dragged across by main force; two others required the same process, but the rest surmounted the obstacle.

* A sort of spade.

Half a mile from this we reached the foot of the ghat, which is cut in the side of a steep hill, and may be about two furlongs in length, and from eight to ten feet broad. The horses being of no use here, were unharnessed, and drag-ropes substituted; a company of native infantry and the Maharajah's sepoys being left to assist us up the ascent. The latter soldiers we found equally willing to work as our own; but, in their careless manner, they more than once nearly allowed the pieces entrusted to their care to topple over the precipice, and, had they once got over, nothing could have saved them from being utterly destroyed, so lofty was the defile.

On crowning the ghat, a beautiful view of the snowy range gradually rose to our sight, the foreground being occupied by an extensive table-land, wild and barren in the extreme. A cool breeze blew from the mountains, and was grateful, as it fanned our countenances, heated by the exertions we had just undergone. The village of Dhamak, where our tents were pitched, was still a mile distant, and we reached it at three P.M., having been eight hours and a half in accomplishing a distance of about nine miles. Both man and beast were thoroughly fatigued, and a quantity of sweetmeats was served out to the sepoys, as they had worked famously on this occasion.

March 12th.—We left Dhamak at the usual early hour, and for some distance travelled along a firm road, free from any obstructions, and a delightful change after the sandy and stony track at the bed of the Buckrala river. Suddenly, however, it descended through a series of ravines, where it became execrably bad, and in parts so steep that the horses had several times to be removed, and the ordnance to be dragged up by the sepoys. We halted at Pakke—a miserable collection of huts, situated close to a caravanserai with walls as black as the fort of Rhotas, and not far distant from a small stream that runs in front of our encampment.

March 13th.—We marched this morning about nine miles, over a country similar to that of yesterday, to Jihliara, a village consisting of some half-dozen wretched hovels, surrounded by a few blighted trees. Our tents were pitched by the side of a clear and murmuring brook with a lofty cliff behind, and a gentle ascent in front, leading to an extensive plain.

March 14th.—A little before daybreak we left Jihliara, and in about an hour reached the top of Manikyala, a large building, supposed to have been erected by Alexander or one of his successors. It is constructed in a circular shape, of large blocks of stone, but has no entrance. General Ventura, some years ago, dug into the top, and had his exertions rewarded by discovering a shaft, which he descended by aid of a rope, and, on excavating the bottom of it, found an urn and some Grecian coins. Quitting Manikyala, we had excellent, though winding road; to Rawut-ke-serai, a large building, rapidly falling to decay, but still forming a very pretty object. Leaving it, we commenced a gradual descent, and passed some very extraordinary shaped rocks, which appear as if they had been smoothed and stained by the action of water, but there is no river in their vicinity sufficiently large to favour the supposition. The scenery on either side of us was now extremely beautiful—the distance being bounded by low ranges of mountains, clothed with woods, and softened to our view through the medium of a transparently blue atmosphere: the intermediate country was thrown up into isolated hills, and the ground nearer to us broken into irregularities by huge rocks boldly starting from the green slope on which we stood, and down which our road was to be traced, eventually losing itself in a jungle far below us. One of the detached eminences, surmounted by a castle, was pointed out to us by Luchman Singh as a spot which Runjeet Singh had much difficulty in making himself master of; and the whole country around is reported to be infested with marauding tribes.

After descending about two miles, we entered the bed of a nullah, filled with large round stones, over which the guns were dragged with much exertion, and following its course, we were, in due time, brought to the river Suhan, on whose banks we encamped, not far from the village of Hurmook. Our position is now encircled by hills, and the sparkling river flows round them with a gentle ripple, where it encounters any obstruction in its progress. Like the Kahun, it can boast of quicksands.

March 15th.—It was our intention, yesterday, to have halted at Rawut-ke-serai, but we moved on to Hurmook, as we had been told there was a difficult pass to surmount on the opposite bank of the Suhan, and for the same reason we commenced our march this morning as early as it was practicable. Following the windings of the river for a mile, we forded it, and immediately after arrived at the foot of the defile, which was so narrow and steep, blocked up with such large rocks, that we were obliged to unharness the horses, and apply the drag-ropes to the guns. In one or two places we had even to make the road, and two hours and a half were consumed before all the ordnance was hauled safely to the top of this gully. From thence, however, we had a capital road, only broken in a few places by inconsiderable ravines, until we reached Rawul Pindee, a large town situated on a level plain, at the foot of a range of mountains, some 4000 or 5000 feet in height. It once formed the confines of the Affghan dominions, and a spacious two-storied house—now the habitation of the chief official—still points out where Shah Shoojah resided after he was driven from Peshawur. A large and good Bazaar runs through the centre of the city, and is stocked with grain and cloths, the latter of which are to be had very cheap, as are also blankets of a good description: but it is narrow, and unfit for wheeled carriages, and we had, in consequence, to go round it. Our camp was formed by the side of a nullah, with steep banks on either side, which we crossed, and thus concluded a march of tolerably severe toil. In the afternoon we had a storm of thunder, lightning and rain, which was severe, and lasted some time. On its clearing off a dark blue cloud rested behind the mountains, and threw them forward with so much prominence, that, seen as they were through a pure atmosphere, they had the appearance of being within a short distance of our camp. In the evening we received a letter from Colonel Wade, who was within a few marches of Peshawur at the time he wrote, and who requested us to hasten our movements and join him as quick as possible, as circumstances had obliged him to move on.

March 16th.—Our road, this morning, was almost parallel to the base of the mountains, and about twelve miles distant from them; occasionally taking circuitous windings to avoid deep ravines with which the plain is cut up, and passing through some very pretty woods of a low and stunted tree, but sparingly covered with leaves. We descended about midway to cross a slight stream, where the track was bad, and the ascent on the opposite side steep and difficult; it was, however nothing to what we had met in the five preceding marches. We encamped on the banks of a rivulet, and not far from the village of Jani-ke-sung, which is situated on a gentle eminence, and has an old caravanserai close to it.

March 17th.—About three o'clock this morning a shower of rain fell; but it cleared off sufficiently to admit of our marching a little after daybreak. At starting, we missed a sepoy of the 20th Native infantry, who after a short search, was discovered at the bottom of a dry well, into which he had accidentally fallen; but ropes having been let down, he was soon got out, happily uninjured. The road at first led us straight to the foot of the mountain, and then turned suddenly to the west, continuing in that direction until we came to a gorge, which we crossed by a causeway, paved with broad flag stones, and very slippery for the horses. This is called the Margulla pass; and as the surrounding country is notorious for robbers, it is overlooked by a small guardhouse, erected by Runjeet Singh for the protection of travellers. Descending through a slight jungle of trees, and subsequently through some execrable ravines, we passed over a bridge that spans a small river, where beneath, and on either side of its arches, the water is of considerable depth and perfectly still. The bridge is roughly paved with large boulder stones, and at either extremity much worn and greatly out of repair. On the opposite side, the ascent is steep and difficult, but not very long, and its summit is on a level with an extensive plain. As we emerged from the ravines, we were considerably disgusted at observing on our right hand a small tree with a few forked branches connected together by means of a cord, on which was strung a number of noses, ears, and hands, lately cut off from thieves, who had been carrying on their avocations in these parts. Nothing approaching to timber was in the neighbourhood, and the tree had been uprooted from some other place, inserted into ground here, and surrounded by thorns and brambles, to prevent the jackals and wolves from getting at these miserable remnants of humanity, hung up as a terror to all future marauders.

For many miles beyond this, we had a road almost uninterruptedly level, passing on our left a large caravanserai, and on our right a "baoli," with 110 steps leading to the water. We afterwards reached a low chain of hills, where there are two roads, and unfortunately our guide conducted us by the wrong one, because the shorter. Several deep nullahs obstructed our progress on this; but we crossed them without accident, though not without considerable labour, and the additional harassment, both to men and horses, is to be regretted as it might so easily have been avoided. A slight descent brought us to a rapid stream, which we crossed, and skirting the base of a lofty hill on our right, we, in half an hour, came to Hassan Abdal, a tolerably large town and still famous for its sanctity. It is, however, composed merely of mud hovels, with a temple or two of burnt brick; but it looks pretty, as its neighbourhood is planted with large pepul and mulberry trees, and a clear crystal stream, which is shaded by them, imparts a coolness to its aspect quite refreshing.

In the environs, an unadorned and by no means elegant sepulchre stands in the centre of an enclosed piece of ground, and points out where the remains of a celebrated dancing girl are interred. A few cypress and other trees are close to it, and a little beyond it is an eminence, on which our camp was pitched, and which we entered with no slight feelings of satisfaction, after a march of sixteen miles, under a tolerably high temperature. Our tents were surrounded on every side by hills, the nearest of which Rattray and I ascended in the evening; but we found it much further off than we had anticipated, and had to climb some 800 feet, ere we stood on its summit. Here a small temple is erected, and is under the surveillance of a Mussulman fakeer, who watches it during the day and retires to the village at night. A pile of sticks was heaped up at one corner, and is collected for a fire that is lighted every seventh day. From our elevated situation we had a most lovely view of the snowy Hindoo Koosh, on the peaks and ridges of which the setting sun was shedding a golden lustre, and causing them to stand out in glittering and brilliant relief against the deep blue of a stormy-looking cloud behind. On twilight approaching, we hastened back to camp, descending by a villanous goat track that led us occasionally across the steep faces of precipitous rocks, on which there was but very insecure footing, and where a slip might have been attended with results fatal to our future researches. We, however, reached the bottom in safety, and proceeding along a hollow, filled with low jungly shrubs, arrived at our tents as it was getting perfectly dark.

I omitted to mention, that when about a mile and a half from Hassan Abdal, we passed the remains of an old garden, near the site of a neglected town, called Wah; and which I have heard is one of the prettiest spots in the Punjab. It was, however, too far distant to visit after our long march; but the view of it we had from the temple on the hill was not very striking; a ruined building, in the centre of a complete wilderness, forming its principal beauties. When on the road between the caravanserai and the baoli, we observed a broad blush of light, coloured with all the tints of the rainbow, and stretched across a large portion of the sky; behind it were to be seen distant hills, which assumed the same hues. It was a lovely sight, and continued visible for some time. Hakim Gilani, a man celebrated for his learning, and a friend of Acbar the Great, died, and was buried here in 1588.

March 18th.—We commenced our journey this morning in a heavy rain, which gradually increasing in strength, eventually obliged us to halt at Burhan, a village about seven miles distant; the roads being rendered so slippery that camels and horses were constantly falling, many of the former receiving severe contusions. Our march at first led us over a succession of undulating hills, covered with a jungle of ber trees, the narrow valley below being marked out into fields, some in the act of being turned up by the plough, others already green with the rising crops. We then crossed a tolerably broad and rapid stream, which must form a large river in the rainy season, and subsequently several deep and awkward gullies, the banks of which being of clay and very steep were extremely difficult to pass. The rain poured heavily all day, and towards evening the wind commenced to blow furiously.

19th. The gale increased last night to a regular hurricane, during which one of my tents was blown to the ground, and the other with difficulty kept up. A pal, belonging to the sepoys of the 20th native infantry, shared the same fate, as did that of my gun Lascars, and the poor fellows' bedding and clothes got thoroughly soaked. The wind moderated during the morning, but the rain continued to fall heavily till four o'clock, P.M., when it blew off, and this evening a streak of blue sky foretels a fine day to-morrow.

March 20th.—Still at Burhan. Though this is a beautiful day, and the country around looks fresh and cheerful after the late storm, four camels died from the severity of the weather during the night, and one of my best horses was taken ill but by copious bleeding and other treatment being adopted at once, he promises to get over it. There is nothing to be seen at Burhan, but Rattray and I were tempted by the fairness of the afternoon to walk to some low hills about two miles distant, and which are cut up into extraordinary shapes. Unknown to us their neighbourhood is notorious for robbers; and when we returned to camp, our mehmindar expressed his surprise at our rashness, and censured us for moving about without either arms or attendants.

March 21st.—Still detained here in consequence of the river Arar being so swollen by the late rain as to be quite impassable. Captain F. and I (this time attended by a small escort) rode in the evening to see it, and found it, though not very broad, five feet deep, and rolling along impetuously. Several men who attempted to ford it were occasionally obliged to swim a few strokes, and were carried down the stream for some distance ere gaining the other bank. Amongst others, we witnessed the passage of the three individuals who, for better security, came over together grasping each other's hands, the strongest bearing on his head their clothes wrapped up in a blanket. They had just succeeded in reaching the opposite side, when suddenly they stumbled into a hole, and, for a moment, disappeared with their bundle under water; recovering themselves, however with much alacrity, they scrambled on to dry land, but had the mortification to find their precautions were of no avail, as their apparel was completely soaked through and unfit to wear. We were convinced there was no hope of our being able to ford the river before to-morrow afternoon, at the earliest; so placing a few stones at the water's edge to mark its decrease, we returned to camp, which was about three miles distant; the road for one-third of the way passing through stony and narrow ravines, in which there are some curious mounds worthy of a closer inspection than we were able to give them.

March 22nd.—We struck camp to-day at twelve o'clock, and proceeded to the river Arar, with the intention of halting on its banks, should the stream have been still too swollen to admit of our crossing it. We found, however, that it had subsided considerably during the night, though it was still running rapidly and more than three feet deep. Our mehmindar had been actively employed all the morning in obtaining Coolies from the neighbouring villages, to assist us across, and had succeeded in collecting about a hundred, who, on our arrival, were busy transporting the baggage-camels, which had been sent on ahead. The scene, confined to the centre of a hollow, was, as may be supposed, one of much confusion, and the bawling of villagers, the shouting of surwans, the neighing of horses, and the groaning of camels, was noise more than sufficient to disarrange the tympanum of any well-regulated ear. The latter animals, as is usual in such cases, from their dislike to water, gave the most trouble; and one unfortunate beast, who had received considerable injury from falling, on the morning we left Hassan Abdal, was almost drowned, the force of the current having knocked him down; on which he commenced to roll over and over, and, at times, disappeared altogether beneath the water. The fellows in charge, however, kept a firm hold of the leading rope, and after some time were enabled to bring him out again on the side he had entered from. He here remained till the last, and was eventually crossed by strong ropes being passed round his body, and some twenty or thirty men supporting and dragging him through the water by sheer force. To guard against accidents the ammunition was removed from the wagons and limbers, and passed over on men's heads; and well it was so, for the last wagon got into a hole, and was, with the polehorses, for some seconds, entirely under water. No damage was done to the shells that remained in them, and but one of the boxes was slightly wetted in the interior; sufficient, however, to have spoiled the cartridges had they not been taken out. We were detained at the river for nearly three hours, and then ascending some ravines partially clothed with jungle, reached an open plain; subsequently passing a Baoli, where we ought to have halted, we encamped at a village about a mile to the right of it, and which unnecessary distance we shall have to retrace tomorrow.

March 23rd.—We marched at daybreak this morning, and had an excellent road almost throughout, bounded on one side by an extensive plain, dotted here and there with villages surrounded by cultivation; and, on the other, by low hills that gradually increased in height as we approached Attock. Amongst other damage done by the hurricane, we were not a little annoyed to hear that its violence had swept away the bridge of boats thrown across the Indus, and that the road which led to it is rendered impassable by deep fissures cutting through it in every direction. With the mighty streams of the Punjab, we had been led to expect much labour and difficulty in crossing them, and consequently grudged it not; but here we had looked forward to the reverse, and our mortification was not a little increased to learn that, independent of having to ferry over this swiftest of rivers, there was a ghat to descend in every respect worse than that of Buckrala, and which would have been avoided had the road to the bridge been left uninjured. At the termination of the plain, instead therefore of proceeding straight to its banks, we ascended an abrupt and somewhat Alpine path, from whence the views on every side are remarkably beautiful. The distance presents a succession of mountains, from the highly elevated snowy peaks of Hindoo Koosh to the more gentle undulations that bound the valley of Peshawur. On the right is the extensive plain of Chuch, covered with a bright

green sward, and intersected by numerous rivulets; on the left (partly concealed by the ridge on which we stood), the lofty and barren ridge of the Khuttuck range in Affghanistan; and, in front, the noble Indus, now swollen by heavy rains, and split into various branches, (one of which flowed beneath our feet,) was bounding onwards with resistless speed, its clear waters, as they dashed against the rocks, being lashed into foam and gleaming with silvery brightness wherever touched by the sun's rays.

A sudden turn concealed these beauties from our sight, and our attention was recalled to objects nearer at hand, the road being execrably bad and requiring pickaxes and shovels to remove the rocks and stones with which it was encumbered. Our tents were pitched on a ridge, in front of a fortified serai, but we did not remain in them longer than to despatch a hasty breakfast, as it was necessary we should cross the river at once. The governor of Attock, on being applied to for assistance, refused to give us any, nor would he allow the infantry to march through the town, unless their muskets were left outside the walls. Regarding this latter stipulation he was not to be blamed, as he merely acted up to the orders of the his sovereign, in denying admittance to armed parties; but he was bound to facilitate our transit across the ferry, which, instead of doing, he appeared to throw every obstacle in our way, and declined to issue an order that the boats should be collected for our use. Captain F., of course, would not accede to the request, (which annoyed him excessively,) and preferred making a circuit of the castle by a path little better than a goat-track, over which he took the companies with the treasure, and all the horses, leaving the Maharajah's troops to assist us with the ordnance.

A precipitous and rocky ravine, situated between the fort and caravanserai, was the only passage by which the guns could descend to the river; and worn as it was to a smooth surface by the action of water, which had also rounded its more prominent masses, it took us five hours of constant and hard labour to lower them down to the ghat; the utmost care and strength being required to prevent them from rolling over a steep declivity on the right hand side. There were but three boats to pass them across the river, and these were small, and so much out of water as to render them but little adapted for the transportation of artillery. Nothing in the shape of a plank to run the wheels upon was to be procured, and the men had to lift the pieces a perpendicular height of from two and a half to three feet, ere they were lowered on board; each boat taking a gun or wagon and its limber. Two trips were made, and I embarked in the last boat. We pushed off from the ghat, formed on the edge of a narrow channel of the river and separated by a stony bank from the main stream, which was flowing like a sluice; and once within its influence we were carried down with great rapidity, in spite of every exertion made by the united efforts of six rowers and two steermen, who struggled hard with their oars and displayed much dexterity in avoiding the huge rocks on either side, and on which, had the boat once struck, nothing could have saved it from being dashed to pieces. We reached the opposite bank far below the spot on which we wished to land; but the "dandies," fastening a rope to the prow of the vessel, jumped on shore and towed us up to the ghat, two men remaining on board to keep us off the sharp crags that here jut into the river and line the inhospitable-looking country. Passing a small promontory, where the current was stemmed with much difficulty, we were dragged into still water, and a short distance above, where the land gradually shelved, we brough to a little before sunset, the boat being scarcely allowed to touch the ground, when, leaping from it, we stood in Affghanistan.

Rattray, who passed through the town in company with the mehmindar, had crossed from the lower ghat by first opportunity, to superintend the landing of the treasure, &c., and to form the new camp at Khyrabad; and Ferris was still busy below the castle in passing over the baggage, horses and other cattle. He had been but little better off than myself, as he could only procure four boats, notwithstanding some twenty others were lying within a stone's throw of him; but as the authorities would not compel the boat men to work, they were not forthcoming of their own free will, and the few at his command were obtained through the instrumentality of Luchman Singh, who, having seized a manjee, took off his slipper and thrashed him until he roared again, and agreed to bring as many individuals as were under his control.

It was not until eight P.M. that everything was transported to the right bank of the Indus, and our camp assumed its usual appearance of regularity and order. As we had left our last ground at five A.M., we had laboured uniterruptedly for fifteen hours, and it was with no slight appetites we sat down, between nine and ten, to a hastily concocted dinner, having tasted but little during the day. Colonel Wade had sent us word, that once in Affghanistan, it would be necessary to keep a stricter guard than usual over the treasure, as the hills around swarm with a population who act upon

————"the simple plan,
That they should take who have the power,
And they should keep who can."

An extra number of sentries have, in consequence, been posted about the camp, and other precautions taken to guard against a surprise.

March 24th.—A little rain fell towards the early part of the morning, though not sufficient to demand a halt, but as the unfortunate prejudices of our Hindoo sepoys had prevented their making anything of a meal yesterday, we deferred our march till the afternoon, to enable them, in some measure, to make up the deficiency. The water of the Indus being — as its name, Attock,. somewhat implies—forbidden to them they could not touch it; speaking in contemptuous terms of its villanous bad qualities, and preferring to use that from a small rivulet which had its source in the hills surrounding our position. Our tents at Khyrabad were pitched about a quarter of a mile from the village, and directly opposite to the fort of Attock, which we quite overlooked; and although in some places it is defended by three walls, pierced with several tiers of loop-holes for musketry, and constructed of stone, it would soon crumble beneath the fire of cannon. Peshawur Singh, an adopted son of the Maharajah's, is the present governor; but he is a young and silly individual, and completely led by those around him. He yesterday, in a very impertinent manner, amused himself by rowing up and down the river in front of the ghat, where Captain Ferris was standing, and evidently with the intention of insulting him by the act; but as that officer seemed to take no notice, either of his pompous appearance, or of his ill-judged proceedings, the youth was most probably disappointed. A report of his conduct, and of his refusal to assist us with boats, will, however, be made to Colonel Wade, who, no doubt, will represent the matter to the Maharajah.

At Khyrabad there is a mud fort, lately erected by authority of Runjeet Singh, and the more commanding positions of the neihbouring heights are crowned with towers and castles. Almost every individual, whom we have seen, has been armed with sword and shield, or in some other manner, and all around bespeaks the unsettled state of the country and its population.

We walked to the banks of the Indus to see its junction with the Cabul river, a stream of equal breadth with itself, but inferior in volume. At their confluence the water was lashed into a sea of breakers, dashing over rocks and whirling in tremendous eddies, sufficient to have swamped a tolerably large boat; but the scene, was as it presented to our view, no doubt owed much of its grandeur to the accumulated rain that had fallen during our stay at Boorhan, and may be very similar to what it assumes during the periodical monsoons. Both the streams were considerably swollen, and opposed strong contrasts to one another, the Indus being perfectly clear and pure—the Cabul river, thick and muddy, the discoloured water of the latter being distinctly traced for two or three hundred yards below the spot where it flows into the Attock. We watched this deeply interesting picture from some over hanging rocks, which bear on their surface such a high state of polish, that they have the appearance of being perfectly wet; but it arises, I conjecture, from the constant trituration of the sand, washed upon them during the rainy seasons. From the sharpness of their angles, and the darkness of their hue, I concluded they were composed of an extremely hard stone, but a few blows from a stick easily separated a portion, the fractures assuming regular shapes of a slaty substance.

Our baggage having preceded us by an hour, under a strong guard, to protect it from the predatory tribes; we commenced our march in regular order, the treasure being in the middle, and a gun in front and rear, with lighted matches to be ready for service at a moment's notice. A mile brought us to the pass of Geedar Gullie, which is a defile, crossing over a spur from the Khuttuck hills, and in two places very difficult for wheeled carriages, being steep and encumbered with loose stones of some size. Its whole extent may be from one and a half to two miles; and in the more exposed parts, Runjeet Singh has erected a few castles, which are garrisoned by troops stationed there for the purpose of securing the pass as well as for the protection of travellers. The scene was one of great wildness, and fraught with excitement: whilst the guards, armed with long matchlocks, and perched on the extremity of a jutting crag, paced to and fro on their elevated and confined posts, and added much to the picturesqueness of the effect. I forgot to mention, that a horse artillery jemadar of General Court's, who had been sent from Peshawur to assist in crossing the guns over the Indus, by Colonel Wade, when he heard that the bridge of boats had been carried away, joined us yesterday evening, with two or three of his men, just after we had concluded our hard day's work. He was then quite drunk, and on one of his sepoys asking him if he had given the purwunnah to the captain, replied, "Yes, you rogue!" and knocked him down. Today, however, he was perfectly sober, and I found him useful in crossing the Geedar Gullie.

After quitting it, we emerged on to a fine champagne country, which, however, bears but few marks of cultivation, a measure soon explained to us by the thousands of tombs spread on every side. These are constructed with much care, and particular attention seems to have been paid to preserve their individuality, each grave being marked out by a row of white pebbles, encircling the mound, and crossed in its breadth by two or three bands of the same; beneath them lie the bodies of countless numbers who have fallen in battle, and the vastness of the collection displays the bold spirit with which the Affghans opposed the encroachments of the Sikhs. Although several years have elapsed since these engagements occurred, the same spirit of animosity still exists between the two nations; but from the circumstance of the Maharajah having obtained the entire ascendancy of the country, nothing beyond a solitary assassination is now heard of, unless when the hill tribes of the Khuttucks descend from their fastnesses, for the purpose of plundering an escort, and then a partial affray is sometimes brought about.

We continued our onward progress for two or three miles, without meeting any interruption, Rattray and myself being a little ahead of the leading gun, when a distant trumpet arrested our attention; and on turning to the direction from which it proceeded we descried a party of horse-men, who had been previously concealed from our view by a slight intervening eminence, advancing down the road in front of us. Bearing in mind Wade's instructions, that we were to be on our guard against enemies, R.

and I reconnoitred; but a few minutes sufficed to show us it was a party of Runjeet Singh's horse artillery returning to their cantonments, which we had left on our right some short distance back. They, equally mistrustful with ourselves, had stopped when we first came in sight, and it was their trumpet sounding the "halt" that had attracted our notice.

About half a mile from Acora, we met the chief, a young man about twenty, dressed in white, with a scarlet chogah thrown over his shoulders, and gold rings enriched with pearls depending from his ears, and who, attended by a large train of servants, had ridden out to welcome us. When within a few paces of Captain F., he dismounted, and advancing, presented him with a nuzzur of two rupees. On being told to remount, he accompanied us to our encamping ground, which we reached some time after sunset. Here, too, we are in the midst of tombs, and indeed I may safely call the whole country on either side of the road, from the Geedar Gullie to Acora, an extensive cemetery. At a place called Syddoo, where a few large trees overhang a small collection of mud hovels, the sepulchres are numberless; and it was here General Court's jemadar related that 8,000 Sikhs had made a successful defence against 150,000 Affghans! A partial shower of rain fell after our arrival; but on the hills around, it seemed to be pouring in torrents. Thousands of the cyrus, (a species of crane,) in regular battle array, flew over our heads, and the number of stragglers betokened that they had come many a weary mile. At night, the sentries around camp were doubled, and I visited them at twelve o'clock to see that all were alert. Happily, there was a bright moon to guide me, as the ground was full of large cavities, caused by many of the graves having fallen in; and I must confess I should have felt somewhat uncomfortable had I pitched headlong into one of these abodes, and found myself embraced by a mouldering skeleton, or welcomed by a ghastly skull.

March 25th.—The rain which fell yesterday evening though not very considerable, was sufficient, in conjunction with a heavy dew, to soak our tents, and we were again obliged to postpone our march until mid day. Meanwhile, the "kamdar" of Acora presented himself to inquire after our wants, and to ascertain if he could be of any use to us; and the village musicians volunteered to amuse us whilst our baggage was going on in advance. This however, as far as regards the harmony they produced, was a complete failure, for a more discordant noise I was never compelled to listen to, except at Chergaon in Kunawar, on the northern side of the Himalayahs, where the concerts are about par. A boy, too, habited in female costume, by way of dancing endeavoured to throw himself into graceful attitudes; and if turning the toes inwards, and the palms of the hands outwards, can be called such, we had plenty of them. The Maharajah's sepoys; however, seemed to enjoy the exhibition much, and one old fellow in particular, whom I had been in the habit of chatting with on the road, was constantly vociferating "Shahbash," "Shabhash!" "Well done," "bravo!" appealing to me at the same time, and saying, "Sahib, razie hai?" "Are you pleased, sir?" and adding, that the music was "khoob nuzzur" or "very sweet." It was quite laughable to observe the eagerness with which an old soldier like him, with a grey beard, entered into such a *puerile* amusement; but a pair of twinkling eyes that lighted up a somewhat handsome countenance, plainly told, that, although age had made inroads upon his frame, it had not entirely robbed him of the spirit and vivacity of youth.

About ten o'clock, a detachment of Runjeet Singh's troops, consisting of some cavalry and a single horse artillery gun, began to form an encampment close to our old ground. The former were irregulars, and appeared as if resolved to act up to their calling, as they marched quite independant of each other; and indeed so wide and straggling were their intervals, that a couple of hours were consumed before all had passed us, and their numbers did not exceed 100 men. The native officer, in command of the artillery, halted a short distance from where we were seated, and advancing, begged he might be allowed to look at the British howitzers. On permission being granted, he touched them with his right hand, and salaamed to them, and after a minute examination, pronounced the workmanship to be faultless—a compliment we could not pay in return, as a more miserable affair than the piece of ordnance under his control cannot be conceived. Powder and shot were indiscriminately mingled in the ammunition box, threatening at any moment an explosion, and the carriages, like those we saw at the Ravie, were frail and but badly put together.

We resumed our march at twelve o'clock in the same order as yesterday; but in consequence of the level state of the country were not so particular in keeping close together. We passed at intervals several small forts erected close to the road side, and garrisoned by a few troops stationed in them for the protection of travellers, as the neighbouring tribes, like those around the Geedar Gullie, are by no means particular in their honesty, and wish to hold all property in common except their own. At one of these fortified posts a couple of Akallies had taken up their residence, and, observing our approach, loudly vociferated for alms, in a tone of voice more accustomed to demand than to beg. Their wants, however, were unheeded by us, notwithstanding their assertion that "Wade Sahib" had made them large presents; and could we have perfectly understood their barbarous jargon of words, I doubt not but that we might have selected from them more than one complimentary sentence indicative of our want of charity, or abusing us for questioning the veracity of their communication. Neither of them had on much clothing, which probably was cast off as the day was sultry; but both wore the conical blue turban peculiar to their sect. In each of their right hands gleamed a naked sword, which they flourished around their heads with much dexterity, dancing and turning about during the operation, and making use of gesticulations and contortions most unpleasant to behold: respecetively on their left arms a shield was suspended.

Our road, the whole distance, extended along the right bank of the river Cabul, occasionally being more or less close to it, and an equally beautiful trip we have not had for many a day. As we neared the town of Nao Shahra, the scene became almost English; the sloping banks on either side of the stream being covered with verdant grass, and fringed with mulberry and other trees, and the distant views bounded by ranges of hills inclosing the expanding valley. The country throughout our march exhibited the same want of cultivation, and a similar multitude of graves, as it did yesterday, until we approached Nao Shahra, where, as at Acora, the ground in the immediate neighbourhood is prepared for agricultural purposes, and promises an abundant crop. The larger portion of the town is situated on the left bank of the river, and not far from the spot where Runjeet Singh fought his last encounter with the Affghans, the victory being so decisive in his favour, that he has ever since held tolerably quiet possession of Peshawur. One mound in particular was the subject of severe fighting. Three times did the Sikhs gain its vantage ground, and three times were they driven back. The Maharajah at length advanced in person at the head of his guards, and drove the Affghans from their position; the day was then his own. Azeem Khan, his antagonist, being on the right bank of the river, was prevented from joining his troops during the action; but he no sooner heard of the reverse they had sustained, than he fled precipitately to save his treasure. An Akalli chief performed prodigies of valour on the occasion, and was at last slain, after receiving several wounds.

Opposite to Nao Shahra, Runjeet Singh has built a large mud fort at the extremity of a low hill, which extends to the brink of the river, and, close to it, a small bazaar, with a good wide street, has sprung up, and is capable of affording supplies sufficient for the garrison, and also for a cantonment of cavalry, situated a few hundred yards distant. Our encamping ground, which we reached a little after four P.M., was not far from the huts of the latter, and, on our arrival, we found the tents pitched and ready for our reception. Numerous herds of camels, which had, during the day, been sent out to graze by the Sikh regiment, at sunest returned to their pickets, carefully guarded; and this precaution is most necessary to ensure their safety, as the Khuttuck tribes, who use the camel for food, are ever on the watch to waylay a straggler; and if, after capturing one, they are pursued, and cannot carry it off, they cruelly hamstring it, in hopes of being able to fetch the carcase at some future period. The Sikhs retaliate, and sometimes succeed in surprising a herd of their hill neighbours, who send their cattle to graze in the vicinity of their haunts, without being careful to watch them very strictly, naturally considering that when so near their own fastnesses, they must be tolerably safe. The result, however, proves they are not so, and the Khuttucks this morning had to bewail the loss of eleven camels, seized upon in their quiet retreat by the Maharajah's people, who carried them off in triumph, and safely lodged them in their cantonment. The Sikhs had sent out this foraging expedition, in consequence of the robbers having despoiled them, a few days before, of three camels, and whilst they were about it, they deemed it only just that their enemies should feel the weight of their vengeance, and have it proved to them, that if their depredations were continued, they, the Sikhs, had at their command ample means to recover their property, as well as to inflict punishment where necessary.

The chief of Nao Shahra, whose abode is on the left bank of the river, crossed it as soon as he had collected a sufficiency of supplies and paid his respects to us. Being attended by a large train of servants and followers, it was the first body of thorough Affghans we had yet seen; and certainly there is a striking difference both in their features and dress from any of the natives of Hindoostan, and their cast of countenance is even more Jewish than that of the Sikhs. Some of their complexions are so fair as to be tinged with colour; and blue eyes, red hair, and carroty whiskers are by no means uncommon. Perhaps, the part of their costume that most strikes a stranger, is the huge turban, composed of vast folds of cloth crossing in front somewhat in the shape of the figure ∞, the colours being principally of blue, white, or checked; and their long flowing garments bound round the waist by a enormous "cummurbund"* which, when opened out, would serve to envelop the man himself, gives them almost a patriarchal appearance. Our visitors were all of the tribe of Eusoff Zhye, the largest in Affghanistan, and the inhabitants of the hills and plains to the north of the Cabul river. Amongst other things in the way of supplies, they brought us a lamb of the broad-tailed species, similar to the breed at the Cape of Good Hope, and which are here called "doombas;" 150 eggs, ghee, flour and other articles in over-abundance, and two-thirds of which we would gladly have returned, but the chief would not permit it, and we subsequently transferred the larger portion of them to our servants.

March 26th.—The country, during the latter portion of our morning's march, exhibited many more traces of cultivation than we have hitherto seen in the valley, but the graves were still sufficiently numerous to remind us of the severe contests that had been fought in it at no very distant period; they were, however, as nothing compared with those of the two preceding journeys. In some parts, where the plain had been left undisturbed and was covered with a thick green sward, it was delightful to observe the profusion of wild and sweet-smelling flowers with which it was bedecked and many of which forcibly reminded us of the fields of England, the most common being the dandelion, which however

* Sash.

does not attain to the size of that at home. Our camp was pitched at Pubbee, and was about eleven miles distant from our last ground.

March 27th. – We left Pubbee at sunrise, and had proceeded about six miles, when we were met by a party of Allard's dragoons, sent by Colonel Wade to escort us to his camp, and who, as we approached them, formed up on one side of the road and saluted us by drawing their right hands to the forehead. We were much struck by the excellent way in which these men were mounted, their horses with one or two exceptions being uncommonly good. The trooper's dress is a red jacket, (by no means new or of a bright colour,) with broad facings of buff crossed in front by a pair of black belts, one of which supports a pouch, the other a bayonet. Round the waist, they wear a girdle, partially concealed by a sword-belt, to which a sabre with a brass hilt and leathern scabbard is suspended, and before the saddle is a small leathern receptacle for the butt of the carbine, which is so attached to the individual as to give it the appearance of being slung across the back. Their trousers are long, of dark blue cloth, with a red stripe; and their turbans of crimson silk, brought somewhat into a peak in front, and ornamented in the centre with a small brass half-moon, from which springs a glittering sprig about two inches in height. Their saddles are concealed by a crimson cloth edged with a border of blue-and-white stripes, and the harness is adorned with brass studs. The officers are attired from top to toe in bright crimson silk, and they merely carry a sabre attached to their persons by an ornamented belt. Altogether, the appearance of the detachment was very creditable, and the men would look remarkably well if a better cloth was used for their jackets.

Not long after the escort had joined us we had to make a detour of some distance to avoid a dilapidated bridge in the direct route, near to which the water was so deep as to be impassable, and to gain a ford where the stream was tolerably shallow, but running with much impetuosity. On its opposite bank, we came upon an encampment of people who obtain a subsistence by exhibiting dancing-bears, monkeys, and other animals, and who most probably were waiting until the river should abate somewhat in its violence, to admit of their transporting the motley collection under their charge. No sooner, however, did they espy us than they set to work at their avocations, and two or three bears were immediately to be seen standing on their hind legs and wrestling with their owners, who were considerably disappointed to find we did not wait to witness a display of their skill. But for this we had no time, and perhaps not much inclination, being anxious to complete our journey. A European officer, the first we had seen since quitting Lahore, just then appeared in sight, and galloping up, I had much pleasure in recognising an old and valued friend in the person of Lieutenant Maule,* of the artillery. We had not seen each other for years, and to meet in a country almost inimical to us and beyond the pale of civilisation, rendered our greeting the more satisfactory. In a quarter of an hour, we reached Colonel Wade's camp, having been two months and seven days on the march, in which period we had travelled over 590 miles, crossed five rivers by boats, and only halted once, except from cases of necessity, such as excessive rain, swollen rivers, or, want of camels.

---

* This most promising and amiable officer was brutally murdered in Kohistan, and was one of the first that fell a victim to the merciless cruelties of the Affghans in 1841. He had often talked of returning to his native land on furlough, but a keen sense of honour kept him in Affghanistan, where, as he had accepted a staff appointment in Shah Shoojah's service, he thought it his duty to remain until the country had subsided into a tranquil state. In him the writer lost an old and esteemed friend, and the artillery regiment a most active and zealous officer. I must again refer the reader to Lieutenaut Eyre's stirring narrative for particulars.

CAMP AT PESHAWUR

COLONEL WADE, with all the officers of the mission, had assembled at the extremity of their camp to receive and welcome us to Peshawur, and as soon as our detachments were arranged in the positions assigned to them we adjourned to a large tent where we partook of the Colonel's hospitality. Accustomed, as we had been, to two or three varieties of food hastily served up on some cracked dishes and plates that had escaped the general wreck of breakage, which a march invariably entails on the crockery, we were scarcely prepared for the change to an elegantly spread table, covered with silver, and furnished with a profusion of delicate viands that would have suited the taste of the most fastidious epicure. Whilst indulging in the art of gastronomy, our ears too were gratified with the sweet warblings of a musical box, and our olfactory nerves were greeted with a delicious perfume thrown forth by a bouquet of flowers plucked in the gardens of Peshawur. Just at the conclusion of this important meal, a drum and fife announced the approach of the Sikh company that had attended us from Lahore, and the men of which, dressed in their best attire, consisting of a red jacket, black cross-belts, white pantaloons, and a crimson silk turban similar to that worn by

Allard's dragoons, were scarcely to be recognised as the rabble, which, for so long a period, had followed in our wake; and whilst, in general, the number of those who *marched* into camp at the termination of each morning's journey, on an average, never exceeded ten or twelve, (the rest being stragglers,) to-day the full complement was present, with the officers and non-commissioned officers in their proper places, who passed by in the full consciousness of being admired and talked of. When in the Punjab, they invariably pitched their tents as far from our encampment as was neccessary to relieve them from all chance of contamination with the Mussulman soldiers in our service; but once across the Indus, and in the territory of their most inveterate foes, — the Affghans, their scruples ceased, and they crept as close to our ground as it was possible for them to do without interfering with our arrangements.

Our junction with the mission has increased its former numbers by one fourth, and it now consists of the undermentioned officers.

Lieutenant Colonel Wade, Political Agent and Chief of the Mission.

Lieut. Cunningham, Engineers; Ist assistant to do.

P.B. Lord, Esq.,* Bombay Medical Service: an assistant in the Political Department, to Mr. MacNaghten (doing duty).

Lieut. Maule, Artillery; assistant in the Political Department.

Lieut. Dowson,† 5th Regt. Native Infantry; do.

Lieut. Barr, H. A.; ditto, and commanding detachment of Horse Artillery.

Lieut. Hillersdon,† 53rd N.I.; assistant in the Political Department.

* Shot at the battle of Purwundurra, 1840.
† These officers formed part of the "Illustrious garrison" of Jellalabad in 1842.

A. Reid, Esq., Bengal Medical Service. In medical charge of the mission.

Capt. Farmer, 21st N.I.; commanding British troops.

Lieut. Corfield, ditto.

Capt. Ferris, 20th N.I.

Lieut. Rattray, ditto. Adjutant to British troops.

All these officers are present, except Lieuts, Dowson and Hillersdon, who are encamped on the western side of the city of Peshawur, superintending some levies lately raised for the service of Shah-zada Timour, with whom the mission has been sent, for the purpose of obtaining the cooperation of the surrounding tribes towards effecting the downfal of Dost Mahomed Khan, and the restoration of his father, Shah Shoojah-ool-Moolk, to the throne of Cabul. Numbers have already flocked to the prince's standard, partly influenced by a regard for his cause, but (it is to be feared) more by the prospect of securing good and regular pay at the hands of the British Government; and it is such individuals as these that have been placed under the orders of Lieuts. D. and H., to be moulded into the shape and form of regularly disciplined soldiers.

The Colonel's camp may well be termed a miscellaneous depot, so various are the materials and so incongruous is the mass of which it is composed; and its strength, exclusive of some Douranee horsemen, under Dr. Lord, and the levies under Dowson, is under 4000 men, and may be classed under the following heads, which will give their number as near as possible:–

	No. of men
British Troops – Detachment of 4th T.2 B.	
Horse Artillery, 2 Cos. of 20th N.I., and	
2 Cos. of 21st N.I., about	380
Shah-zada's Guards – 1 Troop of Horse,	
2 Cos. of Foot	300
Ghoorka Regiment	840
Nujeeb ditto	840
Aligols (Infantry)	840
Poorabies (ditto)	200
Goorcherras (Cavalry)	500
A party of Lancers	50
Grand Total.	3950

The prince's personal guards consist of a risallah* of horse, composed of 1 Rissaldar, 4 Duffodars, 1 Nisanchie, or standard-bearer, Nikarchie, or trumpeter, and 98 troopers; and two companies of Rohillas, each having 1 Jemadar, 4 Naibs, or corporals, 1 Nisanchie, and 99 Sepoys. These are under Maule's superintendence and command, and he also performs the duties of what may be termed the Shah-zada's principal assistant. The other regiments and detachments (except the British) belong to Runjeet Singh, and have been placed at Colonel Wade's disposal. Two guns (6-pounders) are respectively attached to the Ghoorka, and Nujeeb regiments, who, with the Poorabees, are dressed in red, but the Aligols wear white jackets and blue trowsers, and the Goorcherras retain their native costume. Colonel Jacob Thomas, a half-caste, commands the Nujeeb regiment, and is a son of the celebrated General Thomas, of so much notoriety in India, at the close of the last century. He is, I understand, a dull and heavy man, and the efficiency of his regiment, as well as of

* Troop.

his own authority, may be judged from the circumstance that, when his men were ordered, the other day, to move their camp, he came to complain to Colonel Wade, that although he had issued his commands for them to do so, not a single individual would attend to them. At half past seven we sat down to dinner, which was served up in the same profuse style as the breakfast, and speaks well of a political camp life, whilst a few bottles of champagne were opened in honour of our arrival, and added to the hilarity of the evening.

March 28th.—My slumbers were disturbed at daybreak by a villanous compound of sounds, the most distinct of which strongly reminded me, in my semi-awakened state, of the braying of some infuriated jackasses, each endeavouring to outvie the other in the loudness of their most dissonant tones, and attended by a parcel of individuals urging them to the performance by keeping up a continual clatter with pots, pans, kettles, chillumchies,* and other brazen vessels, mercilessly struck together, to create as much confusion as it was possible. There was no sleeping after this, so I vociferated to my bearer to inquire the reason of all the disturbance, and prepared to dress. His reply, however, was immediate, and my senses were somewhat staggered to hear that it arose from the *state band* of his Royal Highness the Shah-zada Timour, whose tent is situated nearly in front of mine, and whose pleasure it is to have the musicians pour forth their inharmonious strains each day at the same unseasonable time, it being a royal custom. I philosophically consoled myself with the reflection that, however I may be inclined to indulge in unnecessary sleep, it will not be in my power henceforth to do so; and I may, hereafter, have occasion to thank the prince for his consideration, in arousing the camp at an hour so beneficial, and so conducive to health.

* Brass washhand basins.

I had no sooner stepped from my tent, than my vision was greeted by an English carriage of the last century, standing opposite to the colonel's tent, and drawn by four handsome mules, indifferently harnessed. I was half inclined to doubt their reality, as my senses had not quite recovered the sudden shock they had received from the Shah-zada's band; but it was useless — there stood the vehicle — the veritable picture of a decayed family coach, its panels painted bright green, picked out with gold, and the very spikes at its back still bristling in formidable array, as a terror to all little blackguards who should attempt to seat themselves behind. It resembled one of those old-looking hackney-coaches, that are yet to be seen flying about the streets of London, although, perhaps, were they placed side by side, preference might be accorded to the jarvey, as a hinder wheel of the carriage is completely out of the perpendicular. The cattle, however, are strong and active, and deserved a better appendage to their tails; and this singular equipage belongs to General Avitabile, the Governor of Peshawur.

I was anxious to see the Shah-zada, for whose, and his father's benefit the British are involving themselves in an expensive war; and I had my wish gratified this evening when he quitted his tent to enjoy the freshness of a declining summer's day, though to him impregnated with a quantity of dust, kicked up by the numerous natives who formed his escort. To overawe the weak minds of the rabble population of Peshawur as well as to protect him from the evil machinations of any disaffected tribes, the prince, whenever he moves beyond the precincts of the camp, is invariably accompanied by the whole of his personal guards, and a large retinue of irregular cavalry. In the present instance a motley crew of Douranees, who had joined him since his arrival in the valley, led the way, and though wild and picturesque in appearance, there is a scampish look about them that tells they would be active enough in a scene of plunder, if any such should chance to fall in

heir way. Their dress is multifarious, each seemingly pleasing
himself as to his costume; but those most to be admired wear a
flexible mail shirt, gauntlets, and casque of steel, or a Kuzzilbash
cap, formed out of the glossy skin of a jet black lamb, and tapering
off towards the top, on which a small red tuft is visible. The
Chupkun, or long Mussulman robe, is very generally used; but its
colours vary with the fancy of the wearer, and the turban, consisting
as it does of innumerable folds of cloth, is heaped on the head in
the most irregular manner, and only kept in unison by the
ummurbund being wrapped round the body in as equally slovenly
way. Many wear high boots of rough untanned leather, or sandals
laced with thongs; and not a few had on shoes with large hobnails in the soles. Their complexions, too, differ as much as their
dress, some being as fair as Europeans, whilst others are as swarthy
as Negroes. A great number dye their beards red, which seems
to be a favourite colour, as it is not unusual with them to stain their
horses' legs and tails of the same hue; and the latter appendage is
very often tied up in a knot. They were all mounted upon a good
and handy description of pony, and generally armed with a light
jezail, or rifle, and a sword and shield; but a few, in addition to
their to other weapons, carried a long spear. Discipline is unknown
in their ranks; and even the necessity of, some measure, keeping
together as a body apparently is irksome to them. Every one strives
to be in front; and now and then an individual would suddenly dart
from the midst of the party and scampering off at full gallop, would
fire off his matchlock and then return to his comrades, at the same
rapid pace. I was much interested in their appearance and
proceedings, as they formed a fair sample of the much-vaunted
Affghan cavalry; and although, no doubt, excellent in their own
country, and in contests with the hordes, they have hitherto
encountered, a charge, on fair ground, from one regiment of
European dragoons, would either annihilate them, or literally bear
them off the field.

Next to the Douranees was a company of Rohillas, who dress in long blue chupkuns, green turbans and cummurbunds, and buff trowsers. They are armed with matchlocks, and have attained to a slight degree of discipline; and although there was a good deal of confusion in their ranks, they looked quite steady in comparison with the irregulars who had preceded them. Immediately following was the prince, in person, mounted on a stately elephant, and seated in a howdah, highly decorated with silver-gilt ornaments. He was simply attired in a robe of dark blue, with a pure white and very neatly constructed turban, and being a fine-looking man about thirty-two years of age, appeared to advantage in a plain costume; but a closer inspection showed that the lineaments of his countenance are stamped with a listless indifference to his situation, and an unyielding apathy to every thing around him. Behind him sat his wuzeer, an old man with silvery hair, and formerly Shah Shoojah's preceptor. His name is Moolla Shukore. A smaller elephant, with two of the Shah-zada's attendants, followed; then another company of Rohillas, and close to them the Risallah, a very well dressed troop, the men wearing a red "chupkun" over a green under-coat, and turbans and cummurbunds of the same colour as the latter garment. They are armed with a sword and shield, and a light spear, to which a small pennant is attached. Their saddle-cloths are chequered with red and green, but their horses are inferior to what they should be. Taking them, however, altogether, they form a very smart escort, and do Maule, who has had the trouble of disciplining them, very much credit. Another detachment of Douranee cavalry completed the guard.

March 29th.—As to-day had been set apart for the Shah-zada to hold his first public durbar in Pashawur, it was necessary that as much splendour and display should be thrown into the scene as was at the command of the mission. The morning was devoted to the reception of General Avitabile, the governor, and of General Court, an officer in the Maharajah's service; and the afternoon to winning congratulations and welcomes from his uncle, the Prince Hashim. A salute of eleven guns, fired from a battery of six pounders, announced the arrival of the French generals in camp; and a guard of honour, consisting of the two companies of the 20th Native Infantry, in full dress, were drawn up in line, to present arms as they passed by to the durbar tent. The time fixed upon for the ceremony was nine o'clock; but, unfortunately, natives of rank have imbibed a most absurd notion that their dignity is much enhanced if they can but manage to keep their visitors dancing in attendance upon them to an indefinite period beyond the hour settled for the meeting. Nor did we find Shah-zada Timour an exception to the general rule. The appointed time arrived, passed by, and yet no intimation was sent of his being ready to receive us; we therefore adjourned to Colonel Wade's tent, and were introduced by him to the French officers.

Mons. Avitabile is a fine tall stout man, upwards of six feet high, with a pleasing yet determined cast of countenance, from which you can see at once he never issues an order without its being promptly obeyed, or woe be to the man who neglects it. He wears his beard, which is of a grey colour, and reaches half way down his chest, and in conversation speaks either in Persian or French. He dresses very magnificently. On the present occasion, his costume consisted of a long green coat, fashioned not unlike a Mussulman's "chupkun," and ornamented with a profusion of lace and three rows of oblong buttons of solid gold; trowsers of scarlet cloth, with a broad gold stripe down the seams, and a green velvet cap, with a band also of gold lace and a tassel of the same material, but no peak. This he invariably retains on his head, whether indoors or not, (as does Mons Court his, both having adopted the native custom of remaining at all time covered;) and out of compliment to them we did the same, although, I must confess, I could gladly have dispensed with the weight of my helmet. General Court was also well dressed; but being a short thick-set man, pitted with the small-pox, he did not appear to the same advantage as Avitabile. The first glimpse I got of him at once impressed me with his strong resemblance to a rough and ready sailor, and I believe the same idea was general throughout our party. He wore an open horse-artillery full-dress jacket, displaying beneath it a red waist-coat, equally profusely ornamented with lace; and his cap and trowsers were similar to the governor's. Both had handsome sabres attached to embroidered belts, the plate of Avitabile's being of gold studded with valuable jewels, as was also his scabbard, a very small portion of green velvet being visible in the centre of it. The blade of his scimitar, which belonged to Akhbar, is a very superb one, and cost the governor 2,000 rupees, which, added to 1,000 more for the setting, may be considered a tolerably large sum for a weapon.

The gong had chimed ten ere the Prince was announced as being prepared to receive us,—a piece of information we were not a little pleased at, as our patience was nigh being exhausted with having waited so long. Wade, with a general on either hand, led the way, and we of the mission followed. On entering the durbar tent, we found the poor Shah-zada, unaccustomed to the royal part he was henceforth to play, *standing* to do the honours, (a piece of condescension, I believe, unlooked for in his station,) but on a motion from the colonel he instantly rectified it by popping with much alacrity on to his guddee or throne. This consisted of a large square ottoman covered with kim-khwab,* in the centre of which and approaching to the front were three pillows, enveloped in a beautifully delicate coloured silk, to support his head and arms. Cashmere shawls were spread in front for us to walk on, and as we did not take off our boots seemed out of place on the ground. On either side of the guddee were arranged chairs, on which we sat, and conformable with Eastern manners did not

---

* Kim khawb: silk worked with gold and silver flowers: brocade.

uncover the head. In front of the prince stood the old Wuzeer, habited in bright kim-khwab with gold ornaments; and behind, on his right and left, were two.attendants. The two French generals having been presented with all due form, we three, who had lately joined, passed through the same ceremony, making a salaam with our right hands as we were named to His Highness, who was pleased to utter a few almost unintelligible gutturals signifying that we were welcome. Beyond these words, and an occasional affirmative expressed by the dissyllable "bulli," he maintained a total silence to the colonel's address, and likewise to a short but loud oration vociferated by Mons. Avitabile. A period was at last put to these uninteresting proceedings by a few menials entering with the "khilluts," or honorary dresses, and presents, intended for the French generals. These consisted of "chogahs," or robes, some trays of shawls, and American rifles; all, of course, furnished by the British Government. The governor of Peshawur received his very graciously; but it was amusing to observe the rough manner in which his brother officer acted, and who, instead of permitting the attendant to envelope his shoulders in the folds of a crimson cloak, seized hold of, and stuffed it beneath his elbow, as it was resting on the arm-chair, and supporting his head. We shortly after took leave, a relief both to ourselves and to our host, who, although he *looked* a prince in every respect, yet, being but lately drawn from comparative obscurity, and unaccustomed, in his new capacity, to the gaze of strangers, seemed but ill at ease with this public exhibition of his greatness, and, I have no doubt, was glad when the ceremony concluded. With the exception of his turban, which had been exchanged for one of a puce colour, tastily and even elegantly arranged on his head, he was dressed in the same simple costume that he wore yesterday, his handsome though listless features, brightening to a look of intelligence as we arose to retire. We all salaamed to him, which he returned, and we then backed out, (or ought to have done so, for, I believe, few of us, except the Politicals, thought of this piece of etiquette,) passing beneath a semiana, or awning, under which trays of flowers were spread out, and thence through the range of kanauts, or screens, that enclosed a large area in front of the durbar tent.

After being kept from breakfast for so many hours, it was not without a great deal of satisfaction that we adjourned to the colonel's tent, and there sat down to a meal, sufficient to have dined some thirty persons; the solid materials of which it was composed being added to the repast in honour of the French visitors, who are accustomed to substantial fare thus early in the mornnig. Champagne and claret formed part of the entertainment, and a second course of pastry and such like articles, was served up on the removal of the first. Behind the governor stood two of his servants, a pair of diminutive Affghan boys, dressed in shawl turbans, gold waist-belts, and spotted "chupkuns," one of whom was an extremely handsome lad, and would even have made a remarkably pretty girl; he, however, looked quite out of place in attendance upon a masculine individual like Avitabile, and would have been better suited for the occupation of a lady's page.

The afternoon must have been entered upon ere we arose from table, and, at three P.M., Maule and I mounted on an elephant, proceeded a short distance from camp to meet and conduct the Shah-zada Hashim to his noble relative. We had not gone far beyond its confines, when a cloud of dust announced his approach, and, on his coming up, we salaamed, and expressed our gratification at his visit, Maule being the interpreter. The prince showed but few traits of his royal birth, being a mean looking old fellow, clothed in a shabby shawl dress, and surrounded by a set of ragamuffins by way of attendants; and, whether the heat was too overpowering for His Royal Highness, or whether he was overcome by the novelty of the scene, or the thunder of the cannonade announcing his arrival, is unknown, but his

handkerchief was seen to be in constant requisition to remove
the perspiration that bedewed his wrinkled forhead, and even
streamed down the furrows of his cheeks. At the entrance to
the durbar, his elephant, of course, had precedence of ours,
and, on his alighting from it and passing through the kanauts that
enclosed the tent, a rush was immediately made by the rabble
to procure admittance with him, which effectually excluded us.
Before a sufficient clearance could be completed to permit our
ingress, the meeting of the Prince Hashim with his nephew, the
most interesting part of the scene, had concluded, and, when
we entered, we found the former seated by the side of the Shah-
zada Timour, on the guddee, which had been brought to the
front of the tent, so as to face the semiana. The latter prince
offered us chairs, which we declined, as we thought he would
prefer to be alone with his relative, and we therefore walked up
and down the area enclosed by the kanauts. Within these limits,
those only who belonged to the royal tribe of Douranee were
allowed to enter; and each individual, as he came within sight of
the Shah-zada, offered up a prayer for his welfare, and then
ranged himself in line along the extremity of the semiana; in this
manner forming an avenue from the entrance to the durbar tent.
Thus placed, the people stood with their hands folded, and their
eyes cast on the ground, agreeably to the custom of the Persians
and Affghans when in the presence of royalty; but, occasionally,
I detected a fellow taking a side glance at his prince when he
thought he could do so unobserved, and one or two even went
so far as to smile; these exceptions were, however, few, the rest
preserving an almost immovable stillness.

The Wuzeer Moolla Shukore and the two attendants who
had waited on the Shah-zada at the morning's durbar, officiated
as masters of the ceremony on the present occasion, and admitted
the select few, allowed to remain in the presence of the son of
their future sovereign; of these, sacarcely any were otherwise than

meanly attired, and their dress, in general; bespoke a close allianc
with poverty. One of the attendants bore the office of physician t
the prince, the other that of the Amla Bashee, a species c
comptroller of the household. A tale is related of the doctor; wh
when at Cabul, a few years ago, was seized by Dost Mahomme
for some offence, and placed in confinement. Here he lingered fc
some time; but not having shown a disposition to escape, his guard
were ultimately reduced to two soldiers, who conversed with hin
and showed him other acts of kindness. One day; both happenin
to complain of illness, the doctor volunteered to provide ther
with medicine, and, as he had the reputation of being a cleve
disciple of Esculapins, they gladly availed themselves of his offe
An opportunity of regaining his freedom suddenly presented itsel
to him, but his plans had to be matured, and he administered only
a slight dose to his patients, which, however, had the effect o
benefitting them so much, that, without any suspicion of his
intentions, they next day requested a repetition of it. Accordingly
another draught was prepared; but. the wily doctor, in whom the
love of liberty was stronger than the welfare of his humane guards
artfully threw a quantity of drugs into the potion, and then quietly
awaited the result. This was not long in being manifested — the
keepers were seized with cramps and retchings that convinced
them they were attacked by that dire disease the cholera, and the
fear of its terminating fatally aided the effects of the medicine.
Their strength was quickly prostrated, and the doctor, who had
been on the watch, observing their helpless state, and the complete
success of his stratagem, left his prison, mounted a horse in waiting,
galloped off as hard as he could, and was forty miles from Cabul
ere his escape was discovered. He eluded all pursuit, and eventually
arrived at Loodianah in safety.

At the conclusion of the durbar, Colonel Wade and the Shah-
zada Timour, seated on elephants, proceeded in state to the
outskirts of the camp, where the latter was to be presented to the

assembled multitudes who had espoused his cause. Divided into tribes, each, as it came up under its respective chief, marched past the prince's elephant — many amongst the horsemen galloping at will out of their ranks, curvetting their steeds, firing their matchlocks, and committing other extravagances to testify their joy. Of all that appeared in this animated scene none claimed so much attention as a band of the notorious Khyberries, whose tall, gaunt figures, high cheekbones, and muscular sinews, betokened a race of hardy mountaineers. Like all hill people, they attend but little to the dictates of cleanliness; and the dirty garments they exhibited to the prince were but in keeping with features equally guiltless of suffering from ablution. Their dress generally consisted of a long chupkun of a light brown colour, reaching to the knees, loose trowsers, and grass sandals, or shoes with hobnails. The turban assimilates with that of the other Affghan tribes. Their usual weapons are a long jhezail, or rifle, with a wooden fork attached to its extremity, on which the piece is rested to secure a better aim; a sword; and a large knife stuck into the sash: some had a pistol in addition. Their appearance was wild in the extreme; and a rude pipe, screaming forth a few shrill notes, heightened the effect, and added to the interest of these celebrated and formidable robbers. A largess of several hundred rupees was scattered amongst the population, and the ceremony did not conclude till some time after sunset. The Shah-zada behaved like an automation on the occasion, never opening his lips, and apparently but little interested in the scene; but the old wuzeer, however, sat behind, was determined something should be said; and making use of the howdah as a rostrum, he arose, and delivered a long oration in the Persian language.

March 30th.—Our late Mihmundar, Luchman Singh, and the Subadar of the Sikh troops, who had accompanied us from Lahore, were introduced this morning to Colonel Wade, who presented them with "khilluts," or honorary dresses, and other gifts. Every sepoy in the company also had a douceur of three rupees; the sums to the native officers being proportionally increased, and all seemed pleased with the generosity of the British Government.

March 31st.—The detachment of Sikh troops that had been so long with us left our camp this morning to proceed to the Punjab, where it will rejoin the regiment to which it belongs. It forms a part of Rajah Gholab Singh's army.

April 1st.—General Avitabile having promised to parade the Maharajah's troops under his command for the Shah-zada, we met at an early hour this morning in front of Colonel Wade's tent, who soon after joined us. It was originally intended that the prince should ride to the ground on horseback, but he excused himself on the plea that his stirrup-leathers were broken, and had now ordered his elephant to be in attendance. After a remonstrance, to the effect that he was to take care this did not occur again, had been sent to him by the colonel, we cantered to the scene of action, escorted by a party of Allard's lancers, leaving the prince to follow, in company with Maule and Cunningham, on another elephant, and attended by all his personal guards. Our party made a direct cut across country; and, for upwards of a mile, was meandering through a cemetery, crowded with countless graves, into which had been cast the victims of a pestilential disease that, a few years ago, had made terrible havoc with the population of Peshawur.

Soon after quitting this burying-ground we were suddenly stopped by an awkward ditch, dug for the purposes of irrigation, and into which a lancer and his horse fell, after a fruitless attempt to leap it. To escape a similar fate, we made a slight detour, where, however, the ground did not prove to be very satisfactory, as a quagmire stretched its treacherous influence for some distance around, and was concealed from view by a coating of dry sand.

Wade and Lord, being in advance, were soon within its limits, and their horses, after plentifully bedabbling the gold-embroidered uniforms of their riders, did not extricate themselves without a struggle. We, who were behind, took warning from their experience, and, by extending the circumference of our circle, avoided a dilemma none of us were very anxious to encounter.

On the arrival of the Shah-zada, the artillery fired a salute of twenty-one guns, the infantry presented arms, and the drummers and trumpeters vied with each other, to produce the loudest sound in honour of the event. This concluded, we rode to the left of the line, and commenced the inspection. Here was a small battery of foot artillery, consisting of a large howitzer, and two small mortars mounted on field carriages, and drawn by bullocks; the men attached to them being badly dressed in old coats of divers colours, and the ordnance not having even cleanliness to recommend it. Two or three regiments of infantry came next: the soldiers being accoutred in red jackets and white trowsers, black cross-belts, and pink silk turbans. Adjoining them ranged some more foot artillery, bad in every respect; about as many more regiments of infantry, and three guns again to their right. We then reached the cavalry, the dragoons occupying the left. These were well mounted, and form a fine body of men and horses. Their dress I have already described. On their right were two regiments of Allard's cuirassiers, the most noble-looking troops on parade. The men and horses were all picked, and amongst the former are to be seen many stalwart fellows, who appear to advantage under their cuirasses and steel casques. Particular attention seems to have been paid in setting the men well up, and their accoutrements are kept in the highest order. Many of the officers wear brass cuirasses, and their commandant is perhaps the finest man of the whole body, and looked extremely well in front of his superb regiment. Lord, who has been some time at Peshawur, says it used to be poor Allard's pride and amusement to review these men, and their present soldier-like and martial appearance is no doubt owing to that officer's constant care and superintendence. A small body of horse artillery occupied ground to the right of the cuirassiers, but beyond the horses there was nothing to be admired about them: they were equally bad with their comrades in the foot. This concluded the whole of the line; and to do the men justice, they were very steady under arms, and, as a body, their appearance was very creditable.

General Avitabile then pointed out a position for us to take up whilst the troops passed by in review order; but it was not without some difficulty the Douranees and other irregular horse of the Shah-zada's guards were prevailed upon, and made to remain still and quiet during the ceremony. The effect of the sun glistening on the cuirassier's casques and breast-plates as they were advancing was extremely pretty; and the regularity and order in which they walked by, could scarcely be exceeded by the Company's cavalry. They were preceded by an indifferent band of trumpets and kettle-drums— the men composing it being robed in long coats reaching below the knees, and having their heads protected by a sort of jockey cap, in which they looked anything but well. The whole of the troops passed in *quick* time, the officers being in front, and *saluting*. The dresses of the latter individuals differed in every regiment of infantry, although all the men were equipped alike. In one they were encased in a tight-fitting costume of crimson silk, from top to toe; in another bright yellow was the predomin nt colour; and in a third, an equally brilliant orange denoted the men in authority; and it was amusing to observe the independent and swaggering manner with which these would-be-gentry stalked by the saluting flag. The step was kept excellently well, but very few of the companies preserved their dressing during the wheel, and only regained it through the exertions of the officers, who turned round and put them to-rights, preserving *their* distance and time by marching backwards; on the lines being rectified, they with the same *sang froid* performed another semi-circle, d being by this time opposite to the Shah-zada, hurriedly saluted m. The foot artillery came last, and even looked worse than nen in line; for a number of buffaloes having been admitted into e service, their sombre hue, and the dirty state in which the llocks were kept, were only more conspicuously displayed.

As the ground did not allow of any manoeuvers being rformed, the columns, as they passed by, filed off to their pective cantonments; the Shah-zada, at the termination of the iew, returning to camp, whilst we adjourned to the Governor's use, where a superb and substantial breakfast was prepared us. A saddle of mutton, cut from off a doomba, flanked one l of the table, and was a conspicuous object from its size, the alone—a solid looking mass of fat, standing a foot from the th, and looking anything but a delicate dish: however, those o tasted it pronounced it to be excellent. The centre was upied by an article of food that puzzled us all amazingly; and it s not till after some time that we discovered it to be a piece of asantry on the part of the Governor, to commemorate the 1st April, being nothing more than a leg of mutton spliced in some nchified style, with a fowl's head stuck where the knuckel of 1e ought to have been. He laughed heartily at the joke, and med amused that he had taken us in.

Breakfast being concluded, we ascended to an upper rtment, where a score of Nautch girls, attended by a couple of nnas, and a band of musicians, soon after entered, and 1menced their avocations of singing, or rather screaming, (as 1 endeavoured to outvie the other in the loudness of her tones,) dancing. Amongst the number were a few children, varying 1 seven to ten years of age, who have already made some gress in their profession, and are gradually being initiated into mysteries of a craft most derogatory in its nature, as carried 1 the East, though unfortunately not considered to be so by the natives themselves. To vary the amusement, the General showed us several long matchlocks, and jhezails, or rifles, which he had just had made up; some of these being seven feet long, and so heavy that it was as much as any of us could do to lift them horizontally; and they can only be manageable with forks (like the Khyberries use) to support them, or as wall pieces, where they would become formidable weapons, as they send a ball to a considerable distance. He also exhibited his collection of sabres, some of which are extremely valuable, but none more so than that he wore at the Shah-zada's levee. One, however, was very curious, from its antiquity, being evidently of Grecian construction, as the blade was covered with figures in basrelief, and of length sufficient to have formed a two-handed sword. It was found in a tank not far from Wuzeerabad.

The house in which the Governor entertained us forms the centre of one of the sides of an old, but spacious caravanserai, the walls of which he has repaired and converted into lines of defence, both for musquetry and cannon; and as there are godowns and store-houses in its interior, where he can lodge ammunition and provisions, the place is easily converted into a fortified situation, capable of containing a large garrison, and of affording strenuous resistance in case of a siege. In choosing a place of residence, amongst the undisciplined population committed to his government, Avitabile was doubtless swayed by these considerations; and should the Affghans at any future period endeavour to cast off the yoke of their conquerors, he would, if such were necessary, easily be enabled to hold this position until succour arrived from the Punjab. Independent of the caravanserai being erected on elevated ground, the General's mansion is raised to the height of three stories, thus completely commanding the city, (the main street of which it faces,) and overlooking the neighbouring ground. An extensive view of the country is obtained from the roof, (which is flat,) and the distance on three sides, backed by a succession of mountains, the most lofty of them being enveloped in snow, is exceedingly pretty, and deserving of a better foreground than is formed by the city of Peshawur, the houses of which being composed of unburnt bricks, and inserted into wooden frames, for the most part unbroken by the usual accompaniments of mosques and minarets, display a mass of ugliness with scarcely a redeeming feature. One half of the area of the caravanserai is now being converted into a flower garden, and the other is set apart for parades, guard mountings, and other military purposes: severel cannon and ammunition wagons were drawn up on the side of the latter. An avenue of young trees stretches from the mansion to the gateway, where the Governor has also a few apartments, still in an unfinished state, but, like the former, decorated with paintings in the native style. The beams in the ceilings of them being constructed of the deodar, (the cedar of Lebanon,) and exposed to the air, threw out a delicious perfume, and reminded me strongly of the abodes of Simla, where this wood is so much used.

CAMP AT PESHAWUR

APRIL 2nd.—Our camp was moved this morning from Chumkunnie to a spot about a mile beyond the eastern face of the city; and as our route lay through the main street of Peshawur, Colonel Wade directed our march should assume the form of a procpssion, in order that the situation of the Shah-zada, surrounded by British, Sikh, and Mahomedan troops, should be more fully displayed to the public, as a means of inducing some to blazon forth the irresistible grandeur of his position, and others to enrol themselves under the Douranee banner. A company of British troops, and likewise one from each of the Maharajah's regiments, under Lieut. Corfield, were sent in advance to the new ground, there to be in readiness to salute the prince on his arrival. Twenty-one guns announced the moment when His Royal Highness mounted his horse, (for after the rebuke of yesterday, he had taken good care to provide himself with stirrupleathers,) and wore also a signal for the procession to move on, the horse artillery leading the way. A line of Sikh troops, stationed on either side of the road, rising from the bottom of the hill on which Avitabile's mansion is situated, up to the gateway, formed a street for the procession to pass through, both the French generals being present to receive the Prince, and conduct him to the city. The eminence being steep, the horse artillery galloped up, and winding beneath the walls of the caravanserai, entered the main street of the town, which was just broad enough to allow a passage for the guns, and no more. Crowds were assembled to witness the scene, and the people in the distance eagerly stretched forward to catch a glimpse of the cavalcade as it appeared in sight. All, however, was orderly and quiet — no boisterous sounds were emitted, and even the hum of conversation was hushed on our approach. Two or three of the governor's orderlies, who preceded us, directed the inhabitants, as we advanced, to sit down — a summons which, wherever it could be obeyed, was immediately attended to. The street was neat and clean; but as a gutter runs down the centre of it, I suspect we did not see it in its usual state, and it is more than probable that the stones with which it is paved underwent an extra purification in honour of the present ceremony. The houses are generally three stories high, with flat roofs, in many instances enclosed by a wooden rail; but they are, with few exceptions, very unsightly, and have a most uncomfortable tottering look about them. The shops, which constitute the lowest stories, were all closed, and the platforms in front of them, where the goods and merchandize of their owners are usually displayed, were now occupied by a dense throng of individuals, who were huddled together as close as it was possible to pack them. We quitted the city by a common-looking gateway, at a few hundred paces from which stands a large fort, built by Avitabile, on the ruins of the Bala Hissar. A royal salute was fired from the cannon on its ramparts as soon as the Shah-zada appeared in sight, and the noise of its thunder had not ceased many minutes ere we reached our new encampment, where the companies under Lieut. Corfield presented arms as soon as the prince approached his tent. On his alighting from his horse, the troops were dismissed, and we adjourned to the house of General Court, who had invited us to breakfast. Happily, as the sun was becoming hot, this was at no great distance; and a breach in his garden wall saved us from the necessity of making a long detour to reach his dwelling, a mud building, of two apartments erected in Ali Murdan's Bagh, where the country seat of that celebrated noble still exists in a habitable state, the family of the French general at present occupying it.

I was disappointed to find the residence of one whose acts of public spiritedness are attested by numerous magnificent works that have survived the ravages of time, to have no pretensions to architectural beauty, and, indeed, scarcely worthy of a passing glance; but the character of its founder will ever throw an interest around the pile. Born in Persia, Ali Murdan's talents soon brought him into notice, and he was intrusted by Shah Sefi, the monarch of that country, with the government of Candahar. This honour he had not long enjoyed, when he received intelligence that the king, who was a monster of iniquity, had designs upon his ilfe; upon which, disgusted at his conduct, and with the revolting acts of cruelty of which he was guilty, Ali Murdan resolved upon transferring his government* to the Emperor of Hindoostan. Shah Jehan, overjoyed at the prospect of this acquisition to his territory, immediately dispatched troops to occupy Candahar, and they succeeded in garrisoning it before the Persian king could offer any opposition — the province long afterwards remaining subject to the Mogul. The supreme command at Cashmere was bestowed upon Ali Murdan, as a reward for his services, and he ruled this valuable domain with so much equity and with such satisfaction to the king, that he raised him to the Subaship of the Punjab, with power to hold Cashmere by deputy. Honour still awaited him, for he was not long afterwards advanced to more important post of Cabul, which he governed for some time, and showed much personal bravery in conflicts with the Usbec Tartars, parts of whose

*The only indefensible act of his life.

territory he annexed to the imperial dominions. He was subsequently promoted to the rank of Captain-General of the forces, and died in 1657, when on his way to Cashmere, after having paid the emperor a visit at Agra. Notwithstanding the amazing sums of money he expended in public acts of munificence — the canal at Delhi, and the Chahar Chuttur, or great bazaar, at Cabul, being amongst the most magnificent, this nobleman died immensely rich, leaving behind him a fortune, in jewels and money, amounting, it is said, to £1,875,000, which came into the possession of Shah Jehan, who always had regarded him with affection, and ever remained his staunch friend.

As General Court had been obliging enough to say he should be happy to parade his artillery for my inspection whenever it would be convenient for me to attend, I, a few days subsequent to this, accompanied by Maule, called upon him for the purpose of seeing it. We found him seated at breakfast, but he immediately issued orders for his men to assemble, and by the time we reached the cantonments they were drawn up in readiness to receive us. On our arriving in front, they saluted, and the general then directed the native commandant, a fine soldier-like-looking man, handsomely accoutred, to put them through their drill. This they performed with great credit; their movements being executed with a celerity and precision that would have done honour to any army. The orders were given in French, and the system of gunnery used by that nation has also been adopted. At the conclusion of the exercise, we walked down the line and inspected the ordnance. The two guns on the right of the battery were six-pounders, and were the same that Lord William Bentinck had presented to Runjeet Singh at Roopur. The rest were cast by himself from their model, and appear almost equally good. The precise number of pieces we saw I forget, but I think nine, including two small mortars for hill service. We then tried some of his fuzees, which are very good, and burn true; and his portfires are also tolerable, but when compared with those in use with every other part of the Sikh army, admirable; as with the latter, they are nothing but cases filled with pounded brimstone indifferently rammed down. All the shot was formed of beaten iron, and cost a rupee each; and the majority of the shells were composed of pewter, which he told us answered uncommonly well. When it is considered that all we saw was the work of the general's own knowledge, and we reflect on the difficulties he has had to surmount, it is a matter almost of wonder to behold the perfection to which he has brought his artillery.

The men dress something like our own horse arillery, except that, instead of helmets, they wear red turbans, (the jemadars or officers' being of silk,) which hang down so to cover the back part of the neck; white trowsers, with long boots; black waist and cross belts; and black leather scabbard with brass ornaments. Both their appointments and accoutrements were kept in high order, and formed a pleasing contrast to the artillery that were present during the inspection on the first of April.

We adjourned to Mons. Court's house, where we were refreshed with a delicious glass of sherbet, more grateful, as the sun out of doors had scorched us with its rays; and after a short time we bade him farewell, having been much satisfied with our visit.

I rode with Captain Farmer to the Wuzeer Bagh, one of the many celebrated gardens in the neighbourhood of Peshawur, and which were in all their loveliness when Elphinstone was welcomed to the court of Shah Shoojah. A change may with truth be said, to have come over the scene, for with the exception of two or three, the rest are neglected, and have run to ruin. We had to traverse a part of the city, which was not at all raised in any estimation by a second visit; the back streets being dirty, narrow, and confined; and the main thoroughfare far from retaining that aspect of cleanliness it bore when we first saw it. The comparatively few individuals we met there did not realise the idea we had formed of a bustling and a thriving bazaar, and seemed a strange contrast to the dense mass of faces that had then lined it. We were, however, at the least frequented end of the city, and, perhaps, may not have arrived at the most business stirring hours. Whilst proceeding along one of the most gloomy streets in the environs, a figure, shrouded to all appearance in grave clothes, crossed our path; and I then beheld for the first time a costume invariably used by the women of Persia and Affghanistan whenever they move beyond the threshold of their homes. A long and loose white robe entirely conceals the figure of the wearer; and a thick veil, with two or three small apertures of net work to breathe and see through, effectually conceals her features from the forbidden gaze of man.

As we approached the garden, we passed a funeral procession, attended by a numerous body of men chanting a dirge, and preceded by others who carried five trays of different coloured cloths, as offerings; but there was no solemnity whatever in the scene; and we, being strangers in the land, attracted more of their attention than they devoted to the ceremony in which they were engaged. Happening to pass the grave on the following morning, I observed it to be surrounded by a number of mourners, all women, who were huddled close together; but they manifested the same indifference as was exhibited by the train who had followed the corpse to its last resting-place.

The Wuzeer Bagh is enclosed by two lofty mud walls, and though much neglected, still retains some impress of its former elegance and beauty. The ground is laid out similar to all Eastern gardens, the square being divided into four equal compartments by fountains and walks; and the never-failing lines of cypress trees, with their dark foliage, looked well, contrasted with the lighter coloured leaves of the mullberry or weeping willow, with which they were intermixed. Beneath them were parterres, in which grew poppies, wall-flowers, and stocks; and the brilliancy of their colours aided in no small measure to increase the lively appearance of the scene. The several buildings that once ornamented the grounds have already been struck by the mouldering hand of time; some of them even will soon be a heap of ruins, and a confused medley of disjointed fragments will hereafter be all to remind the spectator of sites once occupied by the luxurious bath or voluptuous pleasure-house. Years have rolled by since the locality was first used as a retreat from the bustle and turmoils of the day; but its hours of repose and quiet have also long passed, and the clang of the hammer on the anvil, the vociferations of the workmen, and the ribald talk of mercenary soldiers, are now heard where, formerly, the joyous mirth of some light-hearted inmates of the harem was re-echoed, before "grimvisaged war" drove their masters from home and country.

The Wuzeer Bagh, which had been desecrated by the Sikhs, now, in fact, forms our arsenal, and was the spot selected by Dr. Lord for his residence previous to Colonel Wade's arrival; indeed, it is better known to us as "Lord's workshop", than by its proper name. Cannon, rifles, bullets, and all sorts of destructive implements were progressing towards completion during our visit, and are for the equipment of the levies now being raised for the Shah-zada. Those from amongst the Khyberries are quartered in this agreeable spot, and groups of them were to be seen sauntering along the terraces, their thick hobnail shoes jarring the ear as they scraped the smooth surface of the pavement; whilst their rough-looking features, and tall, gaunt, but athletic figures, armed with the jhezail and long knife, or sword and shield, harmonized with the warlike preparations and the existing state of the gardens, in other days, would have been ill suited to appear in a place evidently dedicated to peace, and where all ought to have been lovely, soft, and beautiful. A gateway, in the centre of the wall, on the left-hand side, admitted us within a building now converted into a stable; and hastily passing through it, we entered another compartment of the gardens, equal in extent, and laid out in a similar manner to the first, except that there were no cypresses, and the water had entirely forsaken the fountains. Numerous orange and citron trees however, compensated for the absence of the former; and the deep shades formed by their thick foliage presented retreats too cool and inviting to be unoccupied; but the tenants were horse-dealers, who, seemingly, as a matter of course, had stalled their horses on every available spot.

It was, I think, on the 7th, when the Generals Avitabile and Court were breakfasting with us, that the Shah zada was pleased to transfer from his own royal table to that of the Colonel's a number of cooked dishes, which plainly, show the Affghans to be perfect adepts in the culinary art, although they do not profess to follow Mons. Ude as their model. A sucking lamb, roasted whole, and stuffed with prunes, raisins, almonds, and other delicacies, called forth our especial praises, and the sweet "kabaubs," which were innumerable, were also pronounced to be *more* than agreeable by those who tasted them.

The Governor having volunteered to show us the fort of Peshawur, four or five of us rode there in the afternoon, and found him in readiness to receive us. He was attended by numerous guards and by his two Affghan boys, who were mounted on ponies and armed with small sabres slung round their waists, and with daggers stuck in their belts. After proceeding through a street, formed by a squadron or two of dragoons, and passing beneath a lofty and castellated gateway in the northern face, we turned sharply to the left, and cantered up a paved ramp that leads to the highest of the three stories, of which the fort may be said to consist, the, causeway being of breadth sufficient to admit of the Governor driving his carriage and four to the summit. Troops were stationed at the different angles, who turned out and presented arms as we rode by. In the second tier are ranges of very comfortable barracks; and wells to supply the garrison with water during a siege are to be met with every here and there. On the top compartment, in addition to an incompleted citadel, are buildings for his magazines and store-rooms; the latter he threw open for our examination, and a vast number of ten-inch shells, at one end of a gallery, and a complete hill of bullets at the other, besides lead and other requisites to make up material, plainly prove that a warm reception would be given to an attacking party. Cannons of different calibre were mounted on the ramparts, and numerous workmen were busily engaged in levelling the irregular ground wherever it was necessary. The fort is far from being in a finished state, and the ditch which encircles it has yet to be cleared out and deepened.

Having satisfied our curiosity, we adjourned to some capital apartments of the Governor's, situated over a fine gateway, through which ingress is obtained from the first to the second compartment, and here we found the hospitable General had provided a light refreshment for us. We hastily partook of it, and then, mounting our horses, galloped round the northern and eastern walls of the city to the parade ground, where the Sikh troops were drawn up for Avaitabile's last inspection; the command of the forces being about to devolve on General Ventura, whose arrival is daily expected. The sun had sunk into the far west before we reached the spot, and the rapidly deepening twilight scarcely admitted of our seeing the well-mounted and stalwart cuirassiers, or of noticing the regular step of the infantry as they marched by in review order. Before we neared the city, on our return, total darkness had come on; but the Governor having ordered a number of link-men to be in attendance, their torches were ignited, and we proceeded to come under a blaze of light sufficient to have former an illumination.

Most of the mornings and evenings were now occupied inadmitting volunteers into the service of the Shah-zada; and somany Douranee horse-men presented to themselves be enrolled, that it became necessary to select only those whose steeds and arms were better than of ordinary description. Several chiefs, who came for this purpose, attended by their clansmen, formed fine specimens of the rude and predatory soldier; their manly and tall figures being generally enveloped in the folds of a crimson chogah, embroidered with gold, which, opening in front, displayed a cummurbund studded with pistols and knives, or an arm protected by a steel gauntlet, which reached to the elbow, and was terminated at the hand by a flexible globe of chain rings. To Maule and myself fell the lot of instructing some dozen and a half of individuals in the British method of gunnery, and our crew consisted of a most motley group, enlisted by twos and threes, as we could collect them; the basis of the set being formed by three deserters from Dost Mahommed Khan, to each of whom the Colonel gave dresses of honour as an inducement for others to follow their example. These robes, evidences of their disgrace and perfidy, they were not ashamed to wear; and the bright green colour, of which they were composed, rendered the traitors very conspicuous. Professing to be topchees, or artillerymen, we directed them to go through the gun exercise as it is performed in Affghanistan; and the old jumps and quavers they made when at drill but ill accorded with our ideas of parade decorum. They had evidently been accustomed to serve cannon, and could we have dismissed from our minds the idea of their having been "numuk huram," (lit. unfaithful to their salt,) we might possibly have been gratified with the attainments of our recruits.

General Ventura arrived at Peshawur on the 11th of April, and breakfasted with us on the 13th. He is a gentlemanly-looking person, rather haughty in his manner, and bears a high character as a soldier.

On the 14th, a mutiny occurred in the Nujeeb regiment; which but too plainly showed how slight was the discipline that existed amongst the Sikhs, and very forcibly exhibited to us the qualities of the allies who are to co-operate with us when required. I have already alluded to the little authority possessed by Colonel Jacob over his men. They had now become altogether dissatisfied with him, and, taking the law into their own hands, had turned him and his adjutant out of their camp, levelled their tents with the ground, and declared they would have nothing more to do with either of them. As mark of *respect* for their Colonel, they inverted his chair on the spot where he usually sat, and then, having shotted their guns, quietly awaited the results of their misconduct. Dislike to the officers they had thus summarily got rid of, want of pay, and the unfair manner in which they have been sent to Peshawur, (their present appearance in this province being the third within a very short period,) were amongst the alleged causes of grievance; but to show they had no ill-will towards us, they planted their sentries as usual, at sunset; and when directed to parade by Colonel Wade did so at once. He, however, told them they could no longer form a part of his camp, and in a few days they removed from their ground, I believe, to the Sikh cantonments.

On the 23rd, the sun was rising unobscured by a single cloud, as galloped on to a plain where General Court's troops were assembled in review order for our inspection. After riding down the line, we adjourned to a flat-roofed building, over which an awning had been spread, and where chairs had been provided for our accommodation. This was certainly taking things easy; but as the situation was favourable, and the morning somewhat close and sultry, we did not object to the arrangement. Three regiments of infantry, with a six-pounder gun between each, and a couple on either flank, formed his brigade, which was drilled by a native officer, the words of command being given in French; and the excellent and steady manner in which the manoeuvres were performed, could have been easily surpassed. At the conclusion of the review, the native officers were called up and presented to Wade, who complimented them on the efficiency of their regiments; and one, who was quite lame, from a wound he had received at the action of Jumrood, when questioned about it, was anxious to enter into a long detail relative to the matter; but by a little tact we managed to escape the infliction.

April 26th.—This morning, a thundering cannonade in all directions announced the arrival at Peshawur of Koi-nownihal Singh, the Maharajah's grandson, and commander-in-chief. Colonel Wade having intimated that it was his desire to pay the Prince a visit in the evening, the Rajah Lena Singh, with three elephants and a large train of horsemen, was sent to conduct him to the durbar tent, situated about four miles distant. At six P.M., attended by a large escort, and his officers in full uniform, the Colonel left camp: our cortege forming no inconsiderable body, increased as it was by the presence of the Sikh sawarree. On nearing the royal tents, where a large assemblage of troops, comprising artillery, cavalry, and infantry, was drawn up, the soldiers presented arms, and the batteries fired a salute. The latter, however, was not at all well arranged, as the guns were pointed *at* us, instead of in any other direction; and being at no great distance, we experienced a jarring shock by no means pleasant, either to ourselves or horses; many of the steeds evincing, by their restiveness, an eager desire to escape such near contact.

At the entrance to the durbar court, a deputation, consisting of General Ventura and a party of nobles, received the Colonel, and conducted us to the chief, who advanced to the edge of a white cotton carpet, and shook hands with Wade, who afterwards introduced us. The Prince then motioned us to chairs on his right hand, those on his left being subsquently occupied by six of his chief sirdars, ranged according to their rank. On his extreme left sat Rajah Gholab Singh, one of the best of Runjeet's officers, and second in command. He is a tall, powerful-looking man, very polite and unassuming in his manners, though he has the credit of being wily, and by no means friendly to the English, notwithstanding his professions. Next in order was the Sultan Mahomed brother to Dost Mahomed Khan, the Ameer of Cabul, but at enmity with him, increased, I believe, by the latter having retained one of his favourite wives. He was enveloped in the folds of a long shawl robe, and wore the large Affghan turban; but his dress was by no means handsome. His countenance was dull and heavy, and his complexion stained by the pilled and sallow hue of indisposition. Once the ruler of Peshawur, but now a sirdar of the Maharajah's, he must have felt it peculiarly mortifying to have been seated amidst the conquerors of his country, and compelled, by dire necessity, to take part in their rejoicings. The chair on his left was occupied by the Rajah Lena Singh. He is a youngish-looking man, with a large bushy-black beard, and is spoken of as being a scientific person. Beside him was the Rajah Ayah Singh, a comical individual, dressed plainly in the Sikh costume, and who had such a merry twinkle about his eyes, that on regarding them, one could scare refrain from laughing. Shaum Singh, the father-in-law of Nownihal, sat next him, a stout, easy-going man; and last of all came the son of the late Hurri Singh, some twenty-four or twenty-five years old. Behind the Prince's chair, which was of silver, stood General Ventura, and on his right and left a whole host of the great.

The Koonwur, Nao Nihal Singh, is a young man about twenty years of age, with rather an intelligent, though by no means handsome countenance, and, unlike *our* Shah-zada, appeared quite accustomed to the scenes of royalty. His dress was covered with most magnificent jewels, and on his right arm he wore two bracelets, composed of large diamonds, a necklace of the same precious stones hanging across his chest. His tunic, which was of plain white calico, with skirts, like a flounced petticoat, reached to the knees; his nether man being encased in crimson silk paejamahs, closely fitting to the limbs. He had slipped his feet into a pair of white cotton stockings, but was without shoes; we, however, kept on our boots, which left their prints on the snow white floorcloth as we stepped across it.

The durbar was held in an oblong area, enclosed by high kanauts; at the east and west extremities of which were two small tents facing each other. In front of these were semianas, supported by poles encased with ornamented silver, and under that, to the west, was a smaller one, pitched below the larger, beneath which the Prince sat. Troops were ranged all round the interior of the kanauts, seated on white carpets about four feet broad. These soldiers were armed with matchlocks, and preserved an immovable stillness throughout the ceremony. During our visit, the conversation was kept up entirely by the Colonel and Nownihal Singh, except our occasional remarks to one another, or a word or two which Wade addressed to some of the chief sirdars. At the expiration of half an hour we arose to take leave, on which the Prince conducted Colonel Wade to the extremity of the carpet, and then presented him with an indifferently caparisoned horse, the whole turn-out being worth about one pound sterling.

Our departure was marked by a salute similar to that on our arrival; and, though nearly dark, we proceeded to the tents of the Rajah Gholab Singh, whose visit the Colonel was desirous to return. His encampment was situated about three quarters of a mile from the Prince's, and occupied a garden; at one corner of which a party of horsemen, habited in steel caps, exactly like barbers' basins in shape, was drawn up, and presented arms as we passed by. At the entrance, a company, of infantry also slauted us, and two guns announced our arrival. The ceremonies gone through at this durbar were very similar to those at Nownihal's, though not on such a scale of splendour; but a much better horse than that of the Prince's, with a jhezail, or rifle, and a pair of blunderbuss pistols, manufactured at Cashmere, was conferred upon Wade when he departed. We returned to camp by torchlight.

April 27th.—Sultan Mahomed Khan sent the Colonel, this morning, a dozen of camels completely equipped with jinjalls, a species of small cannon, that carry a ball of about a pound weight; and these are for the purpose of being used against his *brother*, the Ameer of Cabul. The headstalls and harness of the animals being decorated with cowries tastily displayed, and the other appointments being constructed of the brightest and most gay colours, they will make, if not a most useful, certainly a most ornamental addition to our camp.

A number of Mussulmans from Rajah Gholab Singh's regiments were also admitted to-day, and are to form part of an expedition, which is to consist of between 600 and 800 foot soldiers, and about 200 cavalry, to be sent against Sadut Khan a refractory chief, who has thought proper to levy black mail upon an embassy that the Shah-zada despatched a short time ago in his direction. It is expected that matters will be so far arranged as to allow of the force starting in a day or two.

After a long continuance of dry weather, we were favoured in the afternoon with a refreshing shower; but the sun had no sooner set than the rain came down in torrents, and continued to pour without intermission for some hours. It was my turn of duty; and as I went the rounds at night, the state of discipline, or rather the want of it, amongst the Shah-zada's levies and irregulars was most lamentably conspicuous. One half of the sentries had forsaken their posts, and were found snugly ensconced in their tents, whither they had sought refuge from the pitiless pelting of the storm; and it was with the greatest difficulty I could persuade them there was more necessity to be on the alert during such a night than when the elements are calm and serene. On this occasion the lightning was extremely vivid, and quite obscured the pale moon-beams as they shot through an opening in the clouds, whilst the wind suddenly chopping round to the *north*, hurried by with extreme violence, and felt as if emitted from a furnace, although but a few minutes before it had been blowing from the *west*, with a chilliness almost unpleasant.

April 28th.—Whilst at breakfast this morning, the Colonel received a letter from Cabul or Candahar, the contents of which we longed to make ourselves masters of, but it was no use; there were secrets in it only for the initiated, and although he showed it to us, yet being penned in hieroglyphics, our curiosity was doomed to remain unsatisfied. It did not, however, require much of a physiognomist to find out that the news was satisfactory, and so far all is well. It was brought by a spy, who had carried it tied as an armlet wrapped in wax cloth; a precaution most necessary to observe, as Dost Mahomed's people have of late become so suspicious that it is difficult to elude their vigilance. A good method of carrying secret despatches, which is practised in these parts, is to have the letter baked in a chapatie, or cake, as the person, when suspected, can swallow the paper, and thus avoid detection. On such occasions, however, an emetic has been known to be administered, and the individual compelled, though *sorely* against his will, to bring up the communication. Another way is to make the despatch serve as a pistol wad, it can be fired off or drawn as advisable.

The persons whom Wade usually employs as spies are his chupars, or mounted messengers, who disguise themselves inimitably and it was only the other day that two returned from a successful visit to Jullalabad, whither they had gone dressed or rather *undressed*, as fakeers, for I believe they were not encumbered with many clothes. Most of these men are wild and daring fellows, apt to quarrel, and by no means slow at drawing their weapons, especially when their opponents are either Sikhs or Hindoos.

A specimen of the animosity that exists between the chupars, who are all Mussulmans, and these sects, was exhibited in our camp, and was nigh being attended with fatal consequences. It occurred as follows. An order had been issued by Colonel Wade, prohibiting the admittance of any armed person into our encampment,—the interdict being of course only applicable to strangers, when a Ghoorka, who chanced to be sentry on the main street, chose to interpret the order in its literal sense, and opposed the entrance of a couple of chupars, who were returning from some duty or another on which they had been sent. The uniform of Wade's personal guards was well known to every one, and the affray that ensued must consequently have originated in the ill feeling that existed between the parties. The chupars insisted on their right to admittance, which was as firmly denied by the sentinel. From words they came to abuse, till at length one of the messengers drew his sabre. A number of Ghoorka soldiers, whose tents were in the immediate vicinity of the scene of dispute, observing the danger of their companion, flew to his assistance, and a tremendous uproar followed. Being officer of the day, I ran to see what the matter was; and on pushing through the crowd that had now assembled, the first object that met my gaze was the elder of the chupars, stretched, apparently lifeless, on the ground, with a deep sword gash across his head, from which the blood flowed profusely. I immediately despatched a message to the captain of the week informing him of the circumstance, and he too having been roused by the disturbance, was soon on the spot. By this time the friends of either party had come in, and the Ghoorka sepoys, to support their comrades, beat to arms. Without further ado, they loaded their muskets, and presented them, some being levelled at us: and I am convinced, had their opponents but struck a blow, we should have been sacrificed to the blindness of their fury. After being sent for several times, the adjutant of their regiment made his appearance, and being directed to order his men to return to their tents, did so, though with marked reluctance. The chupar was then conveyed to the doctor, who pronounced the wound to be severe, but not mortal, and, having sewed up his scalp, had him carried to the hospital. Thus terminated an affray, which at one time promised to be somewhat bloody, and I believe the Ghoorka who was most concerned in it escaped with merely a nominal punishment.

Somewhere about the beginning of May, the Colonel received intimation on which he could depend, (but not official,) that Candahar had been occupied by the army of the Indus, and he, in consequence, ordered a royal salute to be fired from every piece of ordnance in camp. As we had ten or twelve guns altogether, our rejoicings on the occasion made a most uproarious noise, which was added to by the Sikhs, who, on hearing of the success of our arms, set to work also, and blazed away from the fort as well as from their several cantonments. In the evening the Shahzada held a durbar to receive our congratulations on the victory, and we were each favoured with presents according to our rank, my share being a pair of black Cashmere shawls, and a crimson pashmeena chogah, ornamented with gold embroidery. As the latter articles of dress were thrown over our shoulders, it was well the darkness of night had in some measure advanced, or I know not how long we should have retained our gravity, the figures we cut were so absurdly ridiculous; indeed, a suppressed tittering in the most obscure corner of the tent almost totally upset the Moollah-like solemnity of countenance that those of us in its neighbourhood were striving to conjure up; whilst here and there the convulsive movements of a body would betray the workings that were going on in the inner man to preserve that external appearance of decorum, so necessary for the part we were playing. Some wore cocked hats; others chakoes, which harmonized most ludicrously with bright kim-khwab, or yellow dresses; and it was a perfect relief when we took our departure, and were enabled to indulge in a hearty cachinnation at our pantomime figures, after it had been so long pent up. On examining our presents, when the durbar was concluded, several of us found that both our chogahs and shawls had been worn by their previous owners, and mine more especially, as a black rim round the neck of the former marked where it had come in contact with a greasy beard. We could therefore, make no use of them, and as the Toshah-khanah was in want of such articles, the majority of us sold them, and I for mine obtained 130 rupees.

The weather had now become oppressively warm under canvas, and as the Colonel could only, procure a few kuss kuss tatties; one of which he was kind enough to give to me, camels were daily sent out to bring in jowasa, a species of prickly bush, which, when wetted, makes a capital substitute, though to me it has a rather unpleasant smell. Wade himself has a tent entirely composed of kuss kuss, sent to him, I believe, by General Ventura, and its extremely cool temperature is very delightful when compared with the furnace-like atmosphere without.

Notwithstanding Avitabile administers justice with a strong hand, murders are still committed in the neighbourhood of Pashawur; and the other night, within a few yards of our, camp, a poor grasscutter was cruelly cut off. The foul deed must have been perpetrated from the pure love of shedding blood, as the class of natives to which the victim belonged never possess any money, and wear scarcely a rag; and the hope, therefore, of obtaining plunder, could not in the present instance have instigated the wretches to commit the atrocious act. Such occurrences are, however, far too common in the district to create surprise, and the blood-thirsty disposition of the Affghan is but too manifest in the number of gallows that it has been deemed necessary to erect in the environs of the city. These are constructed of sufficient size to accommodate some five or six malefactors at a time; and after they have suffered the extreme penalty of the law, their bodies, instead of being cut down and removed, are allowed to remain on the gibbets, until they either drop to pieces, or are ransomed by their friends. The number of corpses, stiffened into the attitudes they assumed when convulsed with the last agonies of death, or suspended (as some are) by the feet, that are thus presented to the gaze of a stranger, renders a visit to the suburbs of Peshawur far from agreeable: but disgusting as these exhibitions are, it is to be feared that without them there would be safety neither for life nor property. Indeed, the benefit of this terrible severity is *already* being felt, as the unruly tribes under the governor's control are becoming sensible of the necessity of either subduing their evil passions, or of suffering the punishment that they now see will *certainly* follow the commission of crime; and the monthly average number of murdered victims, though still numerous, is nothing to what it was a few years back.

Before leaving Peshawur, Prince Nownihal Singh returned the Colonel's visit, Lord and Cunningham having been deputed to escort him to camp. A large sawarrie of elephants, on the first of which the Prince and Rajah Gholab Singh were seated, and a numerous body of horse and foot, formed the procession. The Koonwur was received with all due honours, and, led to the durbar tent, attended by the same chiefs whom we had seen with him before. As it was late in the evening when he arrived, darkness soon supervened, and one of Wade's servants, imagining that candles must be necessary, was bringing in a pair at the time the Colonel, General Ventura, and the Prince, were holding a conversation on some important affair in a whisper. "Lejao," "take away," was the colonel's immediate mandate, fearful, it may be supposed, that on this occasion light would prove a conductor of sound, and thus reveal to us the secret negotiation that was going on; but the servant misinterpreting the command, went round to the side entrance, and again brought them in. Again was the "Lejao" vociferated, but to no purpose; the stupid menial returned to the door he first came in at, and was a third time entering with the obnoxious candles, when another and a louder order, followed by a few *compliments* paid to the sharpness of his intellects, at last induced him to take his departure for good and compelled him to cease his endeavours to throw light on a subject with which he had no business. The cortege, as it departed by torchlight, looked extremely well. The jewels of the nobles, and the polished arms of the matchlockmen, glistening with a brilliancy that added much to heighten the splendour of the cavalcade, as it gradually disappeared from our sight. A royal salute marked the Prince's arrival and departure.

Recording this, reminds me of a circumstance that occurred when the Rajah Golab Singh visited Colonel Wade, on which occasion the boasting arrogance of some Khalsa* soldiers met with an unexpected rebuff. On all visits of ceremony, the howitzers, being the only British pieces of ordnance in camp, were used to fire salutes, and though but ill adapted for the purpose, it was deemed more complimentary than employing the Maharajah's guns. As the Rajah Gholab Singh had entered the durbar tent before the salute, with which he was honoured, had concluded, a number of his guards assembled near the battery and freely commented on the *inferiority*, as they termed it, of the Feringee cannon: "What use will such things as these be in the Khyber pass?" remarked one. "Why the roar from one of the Khalsas' guns will drown the sound of two of these together," said a second; whilst a third, more emboldened than the rest, ventured to ask how much powder formed the charge. I had been amused with conceited nature of their remarks, and was too happy in being able to reply: "Exactly *double* the quantity we use in our own provinces, but the cartridges

*Another name for the Sikhs.

are filled with *Sikh powder*, which accounts for the indifference of the reports." They said not a word after this.

On the 9th of May our camp was moved to a spot of ground just beyond the deserted village of Takkal, which is situated about eight miles to the west of Peshawur, and, from its closer proximity to the Khyber hills, it is proportionally warmer, the thermometer having risen the first day to 105° in tent, with *tatties*. At our last encampment I do not recollect it to have exceeded 102°. The right front of our position was formed by the ruins of the Badshah's tope; one of those singular constuctions, which like that at Manikyala, are attributed to Alexander the Great, or his immediate successors.

CAMP AT KOULSIR

MAY 9th.—As it had been confidently asserted on all sides, that, as soon as ever we took up a position at Takkal, the Khyberries would attack us in force, every precaution that is necessary to guard against a surprise has been put into requisition, and it is now in orders, that the subaltern officer of the day shall go the rounds twice during each night. General Ventura has also been appointed to the command of the Sikh auxiliary force, and our camp is, in consequence, formed into two portions; the Shahzada, with the British detachments and his own levies, being on the right, and separated from the Maharajah's troops, who are on the left, by the main street extending between them. The sun had not long disappeared beneath the horizon, when one of those terrible dust-storms, so peculiar to the East, set in with much violence and continued throughout the night. At ten P.M. being officer of the day, (there are but *three* of us for this duty, so it comes round pretty often,) I started on the rounds in a darkness that might have been *felt*, so loaded was the atmosphere with particles of sand, and, by dint of much scrambling and groping, at last reached one of the pickets. Progressing onwards, as I and my escort considered in the most proper direction for another, we were suddenly stunned by the shouts of "Qui vive! qui vive !" on all sides, and up started a guard of the Sikh camp, into which we had stumbled, and where certainly we had no business. It was some moments ere I could assure the Khalsas we were friends, and, as they seemed half inclined, in their sleepy state, to doubt my assertion, the havildar who accompanied me whispered, "Sahib, we had better get out of this as soon as possible, for these fellows are such paguls (fools) that they will, in their fright, shoot us, and declare they took us for Khyberries." I agreed with him; so, once more setting our faces in, as we supposed, a direct line for the second picket, we recommenced our search. It was in vain, however. After the lapse of some time we were brought up by the flag-staff in the very centre of the camp; so giving it up as a bad job, I dismissed the men to their tents, which were close at hand, and, three hours afterwards, met with better success.

A few days subsequent to our removal to Takkal, Lieutenant Mackeson* arrived with about a hundred Moultanies, whom he had succeeded in enrolling for the Shah-zada's service, and who made an equally ragamuffin-like appearance as the other irregular levies. In his capacity of British agent for the navigation of the Indus, he had joined Sir Henry Fane and the army on its reaching; Bhawalpore, but he is now to remain with our camp, and assist Colonel Wade with the political duties.

On the 13th or 14th, we marched to Koulsir, a mile and a half in advance of our position at Takkal; but the Sikhs, under General Ventura, remain on their old ground; an arrangement very much for the better. In front of our new encampment, an arid and stony plain, seemingly unspotted by a single patch of cultivation, extends to the base of the Khyber range, whilst, directly before us, the white citadel of the Sikh fortress of Futtehgurh is occasionally to be seen through the thick haze, and marks the entrance to the celebrated pass.

* Now Brevet-major Mackeson, C.B.

We had not been established many days at Koulsir, when we received intimation that Ghoorkas, who now formed part of General Ventura's camp, had mutinied. It appeared that the General had been compelled to place their adjutant in confinement for misconduct, and as he was a favourite with the regiment his imprisonment was regarded by the soldiers in anything but a favourable light. In the course of the day, they unanimously resolved to release him by force; and to effect their purpose, proceeded in a large body to the quarter guard of the Nujeeb battalion, where the prisoner was lodged, and demanded his enlargement. This was refused, and Ventura happening to come to the spot at the time, determined to repel force by force, and ordered his Goorcherras and guards to load. The Ghoorkas, perceiving him to be resolute in his intentions, abandoned their design, and returned to their tents, which they soon after struck, and, with colours flying and band playing, marched out of camp, taking along with them two guns that were attached to the Nujeeb regiment. No attempt was made to molest them in this nor were they prevented from moving to Peshawur, where they took up a position not far from the walls of the fort, and where they were permitted to remain in a state of open mutiny, without any attempt being made to overawe them, whilst a report of their conduct was sent to the Maharajah at Lahore.

One evening, as we had concluded dinner, and were on the point of returning to our respective tents, the flashes of cannon, followed soon after by their reports, attracted our attention, and as there was no regularity in the firing, and it was evidently in the direction of the fort, we unanimously concluded that orders had arrived from the Maharajah to disperse the mutineers. On the following morning, however, we learned that our opinions were erroneous, and that all this cannonading arose from *authentic* information of the capture of Candahar having been received by the Sikh government, who had directed royal salutes to be fired in honour of the event. The Ghoorkas still occupied their ground, and after a delay of eighteen or twenty days, were allowed to join the Prince Nownihal Singh's camp—one of the object they had aimed at, as they had expressed an unwillingess to move beyond the Khyber pass. What became of the adjutant I never heard.

May 17th.—A sad accident occurred this morning, whilst Hillersdon's levies were at ball practice. One of his men, after having made several ineffectual attempts to fire his jhezail, ceased his endeavours in disgust, and slinging the rifle across his arm, was in the act of turning round, when it went off, the bullet passing through a man's chest, who was standing close to Hillersdon — thence through another individual's arm, and finally lodging in the foot of a third, from which it was extracted with some difficulty.

Much about this time we heard of the defent of the party that had been sent across the Cabul river against Sadut Khan, who, by a successful stratagem, totally routed and discomfited his adversaries. When the expedition advanced against him, he took up his quarters at a certain village, where his plans were to come into operation, and which (after making a faint attempt at resistance) he deserted, leaving the great portion of his baggage behind. The temptation thus given to plunder was too strong to be resisted by his opponents, who forthwith set to work, securing everything they could lay their hands on, never dreaming that their actions were watched, and that they had fallen into the snare prepared for them. The wily Sadut Khan but wanted this, and when he saw that his foes were too intent upon their occupation to regard aught besides, he suddenly, with his followers, dashed into the midst of them, killed and wounded numbers; and dispersed the party. The chief brunt of the action fell upon fifty jezailchees, from Dowson's levies; but many of them met their deaths, and the wounded were, a few days afterwards, brought into our camp in a most pitiable state.

Towards the end of the month, the Sikh auxiliaries took up a position about a mile and a half to our left, and their camp was visited by two Frenchmen, with the singular surnames of *Mouton* and *Boeuf*. When we first heard of these gentlemen being in the Punjab, we naturally enough concluded that these appellations were mere "sobriquets" bestowed upon them by some pleasantly facetious individual; and it certainly *was* curious enough to meet two persons with such extraordinary cognomens, travelling *together* in a country almost destitute of Europeans. Had we heard of them *separately*, their names might not have caused a remark; but the coincidence was too curious to be passed over unnoticed. The former (Mons. M) was a tall handsome-looking man, and a captain in the French cuirassiers; the latter professed to be a gentleman perambulating the globe for his amusement. The Sikhs had not been very long in their new encampment, when several of the grass-cutters having approached too near the pass for forage, were cut off by the Khyberries, who also despoiled them of numbers of their camels, which had been taken to graze in the same direction.

During the month of May, the heat in the middle of the day became most oppressive; the thermometer, between the hours of eleven and four, seldom standing below 110° in our tents. A variety of expedients were adopted to mitigate the effects of this desperately hot weather; some of the officers excavating the earth beneath their marquees; others having only one half of the area dug out, by which means a *change*! of temperature was to be obtained; whilst a few constructed apartments under ground, at the depth of seven or eight feet. For myself I preferred the simple canvas, with a tattie, although much warmer; but there was a dampness in the Surdkhanas, which, in my opinion, is not wholesome: and I also disliked the feeling of moisture that invariably clung to the dress after sitting in one for any length of time. F. whose tent was pitched opposite to mine, had built one of these "vaults for the living," on the most approved principles, and was sitting in it, on a certain sultry day, transacting the affairs of his company with his subadar and havildar, when down came the whole fabric on the top of them; the beams, as they fell, fortunately taking such directions as completely saved them, if not from destruction, at least from broken limbs. I heard the crash, and immediately ran over to assist; but, on reaching the spot, became convulsed with laughter at the appearance of the gallant captain, who, being a stout man, had perspired freely, and the dust from off the clay roof had stuck to his face and plastered it as if with a coating of mud; not a feature was to be distinguished; and besides him stood the subadar, a poor withered-looking old man, who seemed as if he had just issued from a baker's shop.

Two princes of the royal blood, and nephews to Shah Shoojah, joined our camp at Koulsir, but there was no pomp about them; and their tents, which were very small and old, bespoke anything but a state of affluence. One of them, the Shah-zada Salah, was some weeks after sent across the Cabul river, in the direction of Bajour, to watch the movements of Sadut Khan, and the other towards Michnee, for the same purpose. Reports of an intended chupao* upon our camp, at night, by this redoubted chief, were rife, and we were more than once aroused by firing in the direction of the Khyber pass; but beyond these slight alarms we might have been in cantonments, for all the molestation we suffered.

Preparations were at length made that bore some indications of a speedy advance being contemplated. The levies under Dowson and Hillersdon were considered sufficiently *au fait* at their exercise to admit of their joining with the British troops, and taking part in the general duties of the camp. The artillery were busy in constructing ammunition-boxes, to be carried on the backs of mules, and in practising the mounting and dismounting of ordnance

* Foray

from the backs of elephants and, above all, an advanced camp was formed beneath the walls of Futtehgurh, and "sangas," or rude breastworks of stones, were thrown up on the more commanding positions near the entrance of the pass. These rough pieces of fortification, so close to their own haunts, proved very offensive to the inimical Khyberries, who soon evinced a disposition to get rid of them, and, on the 9th, came down in some force with an apparent intention of making an attack. Maule, however, having sent a few shells from a 5½ inch mortar, arrested their progress; but the fellows fired well and true, one of their bullets passing between him and Mackeson, and knocking the turban off the head of the latter's moonshee, who was standing close to them.

On the 10th, I relieved Maule at Jumrood, and took there a 6-pounder gun of the Aloowur Rajah's, in case an opportunity should occur of getting a few long shots. Ferris accompanied me. There was no appearance of the enemy when we arrived; but as the evening advanced, first one head, and then another, and another became visible on the heights in front: until, at length, a small body of jezailchees from Ali Musjid had collected there. The dread of the shells, however, kept them at a distance; but they commenced firing at us with their long rifles, and one of their bullets passed over our heads without committing any damage. It was not considered worthwhile to send a bomb at them, and we contented ourselves with trying the range of some of the 7-feet matchlocks that had been borrowed from Avitabile; but they did not carry so far as the enemy's position, which proved the superiority of *their* jhezails. Shortly after, as night was closing in, and our foes had decamped, we returned to the fort of Futtehgurh, where we slept.

Early on the following morning Wade rejoined us from Koulsir, where he had been for a couple of days, and, on his arrival, we rode to the mouth of the pass, for the purpose of erecting another "sanga" on the right bank of the stream, or rather *bed* of the stream, as the Khyberries had turned the water into another channel, because the Colonel had refused to pay some exorbitant tax they required for allowing it to flow. Runjeet Singh is compelled to give 1200 rupees a month for the little of the "pure element" that is required for the use of the garrison at Futtehgurh; and if the money is delayed beyond the stipulated day of settlement, the stream is instantly stopped, which no doubt proves a certain remedy for the cure of dilatory payment. At the new "sanga" we were occupied till past eleven o'clock, when the heat of the sun drove us to our camp, where we found it delightfully cool, as the Colonel had his kuskus tent, which he gave up for the public benefit.

Our fortifications in front of the pass now consisted of four redoubts—three on the left bank, and one on the right, the latter of which commanded the entrance, and also afforded a good crossfire to the most advanced of those on the opposite side. The largest and most elevated in situation was in the centre, and was occupied by a strong body of friendly Khyberries, under the control of a chief, by name Wahab, a stout and able man, but a thorough rascal. A more complete set of bloodthirsty-looking individuals had, perhaps, seldom been collected together in so small a space, but there was a picturesqueness about their wild costume and muscular figures that harmonized well with the surrounding scenery. I tried to get Wahab to stand for his picture, which he at first agreed to do, and for that purpose put himself into what he termed his fighting costume, done by baring his arms above the elbows, and his legs as far as the knees. He afterwards thought better of it, grew sulky, and moved about so continually, that I was glad do obtain merely a sketch of his dress. I was more successful in securing that of one of his followers, a rough and hardy old dog, who, to heighten the naturally barbarous expression of his countenance, had dyed his hair and beard of a bright red. The other "sangas" were occupied by picked men from Dowson's and Hillersdon's regiments, with a few of Mackeson's Moultanies. Amongst the neighbouring hills, we saw some deserted villages, or, rather, apologies for such, of the Khyberries, consisting merely of caves dug in the earth, in the most rude manner, or as would be seen in the most savage countries. The site of the battleground where the gallant Harri Singh lost his life; was pointed out to us, as well as the remains of the fort of Jumrood, near to which the encounter took place. Little, however, beyond a confused-looking mound is to be seen of the latter, it having been demolished soon after the fatal action, and the stronger and more substantial castle of Futtehgurh erected in its stead.

We again slept within the walls of the fortress, our beds being ranged side by side on the roof of a building in its interior, to which we climbed by an indifferently-constructed ladder. We were joined here by the "gooroo," or priest of the place, whose apartment was on a level with our quarters, and who, with the greatest coolness in the world, dragged his "char-paee," or bedstead, close to ours, and stretching himself on the top of it, was soon in a snore. With nothing but the canopy of heaven for a curtain, we were as cool as it was possible to be at Jumrood, in the middle of summer, or, in other words, we found it unpleasantly warm; and to add to our grievances, the fatigue which the Colonel had gone through at the "sanga" brought on fever, from which he suffered considerably during the night. The next morning, I accompanied him to Koulsir, where he had a smart attack, and was eventually obliged to be bled: but the terrible heat to which we were exposed, was already telling upon most of our constitutions. Farmer had been laid up at Peshawur, and was seriously ill for some days; Rattray followed, and was for weeks on the sick list. Corfield has been so extremely ill, that he is to return to the provinces with General Court, whenever that officer proceeds to Lahore with his brigade. Lord has suffered so much from fever and ague, that he has been compelled to take up his quarters in Avitabile's house, at Peshawur, where he is not so much exposed to the weather. Cunningham, too, has had an attack of fever and been bled and some out of the few that remain have also been complaining. Amongst the rumours and reports that we subsequently obtained from Affghanistan, a most ludicrous one informed us that Wade's illness arose from a bowel complaint, brought on by the anxiety of mind he laboured under when he heard Mahomed Akhbar Khan, Dost Mahomed's son, had arrived at the entrance of the Khyber pass, with a large train of artillery.

On the 2nd of July, official information was received of the death of the Maharajah Runjeet Singh, who, after a long struggle with life, quitted this world on the evening of the 27th ultimo, bequeathing his kingdom to his eldest son, Kurruck Singh, and the famous diamond the "Koinoor," or "hill of light," to the temple of Juggernath, besides distributing above forty lacs of rupees in charity, a few days before his death. As soon as he had ceased to breathe, the chief sultana took the hand of Dhian Singh, the vizier, and inserting it into that of Kurruck Singh, the new sovereign, she placed them in that position on the breast of the corpse, and made them swear to be faithful to one another, and to the late Maharajah's wishes. I think it was on the day following his decease that the body was burned, and, melancholy to relate, no less than four of his wives, and five or seven of his slave-girls, voluntarily sacrificed themselves on the same funeral pyre. On the 3rd, Wade and Cunningham paid a visit of condolence to his grandson, the Prince Nownihal Singh, and found the Sikhs, as is usual with them on such occasions, habited in white robes, without any ornament. To be as similar as possible they only wore white jackets and trowsers, and after a few words of sympathy, took their leave. The Sikhs mourn for twelve days, and during that time, never use a charpaee to sleep on.

A day or two subsequent to this, Wade, and Ferris proceeded to the neighbourhood of the Cabul river, as our inveterate foe Sadut Khan had been busily engaged in inciting the population on its left bank, to arm against us. On the 6th, I joined them with a small Sikh howitzer, escorted by a detachment of the Shah-zada Timour's body guard; and as Wade intended to commence operations that day, and expected me at sunrise, I was obliged to leave Koulsir at 2 A.M. I arrived in the nick of time, as the Colonel had just assembled a number of horsemen who were to accompany us, and with whom we forthwith proceeded to occupy a height which overlooks the river, where it quits the Khyber range, and enters the plain of Peshawur. This view was extremely pretty, the stream, which was far below us, being concealed every here and there by the jutting points of projecting mountains, with a few straggling villages on its left bank, fringed, in one or two places, with mulberry-trees; whilst in the middle of the channel a black rock or two upreared their heads, and broke the force of the current as it flowed swiftly by, causing the water to be lashed into a white foam, and which, as it receded from the obstructions, gradually resumed its unruffled appearance. The Momund country, a mere succession of barren and rocky hills, was to the north; and to the south, and to the east, the valley of Peshawur, over which were spread tracts of cultivation, and clumps of trees, bounded our view; the high range of Khyber mountains being to the west.

The largest of the villages was pointed out by the Colonel as that which he wished to be shelled; but it appeared to me beyond the range of the small howitzer we had brought with us: however, I arranged matters to make a trial. Unwilling to commence hostilities, in the hope that the people might yet be induced to come in peaceably, Wade still deferred proceeding to extremities, notwithstanding some hours had passed by beyond that he had fixed upon as the limit of his forbearance. Presently appeared a couple of horsemen, who were hailed and asked to join us. They replied only by hurling a torrent of abuse at the Colonel, who instantly ordered the riflemen to fire. Ball after ball was sent at them, and although I observed one or two plough up the ground in front of their horses' feet, they managed to escape unhurt; and I was glad of it, as they had displayed much coolness and daring. A party on foot now descended the hills on the opposite bank, and commenced blazing away at us; but without effect, as we were beyond the range of their matchlocks, though a few of our rifles reached one of the boldest of their set, who had crept to the water's edge, and who would have paid dearly for his temerity, had he not been safely ensconced behind a huge rock, upon which the bullets told.

This desultory mode of skirmishing continued for some time, and on it ceasing Wade ordered the remains of an old tower to be put into a state of defence, and lodged a guard there. He then proceeded with Ferris down a narrow cut, which brought them to the margin of the river, and opposite to village, whose inhabitants he previously had warned (in order that the women and children might be sent out of the way) would be attacked unless they consented to acknowledge the Shah-zada. As this cut was no gun road, I was obliged to return by that we had come up, and which, being in many places rather steep, compelled us to have recourse to the drag-ropes, to pull the ordnance, over them. Whilst occupied at one of these eminences, a few stray shots were fired at us from the heights above, but did no injury; and in half an hour I rejoined the Colonel. It was now necessary that the gun should be advanced with much precaution, to conceal it from a party of horsemen, located beneath a tree contiguous to the village; and this having been satisfactorily accomplished, the piece was laid and fired: the shell falling in front of them, and bounding onwards over their heads, exploded just beyond their position. "Sauve qui pent!" was their cry, and away they scuttled to a place of safety as fast as their legs could carry them. Another shot, aimed at the largest house in the place plumped into the midst of it, and raised a cloud of dust that took several minutes to settle. Our attention was then directed to a lofty tower, in which numbers of men had taken refuge; and whilst firing at this, a stray shell happening to descend into a corner of the village, turned out a number of individuals, who proceeded at full tilt across a hill at its back, and behind which another fell, and bursting, drove out a number of women who had taken shelter there, and who now, not knowing where to hide themselves from the deadly missiles, again sought refuge in their houses.

The Colonel, unwilling to make an unnecessary sacrifice of life, but determined to show his threats were not to be disregarded with impunity, now ordered the firing to cease, and we moved along the banks of the river until we reached a small village, in front of which the stream makes a considerable bend, thus leaving an open space of ground, which formed an eligible situation for an outwork. A ditch and mound were forthwith dug and thrown up, but as there was nothing more for me to do, I returned to camp, which was pitched at five in the evening, having been in the saddle, with scarcely any intermission, for fifteen hours. I was as may be supposed, considerably well fagged, and having had nothing to taste since the preceding night, tolerably nigh being amished, and glad to lay hold of a biscuit wherewith to tay the cravings of my appetite. At eight o'clock, Ferris and the Colonel having waited until the position was entirely enclosed by a parapet, and thick brushwood, by of an abattis where such was required, came back, and told me that about an hour after I had left, some marksmen had got on to an island, within range of their situation, from which they blazed away, and killed one man and wounded two others before they could be dislodged. A strong guard was left to defend the village and ground we had occupied.

A day or two afterwards, Ferris having constructed a very fair attempt at a battery in the enclosure, we rode there in the evening, taking with us the howitzer, and also a gun that had been sent from the camp at Koulsir on the colonel's requisition. The left bank of the river was on this occasion crowded with the partizans of Sadut Khan, who was also said to be present; but they were wary and kept almost beyond the range of shot. At Wade's desire a few shells were sent at a building close to a garden, which we saw with a telescope was filled with men, who soon evacuated it; and a few shots from the six-pounder in the direction of Sadut Khan caused him and his train to fall back and take up a more distant and respectful position. Several marksmen again crossed over to the island, and a few of their bullets buried themselves in the parapet of the battery. Night put a stop to our practice, and we returned to our quarters. A trench had been sunk and a breastwork thrown up the previous day as a defence to the Shah-zada Jumboor's camp, situated a short distance behind the enclosure with the battery, and about a mile and a quarter in advance of our own position.

Urgent business now requiring Wade's presence at Koulsir, he left Ferris and myself in charge of the camp near Michnee, and as we had the use of his kus kus tent, we contrived to make ourselves tolerably comfortable in spite of the intense heat. The situation of our encampment was, however, unwholesome, inasmuch as the village near to it was surrounded by rice fields, which being kept in a constant state of moisture, disseminated, a vast quantity of malaria The mosquitoes, too, that were engendered in these swamps, and to whose bite I thought myself quite impervious, attacked us at night in swarms, and stung me so severely that I was obliged to wear leathern gloves. These protected my hands, but my sleeping trowsers were too thin to be any defence against the sharp proboscis which they pushed through at the knee-joints, until they fetched blood and raised large white swellings on the surface. I never suffered from the torments of these insects before, unless I except an onset that was made upon me by a blood thirsty crew when passing through the "Rama Serai," or "happy valley" of the Himalaya mountains, and where I certainly did complain of their treatment but it was as nothing when compared with the annoyance, and indeed I may say *torture* that I experienced at this place.

Of an evening, we used to ride over to the Shah-zada Jumboor's camp, who was always glad to see us, and generally produced a collation of fruit, which he partook of with us. We then commonly adjourned to the banks of the Cabul river, where collecting a few fishermen, we made them cast their nets into the water, and in this manner caught numbers of fine fish, chiefly of a species of trout. As we were returning from these visits, we would often amuse ourselves by trying the mettle of our steeds against the speed of our escort, which consisted of some thirty or forty horsemen, and invariably the jemadar of the troop, who was mounted on a long gaunt racer, succeeded in heading us all. On one of these occasions the Shah-zada promised me a greyhound of the Affghanistan breed, which a few days afterwards he sent to my tent. It was a tall, bony, and somewhat muscular animal, with thick shaggy hair attached to its legs, that on the body being quite smooth; and the Prince assured me I should find it equal to pulling down a deer unaided.

During our sojourn near Michnee, we heard of a serious affray that had occurred at Jumrood between the Mussulmans and Sikhs. How the quarrel commenced is not exactly known, but the latter shut the gates of their fort, (Futtehgurh,) and set to firing briskly on their antagonists. Mackeson, who in addition to the difficult task of conciliating the Khyber chiefs in its neighbourhood, had charge of our camp there, on hearing the disturbance endeavoured to put a stop to it, and for this purpose was advancing to a wicket, when a "Chuprassie" was shot dead by his side, the Sikhs being heard by his cousin, (who had joined him from short time ago Lahore a shout out, "Shoot the Feringee Sahib," or "English gentleman." In spite of the danger to which he was exposed, Mackeson boldly insisted on being admitted with in the fort, where he found the commandant, Boodh Singh, doing everything in his power to quell the tumult. A report of the circumstance was immediately forwarded to Prince Nownihal Singh at Peshawur, who sent the Rajah Lena Singh to inquire into the matter, and ordered the garrison to be relieved forth with. Several individuals besides the Chuprassie lost their lives in this "untoward event."

About the 15th, Wade returned to us, and everything being now in readiness for an immediate advance on Affghanistan, we left Michnee on the 18th, and rejoined our camp at Koulsir the same day. The 19th was a halt, as the Sikh contingent was not quite ready to move; but on the 20th of July, the whole of the force at last quitted Koulsir and marched to Jumrood, where we encamped between the fort of Futtehgurh and our "sangas!" the latter being still tenanted by the friendly Khyberries and levies from Dowson and Hillersdon's regiments. The heights, too, that the Jezailchies had occupied when firing upon us, were now in our possession, and kept by a body of Ferris's irregulars under the personal command of that officer, who had struck across from Michne to Jumrood, instead of returning with us to Koulsir.

The force now at the Colonel's disposal to effect the passage of the Khyber amounted at a rough estimate to some 9 or 10,000 men, 6000 of whom form the Sikh contingent, and are all Mussulmans. The co-operation to be expected from these allies is not of the most cordial description, for it is well known that the Sikhs, as a nation, are extremely jealous of the British power, and nothing would afford them greater pleasure than to see it meet with a reverse. Necessity alone compelled Runjeet Singh to sign the tripartite treaty, but having *done* so, it is but justice to his memory to add, that as far as *he* was concerned, or when his health would allow him to attend to public business, the engagements entered into were observed. Strong, however, as the "Khalsas" dislike to us, I believe their hatred to the Khyberries to be tenfold more bitter; and therefore we have at least the *passions* to work on our side, if we have not their *will*. Of the Affghan levies it is more difficult to speak. Some amongst them have no doubt been led to espouse the Shah-zada's side out of love to his cause, but the majority, it is to be feared, have done so purely for the desire of gain. Many also are secretly of Dost Mahommed's party, and these in their quarrels with the Hindustanees have, on more than one occasion, been *heard* to express their intentions of paying us off, when once within the limits of the Khyber pass. Such individuals *can* only be willing to serve us so long as we continue paramount in power, and *they* are well paid; but were we once to meet with a reserve, it does not require much keen-sightedness to pronounce that their weapons would be turned against us. The British sepoys, the Hindustanee irregulars, and a few of the Affghan levies, amounting altogether to about 2000 men, are therefore the only troops that could be *implicitly* relied upon; but what is this small number to the host that can be brought against them! A whole brigade of our troops *ought* to have been sent with the Sikhs, and no doubt *would* have been, but for the jealousy of Runjeet Singh. The company's "ikbal"* had hitherto been great in the eyes of our opponents, and it is now more necessary than ever that it should continue to be so.

The foes we expect to encounter are the Khyberries in general, and the Afreedies in particular, the most bloodthirsty, and the most numerous of the three tribes that inhabit the country around the pass. When *united*, (which fortunately is not always the case,) it is computed that these lawless marauders can bring from 20 to 25,000 men into the field; but as some had joined the Shah-zada, and others, it is rumoured, are willing to be bought over, we cannot calculate upon meeting a third, or even a fourth of the number. These would, of course, be supported by Akbar

*Good fortune

Khan, who is encamped near the western extremity of the Pass, and can move up to their assistance whenever necessary. A portion of his men, it is also said, garrisons the fort of Ali Musjid. The possessions of the Afreedies lie nearest to Peshawur; those of the Shinwarees being in the neighbourhood of Dhaka, extending from the entrance there to the vicinity of Ali Musjid. The Aurakzyes live more in the interior.

10

THE KHYBER PASS

THE commencement of active operations was hailed by us all with extreme satisfaction, for we were heartily tired of Peshawur and its vicinity, and longed to see what was at the other side of those hills on which we had been gazing for so many tedious months. On the twenty-first we marched in the afternoon under a burning sun to Kuddum, a mile and a half in advance, where we halted and slept. The next morning a strong party, consisting of artillery, cavalry, and infantry, assembled at day-break, preparatory to progressing up the pass, and seizing on some of the heights in front. The Colonel, with Rattray and myself, joined this force, taking with us a small mortar, suspended upon men's shoulders, for the purpose of being carried up the steeps where necessary; the ammunition being conveyed in boxes slung over the backs of a couple of mules. Ferris was, simultaneously, to keep moving with his regiment along the tops of the hills, and Mackeson to penetrate from Jumrood with his Moultanees and part of the Sikh contingent, by a shorter and more confined pass, (the "Shadee Baziar,") only adapted for foot passengers and camels. At dawn of day our cortege was ready, and, as we mustered at the extremity of a lofty mountain, tinged by the grey of morning, with a rippling stream running at its base, the scene was one of extreme beauty and excitement, crowded as it was with a multitude of troops, and the tribes of the various districts in the neighbourhood who were friendly to our cause, and whose infinity of costumes added greatly to the picturesqueness of the display.

After a short interval, everything being reported as ready, we commenced our march, having first sent forward a party of Lord's personal escort as an advanced guard, and who, dressed in long blue chupkuns with scarlet cummerbunds and trowsers, and the pointed kuzzilbash cap, looked extremely well as they appeared and disappeared from, our sight round projecting rocks. We gradually ascended the pass, and soon reached a spot so narrow, and confined on either side with cliffs so perpendicular, that a handful of resolute men might have stayed our progress for some time. Emerging from it, we presently came to Jubbargee, a Khyberrie summer village, constructed on a low and somewhat level piece of ground, jutting from the hills on our right, and composed of rude huts thatched with leaves and branches of trees. It was deserted. On the opposite side was an opening in the mountains, from whence a small stream issued after passing through a very confined valley.

Here our party was divided: Rattray, with the guns and the Sikh contingent, continuing his route along the bed of the main stream, whilst the Colonel and myself, with an escort of horse and foot, and with the mortar, ascended the hills on the right. As we climbed by degrees into loftier regions we felt the temperature becoming more agreeable and refreshing the higher we rose, but the sun was still exceedingly powerful, and produced a good deal of thirst, which we were glad to slake at a diminutive spring that we fell in with two-thirds of the way up. We rested a short time beneath the shade of some trees that had grown up in its vicinity whilst our followers partook of the grateful element, and then, dismounting from our horses to walk up a precipitous steep, we shortly afterwards gained the crest of the ridge, which must have been between 2000 and 3000 feet in height.

From this eminence we had a beautiful view of the pass, with the long-desired fort of Ali Musjid in front of us, about four miles distant, and which, situated on a rocky and almost isolated hill, appeared an exceedingly strong place. It is considered the key to the defile, and our present operations are only preparatory to our endeavours to obtain possession of it. We looked around in vain for Ferris, who was nowhere to be seen; but in half-an-hour he joined us, the deep chasms in the hills having caused him to make several detours, which lengthened his journey considerably. Rattray, too, was descried winding along the bed of the stream, and a messenger was despatched with directions for him to halt and form the camp on a piece of level ground a little in advance, but far below where we stood. We could gain no tidings of Mackeson, and were wondering where he could be, when a man arrived and hastily requested that some assistance might be sent to him, as he had been driven back by a strong force of Khyberries. This, from what we could learn, was consequent on the cowardice of a party of Nujeebs; who had accompanied his band of Moultanees, and with whom he had at first succeeded in chasing the foe from one post to another, even to occupying a height on the opposite side of the pass, when the Afreedies, receiving reinforcements, made a bold sally, which struck such terror into the Sikh troops that they fled at once. Mackeson, however, retained his advantage as long as he possibly could with the Moultanees alone, but increasing numbers having poured in, he had been compelled to fall back upon his present position, where, having thrown up a small breastwork of stones, which in some degree sheltered his men, he nobly maintained the unequal contest.

Ferris was forthwith despatched with his regiment of irregulars to the Lieutenant's assistance, and Rattray having been directed to secure the camp below, the Colonel and I proceeded along the heights by an execrable path that led us over some steep and rugged rocks, and eventually brought us to the summit of a hill, more level than usual, on which a "sanga" was immediately commenced, as it flanked the right side of our encampment. We had not been long here, when a note was received from Ferris, begging that the mortar might be at once sent forward, as the enemy's numbers had considerably increased, and our own men's ammunition was fast failing. Accordingly, accompanied by a small guard, I pushed onwards without delay, and, at the distance of a mile and a half, reached our position; a rising ground in front of a village surrounded by a quantity of brushwood as an abattis and to which our troops could fall back if necessary. The intervening ground was considerably exposed, and shot after shot was sent at our party as we crossed it, but happily without doing any injury.

The enemy, protected by some low stunted trees, were about 350 or 400 yards in advance of the "rising ground" on which Mackeson's embankment of stones had been thrown up, and also occupied the heights of a range of hills that nearly faced it; but, being a long distance off, *their* firing was not very destructive, though occasionally some of their balls told, whilst that from the former was most deadly. Another of their parties, and most probably some of the garrison from Ali Musjid, as they were dressed in a red uniform, lined the crest of a ridge below our left flank, and from thence annoyed our people a good deal. A shell was sent at these fellows, and luckily pitched and exploded amongst them; the success being hailed by our party with a loud huzza, re-echoed again from the surrounding hills; but the enemy nevertheless stood fast and continued to blaze away at us, some of their bullets passing over our heads, and others falling short struck the ground and bounded onwards with a whizz like the twang of a bow-string. The next shell was not so happy, for it flew over the narrow ridge and burst harmless in the hollow on the other side a huzza from the red coats in return being faintly borne to us on the wings of the breeze, as a testimony of their gratification for its innoxious qualities. This kind of warfare continued upwards of an hour, with more or less success, the balls from our foes in front every now and then passing through a small tree close to a hillock that partially sheltered us, and lopping off the more slender of its branches as clean as if cut with a knife. The heat had now become terrific, and the rays of the noon-day sun darted down with an intensity almost insupportable. Meanwhile, the dead and wounded were being carried from the breastwork to the village in the rear, and amongst the former I observed a particularly fine looking man, whose long black hair swept the ground as his corpse was being dragged away. The nature of the dependence we might place on our raw levies was manifested when their ammunition began again to fail, and who one by one, as the individual fired off his last cartridge, left the enclosure on the "rising ground" in spite of exhortation, encouragements, and threats to remain until Mackeson who had gone for some, should return. All was in vain, and it was with the utmost difficulty that either Ferris or I could prevail upon a few to wait until the mortar was dismouned and packed. On this being done, a new difficulty arose as to who should carry it, — for with the exception of one, all the bearers had made off whilst we were too busily engaged to observe their movements, — and some delay arose ere we could persuade half-a-dozen of the irregulars to take it as far as the village. Had the Khyberries at this time been aware of the straits to which we were reduced, and had made a bold dash, there is little doubt but they might easily have secured the piece of ordnance, with ourselves, and the small party that staid with us. They were deceived, however, by a few hardy spirits who still plied their matchlocks from the enclosure with unabated vigour, and whose bold front portended that other troops *must* be at hand ready to support them and take their places.

These were at length called in, and our position was now of necessity being abandoned for want of ammunition. The cessation of our fire soon made our intentions known to the Khyberries, who, preceded by a white banner, were rapidly advancing to occupy the ground we had quitted, when Mackeson happily arrived with re-inforcements of men and material, and perceiving their object, gallantly rushed forward with an huzza, and succeeded in regaining the stockade before the Afreedies, who returned to the clump of trees. As all the shells but one had been expedient to unpack the mortar again, and as it was also thought hazardous to leave it at the village during the night, I was obliged to ride back to the Colonel's "sanga" for assistance to remove it to the camp. Having obtained an order from him for some Coolies, and also received some fresh instructions for Mackeson, I once more retraced my steps to the scene of active operations, and on my way fortunately discovered a number of the deserters, who, in bands of twos and threes, had concealed themselves behind rocks and cliffs. By dint of persuasion, force, and no small proportion of coaxing, I succeeded in getting them to return with me, and having *seen* the mortar perched upon their shoulders, proceeded to give the Colonel's message to Mackeson.

As I crossed the exposed piece of ground *alone*, it was easily perceived from my dress that I was a Feringee, and the shots in consequence flew around me rather thick. I, however, reached the stockade unhurt, where within, I found Ferris and Mackeson comfortably reclining on the ground with their backs against the breastwork; and there I joined them, having first been cautioned to stoop when passing over the interior, as every thing that appeared above the wall was immediately struck. Whilst seated here, the balls occasionally rattled away to our backs, and yielded us the satisfaction of knowing the enemy was wasting his ammunition to no purpose. As it was getting late, I was not able to stay along, so after giving Mackeson his instructions, I took my leave, re-crossed the stockade, and received another salute of bullets as I returned over the exposed spot, one of which struck the ground not a quarter of an inch from my foot. On reaching camp, I felt so exhausted from heat and fatigue, that I threw myself at once on my couch and was soon asleep.

The next day was one of comparative rest to me, as my services were not required beyond the precincts of the camp. Wade, however, returned about a mile down the pass to establish a post, (which was not effected without opposition,) near to where the Afreedies, on the previous evening, had been doing considerable damage to our people, besides plundering the baggage and purloining sundry camels. It was much about the same spot, too, that Rattray's and Colonel Shaik Bussowan's troops were fired on when ascending the pass, by which they lost one man killed and two wounded. As soon as this encampment had been formed, a message was despatched to Farmer, who with the Shah-zada and the main column, immediately left Kuddum and marched to the new ground. As the afternoon had been entered on before the Prince's camp broke up, it was late ere the baggage and tents could be packed and sent forward, and the consequence was some of the more fatigued camels, that had lagged behind, were out all night, and amongst them was one guarded by two sepoys of the 21st, who unwilling to desert their charge remained by its side. It was now reported that these individuals had been slain and left in the pass, on which a strong guard was sent out to bring in their bodies, but who, much to their surprise, found the poor fellows, though desperately wounded, to be still alive. They were carefully conveyed to camp and made over to the surgeon, who sewed up their wounds, one of them having received a fearful sabre gash, which commencing above the left eye proceeded in a slanting direction across the nose, which it separated, and terminated on the chin below the right corner of mouth. The other had three severe cuts over the loins; but neither of the men were considered in a hopeless state.

As the day advanced, reports of stolen and missing baggage rapidly poured in, and amongst other articles carried off by the Afreedies was one of the Colonel's large tents, and what was still more ominous, the Shah-zada's "guddee," or. throne. Camels laden with grain, likewise, fell a prey to the rapacity of our foes, and obliged the horses and other cattle to be put on half rations, — a measure much to be regretted, as not a blade of grass was to be obtained for the former. My commissariat camels, which had been intrusted to the care of a strong escort of Nujeebs, went with the rest, the *brave* guards having fled at the first appearance of the Khyberries, without attempting any sort of resistance. Such, at least, was the tale reported to me by my "gomashta," a thorough *old woman* by the way, and one who, I suspect, was amongst the first that took to their heels. A difficulty of furnishing provisions for the troops also presented itself, and compelled Wade to order Ferris back to Peshawur to bring up fresh supplies.

On the 24th, the Colonel, accompanied by Lord, (who had rejoined the camp at Kuddur with renovated health,) Dowson, and myself, ascended the range of hills on the left, and gradually crowned the heights as we advanced. But little opposition was offered to our progress, for the enemy, who appeared in no great numbers, retreated as we neared, and at length fell back to a respectful distance. I obtained a few long shots at them with a six-pounder of the Sikh artillery, which had been brought to the summit of the ridge on an elephant, and a fire from it was kept up at intervals throughout the day. Mackeson, with Maule, had likewise been progressing on the opposite range, where they had some smart fighting, and the camp was moved forward to ground below the village of Lall Cheenie, near to which our first day's operations took place. At night, Dowson, with a party from his regiment, occupied the heights on the left, and Rattray, with a company of the 20th, those on the right. Mackeson secured his own position.

July 25th.——As the storming of the heights in front of Ali Musjid was to form the chief occupation of the day, a company of the 21st under Farmer, and a large body of Sikh troops under Colonel Shaik Bussowan, were added to the irregulars. We again ascended the heights on the left, Dowson's levies and Farmer's company, with the Khalsa, gallantly driving before them a party of Khyberries, who retreated forthwith to the summit of a lofty and precipitous hill, on which they had erected a "sanga," from whence they soon displayed a flag of defiance. Farmer with the Sikh troops, immediately took up a partially sheltered position directly below them, and commenced a rattling fire, which was returned with equal spirit by the Afreedies. Wade, with Lord and myself, and one of the Maharajah's howitzers, occupied a hill behind them, and an order was despatched to camp for one of the British guns to be sent up the Pass as far as the foot of our situation, to be escorted by the grenadiers of the 20th and a hundred of Kurruck Singh's goorcherras. The firing between Farmer's troops and the Khyberries was incessant, but every attempt to remove the latter from their impregnable stronghold proved unavailing. At last they became emboldened, and were descending somewhat to the left to take Farmer in flank, when a shell from the howitzer had the effect of driving them back to their original station, where they were beyond the range of such missiles. The British howitzer having by this time arrived, I received Wade's instructions, and descending to the bed of the Pass, proceeded to put them into execution.

At this spot, the rocks and cliffs on either side were extremely precipitous, especially those on our right, indeed were almost perpendicular, and surmounted by a tower seized upon in the morning by Mackeson, who had discovered and captured several Afreedies concealed in its interior. The gorge formed by these crags closing upon each other bounded the limits of my advance, and from thence I was to fire on a cantonment of Dost Mahommed's soldiers, situated at the base of the hill on which Ali

Musjid stands, but concealed from my view by a low intervening ridge sloping from the right. The goorcherras were then to gallop forward, plunder the place, and retreat with the spoil behind our position. On emerging from the defile, preparatory to wheeling into action, we were received by a shower of bullets, fired fortunately from too great a distance to cause any serious injury, though sufficiently close to be unpleasant and disagreeable. One hit me on the bridle arm, impressing me for the moment with the notion that some one had struck me severely with a stick, and angrily turning round to chastise the supposed offender I was as instantaneously enlightened as to the true cause of the contusion I had received. Soon after opening our fire, that of the enemy in front ceased, but a couple of Jezailchees, who had ensconced themselves in some hidden position overlooking our left flank, annoyed us a good deal; and as they were beyond the range of our grenadiers' muskets, I was obliged to send to Mackeson for a few of his riflemen to dislodge them. The half-dozen that he ordered for the purpose were, however,. unable to effect this desirable object, and in spite of their new opponents, the fellows still kept blazing at us, one of their balls passing over my shoulder, and striking a fuze mallet which a moment before had been laid down by a havildar or serjeant seated at my side.

Nothing was now to be heard on all sides but the roar of musketry, momentarily drowned by the louder reports of a Zumboor, a mortar, or a howitzer, the discharges from which were re-echoed from the narrow chasms of the pass. Meanwhile, I had explained Wade's commands to the goorcherras' officers, who replied "that it was the custom of their troops, when once they made an advance, never to retreat; that they were quite willing to seize upon the cantonments if it was the Colonel's wish, but they would also retain possession of it or fall to a man." This intimation I conveyed in a pencilled note to Wade for his instructions, but, either unwilling to risk so much when there was no actual necessity for it, or foreseeing proportionate equivalent likely to result from the act, declined allowing them to proceed. After having expended several shells I ceased to fire, but to guard against contingencies, kept several in a state of readiness, to be used as occasions offered; and half an hour had scarcely elapsed, when some ten or twelve individuals were detected endeavouring to escape from their encampment by the left bank. A couple of rounds sent them back rather more precipitately than they had advanced, and subsequently others who attempted the same thing, met with no better success. Affairs remained in this state till the evening, when the Colonel directed two guns of the Maharajah's horse artillery, and two companies of his infantry, to relieve us, as we had been on duty the whole day; and on their arrival about half-past eight or nine o'clock, I sent the howitzer and British troops to camp; and then placing the Sikh auxiliaries in a proper position to guard against surprise, I returned to my tent, which I reached at ten P.M. The firing had ceased on both sides when darkness came on, and all was now as still and quiet as it had before been noisy and turbulent. Between eleven and twelve, the Colonel came back, to whom I reported the arrangements that I had made, with respect to the Sikhs, and who was pleased to express his approbation of them.

Throughout the day, Farmer and Shaik Bussowan, with their troops, had been considerably exposed; the rugged height held by the Afreedies almost entirely commanding their position, and thus enabling them to fire with tolerably accurate precision into our stockade. Many casualties ensued one or two men having been killed at the former officer's side, and several others wounded; but reinforcements having been pushed forward, Farmer was enabled to maintain his ground, notwithstanding the advantages possessed by his opponents. Mackeson and Maule, on the right, had been doing considerable execution; and one of the latter's shells was pitched with so true an aim, that it fell in the midst of a knot of Khyberries, five of whom were either killed or wounded by the explosion.

Being excessively tired and worn out with much exertion, I was soon in a deep sleep; but towards morning was roused by Colonel Wade, to tell me that Ali Musjid was in our possession, a party from Farmer's position having silently pushed forward, and, to their surprise, found it vacated; the first individual to enter it being the adjutant to Ferris's irregulars, a mere lad, though a very gallant little fellow. I of course congratulated him on the event, but feeling very unwell, and not approving of my rest being broken into, I at the moment (with not much politeness) *mentally* wished both him and Ali Musjid at Jericho. As the news was soon buzzed about camp, it was in vain to seek for further repose; and as the dawn was not long in appearing, I arose and dressed. I now suffered from racking pains in my arms and legs, but attributing them to the previous day's fatigue, I bathed as usual, on which a smart shivering fit ensued, and was followed by fever and severe head-ache, which compelled me to have recourse to the doctor, who forthwith transferred me to the sick list: a measure I regretted less, as the fall of Ali Musjid concluded our active operations. Unfortunately for me, the very day on which we had entered the Khyber, febrile symptoms manifested themselves; but unwilling to be absent from my duties at a time when every officer's services were most necessary. I had abstained from having recourse to those more violent remedies which most probably would have cured me at once. The subsequent day's exposure to a burning sun, when the fever was on me,—at times so severe as to compel me to recline on the ground, and in this posture give directions for the proper serving of the ordnance; or when the fire had slackened altogether, to throw myself beneath the leafless branches of a stunted tree, there to seek for the little relief its slight shade was calculated to afford,—did not, as may be supposed, tend to alleviate my sufferings. By abstaining almost totally from food I managed to bear up against the disease, and when I arose on the 25th, to my surprise I felt perfectly well, and congratulated myself on the recovery. The shivering fit and other symptoms that ensued after the bath, too plainly told me that I had been precipitate in my rejoicings, and that there was much to be done ere the evil (which no doubt arose from the unhealthiness of our position at Michnee) could be eradicated from my constitution. Fifty leaches were immediately ordered to my temples; but though the best that could be procured, they were very indifferent, and extracted but little blood. The consequence was, on the next morning I was obliged to be bled from the arm, as I was in a raging fever, greatly aggravated by the intense heat to which we were exposed, and on the third day it arose to such a height, that I again suffered depletion to a great extent, and was also cupped on the temples. I slightly improved after this, but the fever returned daily as the temperature increased, and I then, on the slightest excuse, used to send every individual out of my tent, as I had got some absurd notion into my head, that could I only fall into a swoon for a quarter of an hour, and thus forget my sufferings, I should awake comparatively well. Every exertion, however, to effect this was in vain; for although I was so weak that a dozen or two of strides were sufficient to prostrate me, I was unable to produce a faint.

In some such state as this I continued, during the week that our camp was pitched in the neighbourhood of Ali Musjid, whilst the Colonel was busy arranging affairs for keeping that part of the Khyber open which we had just occupied, and in negotiating for a passage through the remainder, which is subject to the Shinwaries; tribes by no means so inimically disposed as the Afreedies and generally more peaceful in their habits. Meanwhile, Ferris had returned from Peshawur, with the grain for which he had been sent, his march back through the "Shadee Baziar" pass having been disputed by the enemy, who fired on his party, and succeeded in carrying off a number of women belonging to the Nujeeb regiment, who, I believe, formed the rear of his escort, and who could not be induced to attempt the rescue of these poor creatures, their servants and concubines. The result was, that the Khyberries mounted these unfortunate demoiselles on their shoulders, and notwithstanding the scratching, kicking, and biting which they used in their defence, for want of better weapons, they bore them off in triumph, and carried them to their retreats. About the 28th, a couple of Khyberries, who had deserted from us, were caught, and were awarded but a slight punishment to what their crime merited. This was a flogging on the bare back with the "kora," (a native whip) a rather severe weapon, as it fetched blood, and the sufferers nearly fainted before they had received all the lashes they were sentenced to. Perhaps, upon the whole, it was the best punishment that could have been inflicted on them, for the generality of Khyberries, like other Asiatics, regard the approach of death with the most apathetic indifference, merely remarking that it is their "kismut" or fate, and that what is written, must of necessity come to pass; whereas now they were marked for some time at least, which would show to others inclined to act a similar part, that "traitors to their salt" do not always escape detection.

I think it was on the following day, towards evening, that we were visited by a most furious "tofaun," accompanied by heavy rain, which committed a considerable deal of injury. Not above two or three of our tents were able to weather it out, and it was with some degree of horror I saw the "kanauts," or screens, to mine, blown in, by which I got a thorough wetting, a day or two after I had been bled for the second time. The Colonel's kuskus tent being thrown to the ground, he sought refuge in the doctor's, but had no sooner got there, than the tottering appearance it exhibited, obliged him to seek for shelter elsewhere; and altogether, as long as the storm lasted, our camp presented a scene of much confusion.

So many camels had now been stolen by the Afreedies in their predatory expeditions, that, to convey the public grain, it became necessary that all who were supplied with these animals at the expense of the mission; should have the numbers reduced to one half. This occurring in the middle of the Khyber pass, proved rather awkward, but, as there was no alternative, matters were arranged by officers doubling up into one tent; my friend Maule, and I, chumming together on the occasion.

On the first of August, preparations were made for our advance, and Ferris, with the grenadiers of the 20th, and a host of irregulars, was ordered to garrison the fort of Ali Musjid, a by no means enviable situation, as the heat was so oppressive. A depot for stores was also formed in it, and all the spare tents and unnecessary baggage were sent there. On the morning of the 2nd we resumed our march; Hillersdon, who, poor fellow, had been dangerously ill with fever some days before we quitted Koulsir, and myself, being conveyed in doolies; and it was with no inconsiderable delight we found ourselves jostling in the narrow pass with camels, horses, donkeys, mules, bullocks, men and women, bag and baggage, as all bespoke a removal from the dreadful hot-bed into which we had been plunged so long. In a couple of hours we reached Sir-i-chusma, or the Fountain's head, where our tents were pitched beneath the shade of a few straggling trees that afforded a slight relief from the sun. I at first felt better for the excitement, but as the afternoon drew on, I again suffered from fever. On the 3rd we moved to Lali-beg-ghurrie, a village of some size, situated in a more open part of the pass than we had yet seen, and indeed almost deserving the appellation of valley. Two tanks are in its neighbourhood, from whence the inhabitants obtain their chief supply of water, and the quantity required for our camp must have sadly diminished their store. Many other villages, invariably protected by a lofty tower, were to be seen from our position, and when within a mile of Lali-beg-ghurrie, we passed a Grecian tomb, or tope, erected on the summit of a high cliff, and similar in appearance to, though somewhat smaller than, that of Manikyala. A rude Khyberrie tower surmounts it, and, from its elevated site, forms a most excellent watch-tower, which, no doubt, is constantly used. On the 4th we marched to Lundy Khana, the road for some distance being very good; but after crossing the crest of the pass, terminating in a very precipitous and abrupt descent, cut for three miles on the side of a hill. The track here was villanously bad, and in some places, nothing but the bare surface of a rock, down the centre of which a deep groove had been worn by the continued action of water, as age after age the superabundan heavy showe cers had been carried off by this only channel of exit. To lower the guns down this rocky steep proved an arduous task, and, when night closed in they were still a mile from camp; it was necessary therefore to halt the following day, to allow of their being rejoined to the force. At Lundy Khana are the remains of two forts, and tradition assigns them as the residences of two noble "ranies," who erected them at the extremity of their respective dominions, in order that they might enjoy each other's society, and, strange to say, the harmony continued until death separated them. On the 6th we left for Dhaka, passing midway a ruined castle on the summit of an isolated hill, in a more open part of the defile than usual, which again becomes enclosed between rocky and precipitous cliffs, before it terminates in the small and confined valley of the above name: two partially fortified villages are at one end of the latter. Having now got through the notorious Khyber pass, the following order* was issued by Colonel Wade.

*The following paragraph formed the concluding one of general orders by the Governor-general, dated Camp Somalka, 19th Nov. 1839, and, as it relates to Colonel Wade's force, may not be out of place here.

"His Lordship has also much satisfaction in adding, that the best acknowledgments of the Government are due to Lieut. Colonel Wade, who employed on the Peshawur frontier, and who, gallantly supported by the officers and men of all ranks under him, and seconded by the cordial aid of the Sikh government, an aid the more honourable because rendered at a painful crisis of its affairs opened, the Khyber pass, and overthrew the authority of the enemy in that quarter at the moment when the advance of the forces of the Shah-zada Timour could most conduce to the success of the general operations."

"Camp Dhaka, 6th August, 1839.— mission with the Shah-zada having now effected the passage through Khyber, and the fall of the fort of Ali Musjid having been the chief means of removing every opposition to its advance from the place, Lieutenant Colonel Wade (although the heads of the Government, whose officers and troops were engaged in the reduction of that Fort, are the proper persons to appreciate the services performed by them on that occasion) cannot deny himself the personal gratification of expressing his own thanks and acknowledgements to every officer of the British Government for the able and zealous services rendered by them individually, in the operations which led to the attainment of an object, which, after a tedious detention at Peshawur, has mainly contributed to facilitate the progress of the Shah-zada to Cabul.

"It fell to the lot of Captains Farmer and Ferris, and of Lieutenants Mackeson Maule, and Barr, in following the directions of Lieutenant Colonel Wade, to bear the most conspicuous part in the late military operations; and the gallantry and perseverance with which these officers, and the troops in general, acquitted themselves of their respective duties, claim the Lieutenant Colonel's especial notice: but where every officer, whether immediately engaged in these operations, or in other duties which were allotted to them, of equal importance with these which developed on others, vied with each other in a zealous discharge of them, Lieutenant Colonel Wade is conscious that, while particularizing some, his obligations are alike due to all; and in his report to Government he has endeavoured to express his sense of the services of each."

FROM DHAKA TO CABUL

OUR camp was pitched on the banks of the Cabul river, which flowed silently and swiftly by, and opposite to the village of Lallpoora, the principal residence of Sadut Khan, who has erected a small fort close to it. Intimation had been received from that chief, avowing his willingness to come to terms; but the unceasing enmity that he had evinced towards the Shah-zada since our arrival in Peshawur, rendered it necessary to be prepared to act on the offensive, in case he should change his mind. Accordingly, some troops were ordered on this service, and cannon were planted opposite to his stronghold; but no farther acts of hostility ensued, and on the following morning the Colonel was informed that the Momund lord, with his followers, had decamped during the night, and gone off in the direction of Bajore. Wade, on this, crossed the river, and took possession of Lallpoora, and the fort, the government of which he conferred on Toorabaz Khan a chief who had proved a most faithful ally to us. Dowson, with his regiment, was ordered to remain here for the purpose of keeping the western extremity of the pass open, and co-operating with Ferris; and Mackeson's cousin, with a party of from 150 to 200 "bildars," in lieu of pioneers, was directed to repair, or rather re-construct the road, at the Lundy Khana pass.

At Dhaka we staid about a week, my health, at first, being a good deal improved; but this long halt on a swampy piece of ground, and the extreme heat of the valley, brought back my fever, which reduced me considerably. For change of air and scene I embarked on a raft constructed of "mussucks," or inflated skins, on which a charpaee was bound. It was large enough to hold three of us in addition to the two rowers; and the rapidity with which we glided down the stream, and the buoyancy of the vessel when carried into the rapids, was extremely gratifying. I was, however, so weak, that on landing I was obliged to be supported to my tent, but a few yards distant, by Rattray and Maule; and as the fever again returned in the afternoon, I was not sorry to learn we were to re-commence our march on the following morning, when we quitted Dhaka at daybreak, and in half-an-hour reached a narrow and confined pass, called the "koord," or "little," Khyber. The road through this was execrable, and had in some parts to be widened before the guns could proceed; indeed, so many were difficulties they had to encounter, that they did not reach Hazarnow, where we halted, till late in the day. This village is situated in an amphitheatre of hills and being of some size, backed by mountains, with a few trees in its neighbourhood, looked rather pretty than otherwise.

Dawn, the next morning, saw us on our march to Chardeh, a village twelve miles distant from Hazarnow, and the bearers of my doolie, by way of a short cut, carried me along a path surrounded on either side by long feathery grass, that towered far above our heads, and where, amidst occasional openings, might be seen black and turbid pools of water, betokening anything but a healthy state of atmosphere. Quitting this path, which was some miles in extent, we crossed a narrow pass of no length, formed by the spines of two opposite ranges of hills, nearing each other. On its summit, was a cairn of stones, surmounted by a white flag, by the side of which a fakeer kept "tom-tomming" (drumming) and soliciting alms from the passers by. As soon as we had rounded the gorge we entered on an extensive plain, enclosed by distant hills, where, at the base of those to the north, the Cabul river flows; and on our right we passed a couple of small forts very near to each other, and erected in a kind of hollow formed by the mountains, which at this spot assume a circular direction. Chardeh has nothing to boast of; and as my nights were now restless, and almost sleepless, I was glad when the morning broke, and we marched to Ali Boghan, a distance of sixteen miles. The bearers of my litter, on this occasion, had been changed, in consequence of the old set having allowed one of their comrades to desert during the night; and as a punishment, the surgeon had ordered them to be put to other and more arduous duty. I had, however, no reason to be pleased at the arrangement; for their substitutes had not advanced a couple of miles, when first one and then another dropped to the ground, being overcome by fever and heat. This left me with only three men, a number insufficient to lift the doolie; and as the larger portion of the column had already passed by, it became a serious question how I was to proceed. Happily, Reid at this moment rode up, and as the Shah-zada's elephant was approaching, he suggested I should make use of it. I assented, as there was not much likelihood of a more suitable conveyance presenting itself; and, transferring a change of raiment that was being conveyed for His Royal Highness into the litter, I seated myself in the howdah. Here I was exposed to the whole force of the sun's rays, until, through the kind exertions of Rattray, I obtained an umbrella, which in some measure shaded me; but I still found the heat very oppressive; and the jolting motions of the elephant far from agreeable. About three quarters of the way, we passed through a defile of some extent, which is bounded on either side by low hills and rocks, tinged with a reddish hue, and is well known as a notorious resort of robbers. Emerging from it we, in a short time, reached our encampment, from whence we saw the Cabul river on our right, and in front, the city of Jullalabad looming in the distance. The Shah-zada, in the evening, on learning that I had been obliged to make use of his elephant, was not only *not* displeased at the liberty I had taken, but expressed the gratification it gave him to know that the animal had been of service to me. How different would his father, the haughty Shah Shoojah, have behaved! but the prince is kind in the extreme, and has on several occasions sent me lumps of hardened snow to apply to my temples, when throbbing with pain. His attentions to Maule, for whom he has taken a fancy, are unbounded; and, day after day, large trays of fruit and ice are brought to him with the prince's salaam. It is a pity he is so deficient in energy, as his whole nature is replete with the milk of human kindness; and without it, he will never be able to control the tumultuous passions of the turbulent Affghans, should it ever be his lot to rule over them.*

We started at the usual hour on the morning of the 17th, and after passing over a level and uninteresting country, reached Jullalabad at eight o'clock. I was much disappointed at the miserable appearance of this town, composed as it is of wretched mud hovels with flat roofs, and surrounded by a wall of the same material. The main street was almost empty, and yet there must have been a considerable number of inhabitants somewhere, as I noticed the butchers' shops were most numerous, and all well stocked with provisions. Most of the residents we fell in with had their complexions stained with the yellow tinge of sickness, which did not say much for its situation; but we soon ceased to regard this with any surprise, when, during the four days of our sojourn in its neighbourhood, we found the changes of temperature to be so

---

* Consequent on the events that have lately occurred in Affghanistan, the prince is again a pensioner of the British Government in India.

considerable. At noon the thermometer never stood lower than 102°, and a hot wind blew all the day; but at night it became so cold, that counterpanes and blankets were absolutely necessary to defend us from its influence. Under such a climate I did not rally much, and, in addition to one third of the several regiments and detachments being on the sick report, numbers were daily swelling the list, and, amongst others, the surgeon, who, about this time, was laid up with fever, brought on by exposure and attention to his arduous duties. Amongst the levies the deaths were frequent; and to such a height did the sickness at last attain, that it became necessary to make arrangements for the reception of the invalids at Jullalabad, as there was no carriage to convey them further. Hillersdon's regiment was also ordered to remain with Mackeson, who has been appointed to perform the duties of political agent here.

On the 21st we marched to Charbagh, which, from its proximity to some hills, we found remarkably warm; and, on the 22nd, moved to Balabagh, about eight miles distant from the former. I had benefited so much by the change from Jullalabad, that I resolved to mount my horse on the following morning, and though it was with some difficulty I threw my leg across the saddle, I managed, before I took to my litter, to ride some three or four miles. The sun was by this time up, and we soon after descended to the bed of a clear stream, where the road was very bad, and continued to be so, with sundry ascents and descents, till we reached a prettily situated village at no great distance from the gardens of Neemla, near to which Shah Shoojah lost a battle, which terminated in his expulsion from Affghanistan. Opposite to the village we commenced a steep ascent that lasted for some distance, and then terminated in a tolerably level road that ran along the ridge of hill, where the pure breeze was blowing with a freshness that we had not tasted for months, and which was really delicious. Three or four descents ensued before we reached Gundamuck,* and one of these led to a stream, over which a picturesque bridge, now in a dilapidated state, had been thrown by some of the Mogul emperors. We had to ascend from this to Gundamuck, where the temperature was delightful when compared in the excessive heats we had encountered in the valleys of Peshawur and Jullalabad, and the quantities of peaches, melons, grapes, and other fruits which the natives brought for sale, showed that we had come into a more genial clime. So abundant were the grapes, that they sold us a donkey's load of them for one rupee, or two shillings, and the quantity was more than enough to satisfy ourselves and servants — indeed had we been possessed of a smaller silver coin, the vendors would have considered themselves amply remunerated with it in lieu of the larger. Night closed in before a report reached us that the guns had only succeeded in crowning the heights above Neemla, and a halt was, in consequence, called for the 24th, when they reached camp at noon, most of the horses being knocked up, and two of them killed by the fatigue they had undergone. Notwithstanding I had suffered from an attack of ague in the morning, I was able to *walk* (my first essay for a long time) a short distance to inspect some ordnance that had been abandoned by Mahomed Akbar Khan during his flight from the Khyber, and which fell into our hands here. It consisted of ten or twelve brass cannons, mostly of small calibre, and omitted to mention, that between Jullalabad and Charbagh, we passed a very large brass gun, mounted on a most rudely constructed carriage, the naves of the wheels being about

* It need scarcely be remarked, that, during the late disastrous retreat from Cabul, the last stand made by the British troops occurred in a neibourhood of Gundamuck, where nearly the whole of the little resolute band were cut to pieces. From hence to Cabul the passes must ever be associated with the dreadful massacres that took place on that fatal occasion.

two feet and a half in diameter, and the felloes thick in proportion, which he had also been unable to carry away in his retreat.

Soon after leaving Gundamuck, we descended a steep bank to the bed of a crystal stream, which we forded, and then climbed a more gentle slope on its opposite side. The road was subsequently confined between low ridges of hills, and though narrow, was tolerably good. A gradual descent eventually brought us to Soorkab, a name the spot enjoys from the deep red colour of a small river that flows by it, and which is spanned by a stone bridge. The heat here was dreadful, our encampment being enclosed on all sides by steep and rocky hills, which re-cast the sun's rays upon us, and prevented any breeze that might be blowing from reaching us. My fever again returned, and I felt extremely ill. The next morning we crossed by a succession of difficult passes and defiles to Jugdulluck, where, beneath the shade of a pretty clump of trees, we managed to spend a more agreeable day. The march must have been at least thirteen miles long, and the road in parts was very steep and rugged. After gaining the crest of the last ghat, we had a gradual descent of about five miles to the village, the road being nothing more then the bed of a stream, enclosed by hills covered with dwarf trees, that opened out as we neared the termination of our journey. Jugdulluck is celebrated as the spot where Shah Zeman, the elder brother of Shah Shoojah, and now a pensioner at Loodianah on the British Government, had his eyes put by a lancet. We left it early on the following morning, and crossing another series of steep ascents and deep descents, reached Bareekhab, where our camp was formed in a close and confined hollow, into which the rays of the sun appeared to be concentrated. During the march an attempt was made to murder a Chuprasee attached to the mission, but fortunately his cries were heard, and one of the miscreants being secured was made over to the Shah-zada for punishment. The guns having to make a longer circuit, and descend the Paraderie Pass, did not reach Bareekhab till late in the evening.

The next day we passed over a succession of bare and rugged hills, until on crossing a gorge, we descended by an abrupt steep to the bed of a stream, and close to a curious rock, beneath which a fakeer had taken up his residence, and where he no doubt finds a profitable employment, as the trees in its neighbourhood are covered with pieces of rag, the offerings of the superstitious. At this rock I once more mounted my steed, and rode for three or four miles along the bed of the stream, (our only road) which was encumbered by huge boulder-stones, and enclosed by steep hills, on which grew some struggling trees, but partially covered with foliage. After returning to my doolie, we passed on our right an old and ruined fort, around which were vestiges of a village and thence continuing up the defile for three or four miles further, we reached Tezeen, our halting-ground. Being of some considerable altitude, we were favoured with a cool breeze throughout the day, and the change of temperature benefited me so much, that I was enabled to ride on the following morning, when we continued our march. After quitting the valley of Tezeen, we entered a very confined and narrow pass, with prependicular crags towering up on either side, and a small rivulet forcing its way between them. At its termination we reached the foot of an extremely steep hill, which having ascended, we were greeted by a keen and cutting wind, that betokened the loftiness of its situation, its summit being upwards of 8000 feet above the level of the sea. We then crossed over a succession of ascents and descents, I conclude to the number of seven, as they are termed the Haft Kotul, or Seven Passes, the road being tolerably good, and unencumbered with stones. From thence we had a gradual descent to our encampment, pitched on some fields from off which the harvest had been carried, and nearly surrounded on three sides by hills at no great distance.

On the 1st of September we moved to Dhootkhak, our road for the first five miles being confined to the Khoord Cabul pass, a narrow defile bounded on either side by precipitous and lofty mountains, whose frowning summits darkened the chasm, as in the early morning we crossed and recrossed a small rivulet that rapidly sped down its shingly bed. We then entered on an open valley, bounded on the west by a low range of hills, which concealed the long-desired city of Cabul from our sight, and in half-an-hour arrived at our encampment. Some stragglers having lagged in the pass, were attacked by the Ghiljies, who killed one or two and bounded the remainder, before they could effect their escape. In the evening we were rejoined by the guns that last night had remained near the Huft Kotul, the men having with the greatest difficulty, succeeded in dragging them up the stupendous ascent of the pass, under the superintendence of Maule, who has had charge of them ever since leaving Gundamuck, and to whom, therefore, much credit is due. Despatches intimating our approach were sent in the course of the day to the envoy at Shah Shoojah's court, and to the commander-in-chief, Sir John Keane; and on the following day we halted to be in proper trim for our march into Cabul, when in the evening the Sikh troops were inspected in full dress, and their appearance brought forth the Colonel's encomiums. At length the day arrived on which we were to reach the long desired goal, and as my health had considerably improved, I resolved, with the doctor's permission, to take part in the procession. Accordingly on the morning of the 3d September, I stepped into my litter, and having been carried halfway, mounted my charger, and drew up my detachment on the right of the road. On the Shah-zada's appearing in sight, we saluted him with twenty-one guns, also a signal for the troops at Cabul to get under arms; and as he neared us we wheeled into column and headed the procession.

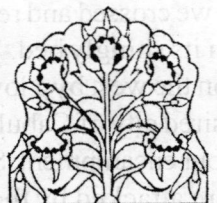

FROM CABUL TO FEROZEPORE

AFTER gaining the summit of rather a steep eminence, the city of Cabul suddenly burst on our sight, and being situated between a couple of fortified hills, formed an extremely pleasing picture. It was about three miles distant: the intervening space presenting an animated scene, covered as it was with innumerable tents, and crowded with soldiers of every description that composed "the army of the Indus." The road from the eminence to the city was lined with troops from Bengal and Bombay, the several regiments presenting arms and the artillery firing royal salutes as the Shah-zada passed. It was late in the day ere we reached the walls of the town, close to which ground had been marked out for our encampment, but my friends D. and Dr. M. who had joined me on the road, observing the weak state I was in, persuaded me to enter a tent until my own should arrive. Here I unrobed myself, and was accommodated with a comfortable dressing-gown in lieu of the stiff dress-jacket; but I was a good deal knocked up by fatigue, and M., on feeling my pulse, found it pelting away at 130 per minute. On the following morning I visited the city in the colonel's "tonjon," and was very much struck with the handsome appearance of the chief bazaar, called the "char-chattur." from its being enclosed or covered in. Here and there, however, octagonal areas which formerly possessed reservoirs of water, now choked up, broke the line of roof, and not only admitted light, but caused a free circulation of air to pass underneath the arcades, which without them must otherwise have been confined and unhealthy. Of all the shops, the most attractive are the fruiterers', and they arrange with taste the numberless luscious edibles that they offer for sale. Grapes of every variety and size, water and musk melons, (the pride of the Cabulies,) apples, pears, quinces, pomegranates, &c., are piled up in front of their "dokans," and are in such profusion that it seems astonishing there should be found customers numerous enough to purchase the *hills* of fruit that everywhere catch the eye. Next to the fruiterers the trades that predominate are the leather, sellers, furriers, braziers, butchers, and cooks, and the constant ingress of individuals to and from the shops of the latter bespeak it as a thriving profession.

Soon after my return to camp, I was seized with a violent fit of ague, a circumstance by no means surprising, as the ground below us was so moist that on pushing a stick into it to the depth of a foot and then withdrawing it, water oozed out of the hole. To hope for recovery when in such a situation was useless, and I was therefore instantly removed to higher ground, occupied by the Bengal horse-artillery. The next day, at the same hour, a similar attack followed, and I was then bled in the cold stage without deriving those immediate benefits it was thought I should have done, and subsequently it was not expected I could survive the night. From it, however, I date my recovery, as the following morning passed over without an attack, and I gradually regained sufficient strength to move about in a few days with the aid of a stick, and in due course of time to convalescence.

About the 5th of September we received intelligence of the murder of Colonel Herring, who was on his way to Cabul in command of a treasure party, and who one evening, having incautiously ascended an eminence, a short distance from his camp at Hyder Khel, accompanied only by a couple of officer as and two or three sepoys, was suddenly and unexpectedly attacked by a number of robbers, who succeeded in killing the Colonel and wounding one of the officers, Lieut. Rind. The latter individual, with the rest of the party, made good their escape to camp, on which a large detachment started off in pursuit of the villains, who were, however, nowhere to be found. The body of their victim was recovered and brought on to Cabul, where it was interred in the Armenian burying-ground, beside the remains of Brigadier Arnold. Captain Fothergill, of H.M. 13th, was buried the same evening; and a few days afterwards Captain Timmings, of the Bengal horse artillery, was laid by his side.

On the 16th the Bombay troops moved their camp to the westward of Cabul, preparatory to commencing their return march, and the night previous to their departure M. and I were aroused by loud vociferations of "Choor, choor!" (thief, thief;) On inquiring into the reason of all the noise, it was soon ascertained that some rascals, under the cover of a dark night, had succeeded in opening one of my boxes, placed *between* a couple of my servants, (fast asleep at the time,) and abstracting therefrom some two hundered rupees' worth of property. There is but little doubt the thieves were from the Bombay column, and most probably some of the camp followers, who, knowing they were to be at a distance next morning, hoped to escape without detection and, what was worse, they did.

Towards the end of the month a review of the Sikh troops under Colonel Shaik Bussowan took place, for the inspection of His Majesty Shah Shoojah. I rode to the parade ground, and saw, for the first time, the King of Cabul. He was seated in a highly-ornamented litter, dressed plainly, in the royal purple, and had a handsome expression of countenance, with a long flowing black beard that derived its colour and glossiness from the hands of a barber. He was attended by a long train of servants, habited in the costume of the days of Baber and Timour, and a more outre apparel can scarcely be conceived; some wearing a species of horn growing out of each shoulder, and others, a head-piece not very unlike a fool's-cap: H.M. executioner, was one of these. Sir W. Cotton, Sir Alexander Burnes, Mr. MacNaghten, and other men of celebrity, were also on the ground.

Beyond Baber's Tomb, there was little to interest one in the environs of Cabul; but there was much in the city, which I often visited, and the loud hum and busy crowd of people appeared each successive day to be rather increased than diminished; indeed, at times, it was absolutely difficult to push one's way through the dense population that filled its streets, and choked its bazaars. I passed through the Bala Hissar, a sort of interior fort, in which stands the king's palace, a building of no pretensions to architecture, and only to be distinguished from the neighbouring houses by its size. A diminutive town has sprung up by its side. Above the gateway through which I made my exit his Majesty's band was playing, and reminded me strongly of his son's at Peshawur, except that the instruments being more numerous, the discord was the greater. Opposite to the Bala Hissar, but outside the walls of the fort, is a small mosque, of no great antiquity. Sheltered by a few trees, and close to it, lies a small tombstone, (evidently removed from its original situation,) which bears an inscription purporting to cover the remains of John Hicks, son of "John and Edith Hicks, who departed this lyfe in 1666," or to that effect; the words being carved in plain letters, and carried round the slab without any attention being paid to their division into syllables. It is a curious relic, and at some future time we may possibly learn who this individual was that found a grave in so distant a country, at a period when little or nothing was known of the existence of Affghanistan. The Armenian burying ground is situated about a mile to the south of the mosque, and is likely to form the English cemetery as well. Returning from it, there is a pretty view of the Bala Hissar to be had although a vista of trees, from whence a portion of it is to be seen standing as if by itself, and appearing not unlike an English castle.

The objects of Colonel Wade's mission having been brought to a conclusion, and the Shah-zada safely lodged in the palace, a report was made by the Colonel to Sir John Keane, that he no longer required the services of the British troops; on which they were transferred, on the 1st of October, to "the army of the Indus," and I joined Captain G.'s troop of horse-artillery; the howitzers being left with the assistant-commissary of ordnance, who was to remain at Cabul. Rumours were now rife that the troops destined to return to Hindoostan would soon march; but as pay was a very requisite article, and the treasure chest was nearly empty, it was necessary we should await the arrival of Captain Hopkins's detachment, which was convoying some thirteen lakhs of rupees for our use from the provinces. To protect it from the predatory Ghiljies that infest the passes between Jullalabad and Cabul, the 3rd cavalry were sent to escort it from Jugdulluck; and, after a harassing march, they returned to camp on the 8th, with the long-expected remittances, a portion of which was immediately disbursed to the troops, who were in much need of it. Unwilling to quit Cabul without seeing the tomb of the celebrated Baber, which was at the western side of the city, I rode there in company with M., and attended by an escort of troopers, as it was not considered safe to move far from the limits of our position without a guard. Our route took us through several streets in the city that I had not visited before, but they were by no means equal to the main thoroughfare in appearance. We crossed the river by a bridge, and skirting its banks, passed through a stony defile, formed by an opening between the for to fied hills, down which the stream flows. The scenery here is strikingly pretty, lofty and precipitous crags rise on either side of the water, which is fringed with mulberry, willow, and other trees; the rocks above momentarily threaten to topple from their lofty situations and block up the road below, or overwhelm the passing travellers; and in front, an old bridge, picturesque in decay, obstructed the progress of the stream which rolls against it, before seeking an outlet through its ruined arches. The morning was clear and frosty, and a cutting wind greeted us, as we passed up this valley. We crossed the bridge, and cantering along a good road, reached a respectable and clean-looking village. A short distance beyond, we came to an enclosure, crowded with mulberry, plane, and other trees, whose spreading branches were well calculated to afford a grateful shade during a summer's day, but which we would have gladly exchanged for a little sunshine, as our fingers were nipped with the cold. We entered the garden, a series of terraces that had once been planted with flowers and shrubs, but now overrun by a jungle, and ascending a paved walk, by the side of which a rippling stream came purling down, we stood at the grave of the conqueror of the East — a small slab of marble, with a Persian inscription. It was simple, and would be passed unnoticed, but for the celebrity of the remains that lie beneath it. Other and more costly monuments are in its vicinity, but they are comparatively unheeded, and the eye turns from them to rest again on the more humble sepulchre of the monarch who, less honoured in his death, has left a name that will perish only with the earth.

On returning we made a slight deviation in our route, and instead of crossing the bridge near the entrance of the defile, we kept on the right bank, and passed a large mausoleum, where an ancestor of Shah Shoojah's is buried. As we went through the city we resolved to taste the far-famed "kababs," and accordingly adjourning to a cook's shop, where we paid a couple of annas, (or three pence,) *beforehand*, we were ushered into an upper apartment on the floor of which we discovered an Affghan seated, and busily engaged upon the art of gastronomy. He was so polite as to offer us a portion of his food, which M., to show his fellow-feeling, tasted, and on our own fare being brought in, piping hot, a large quantity of it was transferred to our new acquaintance, who readily received it from our hands. Having got our breakfast before us, we were now at a loss what to do with it, as knives and forks there were none, and instead of plates we each had a long flat piece of unleavened bread, on which the "kababs" were placed, and which required a steady hand to keep them in their position. We looked at them for a moment, but it was no use sticking at trifles, so boldly seizing the end of a skewer, on which the lumps of meat had been spitted, we commenced work, our *plates* gradually diminishing in size, and disappearing as fast as the viands on the top of them. In spite of the visions of dead camels, cats, dogs, and other villanous compounds, which we were assured formed the ingredients of these savoury messes, (an officer having *seen* a leg of the firstnamed beast carried into a cook-shop at Candahar,) we got on admirably well, and not only enjoyed our meal, but at its termination pronounced an encomium on the cookery of the Affghans.

On the 5th or 6th, Wade departed with the Sikh troops; and on the 15th the first column, consisting of H.M. 16th Lancers, two companies of Sappers and Miners, a guard of Infantry and local horse, and head-quarters' staff, with Sir John Keane, commenced their march for the provinces, and we of the second column followed on the 16th. The feeling of delight that pervaded the army when, after so many hardships, it once more turned its face towards Hindostan, was universal; and I may say the regret that filled the breasts of those who were destined to remain in Affghanistan was as unanimous. Many appointments in the Shah's service had been offered to officers, and declined by them; and even soldiers who could have got salaries of 100 or 200 rupees per mensem in lieu of their comparatively trifling pay, refused to remain behind on even these (to them) splended terms. The paradise that all expected to see in the beauties of Affghanistan had faded as we advanced, and a dreary spectacle of barren mountains and swampy valleys occupied its place. True it is, a few bright gleams of scenery do occasionally meet the eye, but they are scarce, and travellers in their hasty journeys have allowed their thoughts to dwell on these lovely spots, rendered more beautiful by the contrast of the surrounding country; and, in their descriptions, have forgotten to mention the more marked features of the province, which consists of desolation and barrenness.

The rendezvous of our column was at the foot of the hill I spoke of as having obscured our view of Cabul when at Bootkhak, and here we had to wait some time for a squadron of the 3rd cavalry, that had been despatched to the Bala Hissar, for two state prisoners, Hyder Khan, the Governor of Ghuzni and Dost Mahomed's third son, and the traitor Hadji Khan Kakur. On their arrival, we commenced our march in the following order the column being commanded by General Thackwell:—3rd light cavalry — state prisoners — Captain Grant's troop of horse artillery — Lieut. Barr's detachment of ditto — 4th local horse — Drafts from the European regiment, and native invalids returning to the provinces. On crossing the Logar river spanned by a narrow bridge without a parapet, a gun was capsized into the water, with all the men and horses. Fortunately the stream, though of an icy coldness, was of no great depth, and the gunners, with four horses, were soon rescued from their uncomfortable situation. The police horses had unluckily got entangled the harness as they fell, and notwithstanding every exertion was made to save them, they were drowned. A havildar of the Lascars, who was seated on the gun, had a narrow escape, as he was for several minutes under water before he could be removed from his dangerous position, and, wonderful to relate, he had only received a severe contusion on the back. Our encampment was at Bootkhak, where, as the advance column had been fired upon the previous night from the heights above, it became necessary to use more than ordinary precautions to guard the prisoners, lest any attempt at a rescue should be made; and extra sentries were planted round their tents at the suggestion of Captain M'Sherry, who had the immediate charge of them. On the 17th we moved to Khoord Cabul, the ascent of the narrow defile leading to it being accomplished in a cold wind, that cut us to the skin, whilst the splashings from the water, as we crossed the stream, froze before it could drop from the skirts of our cloaks, or the tips of our steel scabbards. The next day we marched to Tezeen, and as we neared the summit of the lofty "Huft Kotul," we passed the dead body of a native, who had evidently died from the weather, and who, without-stretched arms, was lying flat on his face, apparently having fallen in that position while making a last struggle to gain the top. He had been stripped of every rag; and not far distant the corpse of another was seen in the cleft of a ravine, which the poor fellow had entered with the vain hope of screening himself from the keen blast that hurried up the pass, and where, instead of the repose of sleep, he had found a more lasting rest in death.

Camels that had dropped whilst carrying the baggage of the preceding column dotted our path; some in the agonies of death, others insensible or perfectly stiff; and these, strange to say, were not the most attenuated and sickly, but the hale-looking and stout, and such as would be expected to travel for many a day to come. Each individual thought that a similar fate must, of necessity, attend his own beast of burden, and the inquiries as to whose camels had *sat* down (for it was remarkable, that when once they assumed this posture on the line of march they might be abandoned, as few ever rose again) was constantly to be heard. From Tezeen we proceeded to the Fakeer's Rock, where we halted on a shingly bank nearly opposite to it, and not far from the entrance to the

Luttabund pass, a shorter route to Cabul, only fit for horse-men and foot-passengers. We encamped on the 20th at Kutta Sung, a mile or two beyond Bareekhab, and, on the march, again passed the body of a camp-follower, whose energies had been clasped by the cold hand of death just as he had succeeded in climbing to the summit of a steep pass, his emaciated frame betokening that disease and famina had previously made sad inroads on his constitution. Jugdulluck was our next halting-ground, but instead of traversing the range of hills, over which I had been carried in the litter, we ascended the wonderful "puree duree," or "fairy pass", formed by a deep cleft in the mountains that extends between three and four miles in length. The scene was savage and wild in the extreme, and the defile so contracted at times, as barely to allow a passage for the guns. In one part the cliffs even met within seven feet of each other, the space between being occupied by a stream that narrowed as it forced its way through them, and then widened out again as it left the obstruction behind. The loftiness of the precipices prevented the sun shining into the pass, and the cold was consequently so intense as to cause numbers of camels to lie on the ground, or in the water, wherever they chanced to drop; and in this position they remained, never to rise again.

On the 22nd we were at Soorkab, at once more encamped on the banks of the "red river." During the day a portion of the rear ground was attacked by a large body of robbens, whose numberss compelled the sepoys to intrench themselves behind a bank, where they gallantly maintained the combat, and had several of their party killed amongst the rest was the Jemadar, or native officer in command, who was shot when in the act of stopping to draw a cartridge from the pouch of one of his dead soldiers, whose musket he had seized and had made active use of. On the news reaching camp, a squadron of cavalry and the 4th Locals were sent back, but to no purpose, as the rascally Ghiljies had meanwhile decamped. On the 23rd we arrived at Gundamuck, and halted there on the 24th, and, on the 27th, entered Jullalabad, where the army remained two days. I formed one of a committee of officers to valve the guns that I mentioned had fallen into our hands at Gundamuck, and which had since been brought to the last-named town; and, having regarded them in the light of old brass, we estimated their price at 5,000 rupees, (£500,) all the prize-money that we, of the mission, will be entitled to a share of. On the 30th we quitted Jullalabad, and on the 2nd of November arrived at Dhaka. The 4th, from day break to nightfall, was occupied in dragging the ordnance up the steep pass of Lundy Khana, which Mackeson had considerably improved, and in marching to Ali Musjid, or rather a mile beyond it, where our encampment was formed. None of the baggage of our immediate party come up that night, and were fortunate in obtaining possession of some hospital litters that answered in lieu of beds, though, from their shortness, they were anything but comfortable. The next day, as we halted, I took the opportunity of visiting the fort, which illness had prevented my doing before, and I was surprised to find its interior so small, being only eighty yards long by twenty broad. It, however, has an enclosure, which comprises a large area, and takes in all the little irregularities in its neighbouthood that are capable of being turned to account in its defence. I afterwards breakfasted with. Ferris and Dowson, who had moved up with their troops in consequence of an endeavour made by the Khyberries to repossess themselves of this stronghold, and rumours of which had reached us at Jullalabad. The former was looking extremely ill, and had for weeks been at death's door; the unwholesome climate of the pass not only having driven him, but the whole of the grenadiers of the 20th N.I., to Peshawur. When they marched from Loodianah, in February last, they were as fine a body of men as over trod ground, and their lively song, as they celebrated the Hoolie festival on the line of march, told of a set of fellows that were going to the wars with a spirit bordering on that of British soldiers. Now a few miserable men, worn with disease, and scarcely able to shoulder their muskets, or drag their legs behind them, formed the company; fever and dysentery having carried off nearly half of them, and those the finest-looking of the band. On inquiring after some whom I had more particularly remarked, the answer I received was invariably, "He is gone too," and the loss of none I regretted more than of a havildar, (sergeant,) by name Gooman Singh. He was havildar-major to his regiment, and consequently exempted from the present duty, but being a high-spirited man, anxious (unlike most natives) to visit distant climes, he had volunteered to join his company, and fell a victim to his zeal. Ferris was long despaired of, and having only a native doctor to attend him, (who proved worse than none,) his recovery was miraculous, and mainly to be attributed, under Providence, to the fatherly care shown to him by General Avitabile.

From Ferris I received the particulars of the late assaults of the Khyberries, who commenced them by attacking a post at Lall Chenie, garrisoned by 500 Nujeeb soldiers, the majority of whom they succeeded in slaughtering: the rest with difficulty made their escape to Jumrood. Having committed this terrible masscre, they proceeded to attack Ferris's position, at the fort of Ali Musjid, but were repulsed with some loss; and night drawing on, compelled them to desist. The next day, F. went to Lall Chenie, and interred no less than 300 bodies of the Nujeebs; and when it is considered that many of those who reached Jumrood must have been severely wounded, it is very probable no more than 150 survived that terrible onset. Another attack on the part of the Khyberries was expected, and, as the sequel proved, was not long in being made. F. had, however, prepared a warm reception for them, and he described the appearance of the pass, as they advanced, to be nothing but a sea of heads. Onwards they came till within thirty or forty yards of a low wall, behind which a party of picked men had been reclining with their matchlocks in readiness, and who, starting up at the

word of command, poured a deadly and unexpected volley into
the midst of the foe, which caused them to send forth an unearthly
and terrine yell, heightened by the shrieks and groans of the
wounded. Ferris, then, at the head of a party of horsemen, at
hand for the purpose, boldly galloped forward, and was in the act
of turning round to give a shout of encouragement to his followers,
preparatory to charging, when the discovered he was, with one
exception,* *alone*, the cowardly sowars having hung back. He
was, by this time, close to, and partly intermixed with the
Khyberries, who could have killed him in an instant, and how they
allowed him to escape he knows not to this day. They, howawer,
bad suffered enough, and only thought of making off with their
dead and wounded; and thus affairs remained when the returning
army reached Ali Musjid. As F. had only irregulars to depend on
for the defence of the Khyber, he applied to to Sir John Keane for
two companies of infantry, which were granted to him; and those
of the 27th Native Infantry, under Lieutenant Laing, that had
escorted the treasure to Cabul, were ordered on the duty.

On the 6th we moved to Kuddum, a few stray shots having
been fired at the guards in charge of the baggage; and on the 7th
we halted at Koulsir, close to the ground so long occupied by the
mission, and which was now covered with fields of grain. The
next morning we marched to Peshawur, and encamped on the
eastern side of the city, where we were only to have remained a
couple of days; but a longer sojourn was rendered necessary, as
the Sikh troops could not be prevailed upon to convey grain to
the garrison at Ali Musjid, who had but a day or two's provision
left. To effect this desirable object, it therefore became necessary,
on the 10th, to send two companies of the 21st Native Infantry
under Farmer, and one of the Sappers and Miners under Lieutenant
Macleod, of the Engineers, on that duty, accompanied by 500

* The exception, if my memory serves, was the jemadar, whose gaunt
mare used to outstrip our steeds at Michnee.

Sikh soldiers, and escorted by a squadron of cavalry and two guns to the entrance of the pass. They succeeded in making over their charge in safety; but on their return were opposed by the Khyberries in force, who boldly attacked them as they were threading the hills. The Nujeebs, without attempting resistance immediately took to flight, hamstringing such camels as obstructed their progress: and, at last, our own sepoys, having expended all their ammunition, were obliged to follow the example thus set them of showing a quick pair of heels. The Afreedies, perceiving the dismay they had created, threw down their matchlocks, and advanced to close quarters, with their deadly knives; and the ferocity with which they used these murderous weapons was spoken of as being quite fiendish. A large booty and a vast number of camels fell into the enemy's hands, and were forthwith transferred to their strongholds. The conduct of the Sikh troops on this occasion gave so much offence to General Avitabile, that he, in his capacity of Governor, denied them admittance into the town of Peshawur, and ordered any of them that should be seen in it to severely beaten with a slipper, the most derogatory punishment that can be inflicted on a native.

After this defeat, it was necessary for the returning army to remain at Peshawur until Colonel Wheeler, who, with the 48th Native Infantry, had been sent for from Jullalabad, should arrive to the succour of the garrison of Ali Musjid, as that fort was now sure of being attacked by the Khyberries. Meanwhile balled ammunition was being made up in our camp as fast as possible, and all the available infantry, including the drafts for the 2nd European regiment, were sent to Jumrood on the 14th, to proceed from thence to the assistance of our troops in the pass, whenever such a step might be necessary. At twelve o'clock the same night, I was ordered off with a couple of 6-pounders and a resallah (troop) of Locals, to escort a quantity of ammunition to the troops at Jumrood, who were to take it on to Ali Musjid. There was no moon to light me on my progress, and the faint gleamings of the stars were barely sufficient to guide me over five extremely narrow bridges that had neither parapet nor wall to prevent one from falling over the side. When we reached the sixth and last, the first dawn of morning was visible, and as it gradually brightened into open day, only served to display more vividly the melancholy accident that occurred at this spot. A few yards beyond the bridge, and nearly running at right angles to it, was a deep and narrow cut, which it was necessary to avoid but, unfortunately, the troopers in the leading gun turned too suddenly to the left, by which means a wheel of the carriage got off the bridge, and the ordnance was immediately caps zed. A Lascar, who, under cover of night, had seated himself on it, fell at the same moment, and was, sad to relate, underneath, and buried in the water. Every exertion was made to rescue the poor fellow, but in vain; the ordnance had fallen so awkwardly, and the ditch was so deep, that upwards of ten minutes or a quarter of an hour had elapsed ere he was dragged out. On subsequent examination, by a surgeon, it appeared he had received so many contusions about the head and chest, from the gun tumbling on him that death must have been almost instantaneous; but if such had not been the case, I fear he would have been drowned, as we had no means at our command wherewith to have restored suspended animation. We reached the camp at Jumrood, at nine A.M., and immediately on arrival made the ammunition over to Captain Prole, 37th Native Infantry, who commanded.

My tent was once more pitched amidst scenery with which I was familiar; but the landscape, though the same, had been changed in some of its accompaniments. It is true, the Sangas still existed; and were even occupied by the friendly Khyberries, who, to show their zeal for our service, had kept up an incessant fire (whether necessary or not is unknown) during the previous night; but the immediate camp was altered, and in lieu of Dowranee horsemen and raw Affghan levies, it was filled with British sepoys and European soldiers. I had not long retired to rest, when the report of a musket, followed by the sharp whiz of a ball, told that something had occurred; but I had been so often disturbed by false alarms, when the visitations of Sadut Khan were expected, that I had ceased to give them any serious attention; so, pricking up my ears for some time to ascertain if anything would follow, and hearing nought, I turned round and was soon asleep. The next morning I was told that the shot was occasioned by a sepoy having incautiously placed his musket too near a fire, by which a spark had ignited the priming, and set it off. A day or two afterwards it seemed as if the circumstance had been premeditated, for the man being slightly wounded in the thumb, but perfectly fit for duty, begged he might be admitted into hospital, which would have exempted him from proceeding to Ali Musjid; and as he was one who had *distinguished* himself in the former flight, there is reason to believe he was only a malingerer.

It was at noon, the day after I joined Prole's camp, that the political agent, (Mackeson,) having received no tidings from Dowson; (who commanded at Ali Musjid, consequent on Ferris's departure for Peshawur, again very ill,) and being anxious about his safety, ordered us to move forward; but a letter from D., in which he stated that he thought he could yet hold out without assistance, having reached as after we had advanced about a mile and a half, we returned to our old position. Mackeson had on this occasion directed the Sikh troops to enter the pass by the main route, to create a diversion; but in spite of his arguments, and those of Colonel Courtlandt, an officer in the Maharajah's service, who was to have gone with them, they refused to do so; shielding themselves under the excuse, that their orders were to *accompany* the British troops, and that, therefore, whichever way *they* went, the Khalsas would follow.

Negotiations were now set on foot with the Khyberries, and it was hoped some amicable arrangement would have been entered into, when a communication from Dowson informed us that they had appeared in considerable numbers, and had hoisted a black flag close to the tower above the gorge near Lall Chenie. Mackeson fearing that Colonel Wheeler had, at his requisition, taken a more circuitous route by Choora, and would not therefore be in time to succour Dowson, ordered an advance to take place the following morning. Accordingly, at daybreak we commenced our march, my own duty being merely to accompany the troops to the entrance of the pass, (the Shadee Baziar, where there is no gun road,) as it was thought a small "sanga" which commanded the gorge, might be in the Khyberries' possession, and if so, they were to have been dislodged by a few shrapnels. Before reaching this defile, a sort of council was held to consider whether it would be most advisable to trust the baggage to the case of the Sikh regiments, or to a small party of peasants who lived in the neighbourhood of Peshawur, as the British troops were only sufficient to guard the long line of camels that carried the ammunition. So meanly was the courage of the former thought of, that it was unanimously resolved to commit it to the charge of the villagers, and this disposition having been completed, the column again moved on. As we neared the entrance, it became evident that the "sanga" was unoccupied, and a party under Farmer having been pushed forward to secure it, I wished them all a successful expedition, and, agreeable to instructions, commenced my return march to Peshawur, accompanied by the resallah of Locals.

On reaching Futtehgurh, I halted beneath its walls for the purpose of giving the troop horses a feed; and whilst here, a scene most revolting to human nature occurred within twenty yards of my position, and which I grieve to say I had no means of preventing; indeed, the tragedy had well-nigh concluded before I was aware of what was going on. It appeared that, the previous evening, a party of Khyberries had made a successful foray, and had carried off a number of camels belonging to one of the regiments that formed the garrison of the fort, and also a couple of Sikh soldiers, who had the care of them. Immediately it became known, a detachment was ordered out in pursuit; but, meeting with none of the marauders, they had, in their stead, captured two of their enemies' tribe, who were quietly pursuing the "even tenor of their way," and had nothing whatever to say to the robbery. These unfortunates, having been kept in close custody the whole of the night, were next morning, when I halted at the fort, removed from the place they had been confined in, and dragged by their ferocious captors to a spot at no great distance from where I was standing. I saw the crowd advance, but imagined the Sikh soldiers who composed it were *mutineers* on their way to Peshawur, though I was at a loss to guess the meaning of the dried bushes that they were carrying with them, and as for the wretched prisoners, I did not observe them. The Sikhs, on stopping, immediately formed a circle, which was too dense for my vision to penetrate, and not caring to know what was going on I had turned away from the scene. Presently loud vociferations of "Putthur se maro" — "Stone them to death," caused me to look in this direction again, and then a fierce flame was lapping the air far above the heads of the spectators. Convinced that some cruel work was going on, I accosted a respectably-dressed Sikh, who was standing in a most unconcerned manner near me, and to my question as to what they wire doing, he replied with perfect indifference, "Burning a couple of Khyberries," and then related how the miserable wretches had fallen into their hands. I expressed my detestation of the cruel punishment, when he added, "Why should we not? the same fate has by this time attended the two Khalsas that were captured last night." Such are the consequences of the bitter hatred that exists between these nations; but I was afterwards glad to learn that the sufferings of one of the victims, had terminated most speedily, for in his agony he had burst his bonds, and madly rushing against his enemies, was instantly felled to the earth by a dozen sabres. The other was not so fortunate, but *his* torments were less than five minutes in duration, (then, *what* torments!) as the dried thorns produced a fire of exceeding fierceness, that must have destroyed him almost at once.

Anxious to leave a place that had been polluted with such barbarity, I recommenced my march as soon as I possibly could, but at Koulsir another met my gaze in a lifeless corpse stretched on the high-road. Two deep gashes across the thighs, which were nearly separated from the body, pointed out the cause of death; and a finer proportioned man (such an one as on fair ground would have beaten forty cowardly antagonists) never fell beneath the blows of robbers. He had been stripped of every rag.

At 4 P.M. I rejoined the camp at Peshawur, and in the course of a day or two we received accounts of Prole's deteachment, who had safely convoyed the ammunition to Ali Musjid. For the first three quarters of the distance our troops were allowed to pursue their way unmolested, but on approaching the heights near Lall Chenie, (a favourite spot of the Khyberries,) they were fired on, and met with considerable opposition. The majority of the officers being in blue surtouts, were very conspicuous amongst the soldiers, and the Afreedies took good care to select them for their marks, and with such true aim, that Prole and Macmullen fell almost at the same moment, both severely wounded in the thigh. A party of sappers, under M'Leod, immediately rushed up the hill, and gallantly drove the enemy from their position, and the convoy eventually arrived at its destination, with the loss of several men killed and wounded. Colonel Wheeler, with the 48th, having been obliged to abandon the Choora route on account of the load being impracticable for guns, reached Ali Musjid the next morning, and the following day, after having strengthened the garrison, marched for Jumrood by the main pass. Negotiations of an amicable nature having been made with the chiefs, it was thought there would be no opposition. Still, the crowds of Khyberries that occupied the heights, and the known treachery of the tribes, rendered it necessary to move with caution. The Colonel had not advanced very far, when the true intentions of the Khyberries were manifest, for they made a desperate attack on the baggage, and such camels as could not be carried off they hamstrung by which means the loads eventually came into their hands. Colonel Wheeler immediately moved up his force, and drove the enemy from their plunder; but, in consequence of so many camels being mutilated, he was compelled to abandon a large quantity, as there was no conveyance to remove it, and several officers thus lost all they possessed. The 37th and 48th regiments, and the sappers, behaved most gallantly.

Colonel Wheeler's arrival having obviated the necessity of a longer detention at Peshawur, the Commander-in-chief, with the first column, broke ground on the 23rd, and on the 24th the second column encamped at Pubbee. On the 27th we reached the Indus, and crossed it on the following day by an excellent bridge of boats. I then visited the fort of Attock, to which, in the month of March, we had been denied admittance; but beyond its exterior there is nothing to interest one. The governor of it at that time was Peshawur Singh, whose behaviour was so insulting to Ferris, that it became necessary to make a report of it to Col. Wade, who, on hearing of it, immediately acquainted the Maharajah with the circumstances, and requested that some notice should be taken of his conduct. A reply was, in due course of time, received, and conveyed the intimation that a fine of 100 rupees had been imposed on the young scoundrel. This was deemed a mere subterfuge, and a stringent letter was forthwith penned, hinting that a more suitable punishment was required: the affair ended by Peshawur Singh losing his governorship as a requital for the brief amusement his pranks had afforded him. On the 1st of December we halted at Wah, and I thus had an opportunity of seeing its much-vaunted beauties, which consists o f a d ilapidated country-seat o f Jehanguire's, imbedded in what had once been a very pretty garden, but now a perfect wilderness. A large and beautifully clear sheet of water faces the ruin, and is tepid, notwithstanding which a few fishes were to be seen playing about, and did not appear to find it too hot to hold them. I can easily conceive this spot to have formed at one period a most delightful retreat; but the house is now in so ruined a condition, and the gardens so overgrown with jungle, that little pleasure is produced by contemplating them in their present state.

On the 3rd we reached Rawul Pindee, and halted there on the 4th; when, under cover of night, an Akalli inflicted with a sabre a severe cut on a private of the Lancers, who had charge of the regimental pack of hounds: it is supposed in revenge for the dogs having the day before seized upon the carcass of a *dead* bullock. A horse-artilleryman was also wounded in the arm, having beer attacked whilst playing his pranks in the city; and so he, in measure, only reaped his desert. The 11th saw us again before Rhotas, and on the 12th we marched to the town of Jhelum. situated on the river of the same name. Here was heard of the sad and melancholy accident that had occurred the previous day, wher the Lancers were fording the stream, by which Captain Hilton corporal, and nine private met with a watery grave. The fore, being somewhat in form to the letter S, was difficult to follow; and in some way or another a squadron gradually shelved off into deep water, on which the sad catastrophe ensued. Our column crossed the next day by boats,—the horses being taken over the ford by their grooms, or such soldiers as could swim; and it being properly defined, no loss was sustained. On the 15th we were at Kohar, near to which we had been ferried over the Jhelum when going to Peshawur; and shortly after arriving there gunners took it into their heads to administer a trifle of Lynch law. For some days previous they had been thoroughly disgusted with the bad quality of the bread issued to them by the baker, (who had been often reprimanded for it, and had it returned on his hands by those in authority,) and on the morning in question having learned that none had been provided for them, but that chupatties, or unleavened cakes, were to be distributed instead of the loaves, they resolved to be revenged on him. Unfortunately this intimation had been conveyed to them just as the man of dough was ambling into camp upon a wretched pony; and no sooner did they espy the object of their wrath, than, without further ado, they dragged him from his saddle, tied a rope round his neck, and ran him up to the branch of a tree. Here the unfortunate, but rascally offender, was to allowed remain a few seconds before he was lowered down, and (not willing to carry their frolic too far) before the breath had quite oozed out of his body. Of course such conduct on the part of the men was not allowed to pass unnoticed, and a parade was ordered as soon as the circumstance became known. The half-hanged baker was then taken down the line, and having identified two individuals as the ring-leaders on the occasion, they were ordered into confinement. Sir John Keane subsequently directed a court of inquiry to assemble, but it elicited nothing, as the two supposed rogues satisfactorily proved an *alibi*, and were in consequence released. The lesson, however, was not lost upon the baker, and soldiers henceforth had satisfaction of receiving a better description of bread.

From Dingee, instead of proceeding by the large towns of Gujrat and Wuzeerabad, we pursued a more southerly route, as the Sikh rulers had expressed a wish that the troops should not pass through Lahore. At the city of Rainuggur we crossed the Chenab, not above a quarter of the breadth it was at Wuzeerabad, in March, and passing over a rich and fertile country, forded the Ravee on Christmas-day, when Major S —— and I, to keep up old customs, indulged in a plumpudding that had been boiled in a *tea-cup*! A day or two previous Sir J. Keane, having received an invitation from the court of Lahore, marched for that city, taking with him, in addition to the Lancers, Grant's troop of horse-artillery as an escort. I had the option of going with them, but as I had seen the capital of the Punjab, I preferred remaining with the second column. On the 28th we arrived at Kussoor, a large and ancient town, that in former days must have covered an extensive area, as its ruins are interminable; and, on the 29th, crossed the Sutledge, and once more trod the soil of our own provinces. The delight which every one, from the General to the lowest campfollower, experienced on arriving in Hindoostan, was manifest in their countenances; and the congratulations offered and received on the occasion, were given and accepted with the hearty good-will. The next day there was a halt, to allow the baggage, &c, to be ferried over; and on the 31st of December, 1839, we closed the year by marching to Ferozepore, the rear of the army of the Indus (in our column, at least,) being brought up by about two dozen sepoys of the 20th N. I., (under the command of an officer of the 48th,) worn out and ragged, and preceded by a single fife and drum, playing the Grenadier's March. It appeared almost a lible on the grand army that, little more than a year before, had assembled on these very plains, and astonished the "Lion of the Punjab" by its magnificence and strength; but which, from the numbers of regiment that had been left in Affghanistan, and the casualties, that had occurred, was now reduced to two or there regiments and detachments, the men with their clothes worn out and patched, and the horses with little to boast of but skin and bone. On the 1st of January, 1840, the Commander-in-chief returned from Lahore, and on the following day having issued a very flattering order, the "army of the Indus" ceased to exist. In the course of a few months we received intelligence of the honours that had been conferred on various officers engaged in Affghanistan;

and amongst the number were three who had belonged to our mission. Colonel Wade was knighted, created a C. B., and promoted to the rank of Lieutenant-colonel in the East Indies, besides having the Royal permission to receive and wear the first class of the Douranie order; and Dr. Lord and Lieutenant Mackeson were rewarded with the third class of the same order.

FINIS.